PRECARIOUS INTIMACIES

Generation, Rent and Reproducing Relationships in London

Faith MacNeil Taylor

BRISTOL
UNIVERSITY
PRESS

First published in Great Britain in 2024 by

Bristol University Press
University of Bristol
1–9 Old Park Hill
Bristol
BS2 8BB
UK
t: +44 (0)117 374 6645
e: bup-info@bristol.ac.uk

Details of international sales and distribution partners are available at bristoluniversitypress.co.uk

© Bristol University Press 2024

British Library Cataloguing in Publication Data
A catalogue record for this book is available from the British Library

ISBN 978-1-5292-2485-6 hardcover
ISBN 978-1-5292-2487-0 ePub
ISBN 978-1-5292-2488-7 ePdf

Cover design: Andrew Corbett
Front cover image: Alamy/Mike Read
Bristol University Press uses environmentally responsible print partners.
Printed and bound in Great Britain by CPI Group (UK) Ltd, Croydon, CR0 4YY

FSC
www.fsc.org
MIX
Paper | Supporting
responsible forestry
FSC® C013604

Contents

Acknowledgements   v

1   Introduction   1
2   Precarious Intimacy   23
3   Obstructing Reproduction   60
4   Labours   80
5   Feeling Space   101
6   Conclusion   124

Bibliography   129
Index   150

Acknowledgements

I am indebted to every person I met and interviewed for this project. Thank you so much for trusting me with your stories. I am forever grateful to Catherine Nash for her supervision, mentorship and friendship. Thank you also to Cathy McIlwaine and Philippa Williams for helping the study come to fruition, and to Cindi Katz and Kendra Strauss for your comments and support. To human geography colleagues at Queen Mary and Royal Holloway, thank you for your support, encouragement and friendship. To Siân, Zack, Caroline, Jess, Steven, Alex and Andree at the Green Group, thank you for helping me to understand more about housing and planning policy in London, and for the laughs along the way. Anisha: thank you for all the listening and loving. Thank you to colleagues, co-organisers and service users at adventure playgrounds and at Akwaaba: turned out I hadn't done urban geography until I had done playwork. To friends who have supported this work's birth, thank you for being there. Jen, Fae, Janey, Sasha, Sofia, Clare: I am blessed by your presence in my life. Mads, your calm, steady presence is so healing for me. Tasmia, you are my rock and my kin. No pressure. Joey: thank you for being my family, for all the care and curiosity and commitment. You have given me so much safety. Big up creative collaborators and friends: Jacob, Mike, Theo, Phil, Clare (again), Owen, Deanna, Milly. Special thanks to Sarah. Meghan, thank you for all the love, laughter, safety, beauty and support while I did my PhD and embarked on yet more punishing toil. I'll never stop thanking the universe for you. Amy, thank you for reading so much of the first typescript, and for the encouragement, real-talk, peace, grounding, and the tender sweet love. Hannah, thank you for the hours of reading and soothing, the deep engagement, the passion, fire, the cool open water, for loving me fiercely and holding me gently. Thank you to my spirit guides for keeping me aligned and strengthening my forcefield: A, M, A, GM. I'm grateful for my parents, Sandra and Peter, and my sister Georgia. Thank you to Japa Dasi for the spiritual mentorship. Thanks to the rave crews, river neighbours, queer DIY punks. Endless gratitude to my non-human loves, Claris and Willow. This project would not have been possible without financial support from Queen Mary, University of London. Thank you, finally, to the team at Bristol University Press for supporting, working on and publishing this book.

1

Introduction

This book is about the reproduction of relationships amidst economic precarity. In it, I focus on the precarity that is generated by neoliberal rentier capitalism in Britain, homing in on the experiences of millennials living in rented accommodation in London. I focus on millennials because I am fascinated by the intergenerational ruptures that have accompanied the advancement of neoliberalism in Britain in the 40 years preceding this book's creation, whereby the nuclear family model that so many of us grew up within is no longer as economically viable owing to the scarcity of affordable housing. Taking this phenomenon as its premise, albeit critically, this book explores the different ways that relational reproduction is imagined and practised by millennial Londoners living in both privately and socially rented accommodation, with a particular focus on the Borough of Hackney, where I have lived for over a decade.

This book is the result of interviews with scores of residents. Forty interviews were conducted as part of doctoral fieldwork in 2018 and 2019. These conversations have been supplemented and preceded by discussions with many more residents from 2016 to 2022. I have had these discussions in professional capacities, for jobs – as an academic researcher based in universities and as a housing and planning researcher at the London Assembly in 2021 and 2022 – but I have had many more of them as a community member, artist, political participant, playworker and millennial renter myself. There have been conversations at organising meetings and at dinner tables, discussions over Zoom and text message, chats with audiences from stages I've been singing on, conversations with young people on playgrounds, exchanges with partners, lovers and friends. While the only accounts I directly discuss in this book have been gathered through formal methods and written consent, all these conversations show up in this text, because all of them have shaped my thinking about the precarious intimacies assembling rented home space in the city I live in.

In the chapters that follow, I write about people living in both privately rented and socially rented accommodation. I do this for a few reasons. First,

I want to challenge the idea that socially rented homes are less precarious than tenancies in the private rented sector. This is a commonly held view across the movement for renters' rights, but it does not adequately reflect the different types of insecurity that people living in social housing face, especially owing to years of degeneration, corporatisation and displacement. Second, I want to challenge the idea of a typical millennial living in rented accommodation being a private market participant. Braiding our understanding of 'generation rent' with the private rented sector erases the experiences of millennials from low-income backgrounds who may continue to live in the socially rented housing they grew up in owing to economic barriers to market incorporation, or millennials who have been housed in temporary accommodation, or millennials parenting children in overcrowded flats rented from housing associations. These, too, are stories of millennial experience. Third, the deliberate erosion of social housing in Britain is key to understanding the state's broader attack on the relational and reproductive lives of low-income communities. Without including the experiences of people living in socially rented accommodation, a key part of the neoliberal story of precarious intimacy is missing.

This chapter begins with an account of my own housing experiences, and then moves into a discussion of the ways a broader prefigurative politics of relationship anarchism shapes my approach to reproduction and relatedness in this book. I subsequently discuss the generational and reproductive disjunctures that have unfolded from British rentier capitalism. The second half of the chapter discusses the politics of academic knowledge production, positionality and methods, closing with some thoughts on the psychic dimensions of financialised life. In the chapter that follows, I first present a review of the conceptual literature, academic research and cultural texts to which it contributes. This review offers a fresh multidisciplinary synthesis of literature on precarity, reproduction and intimacy that, I hope, makes some interesting connections between thinking on everyday neoliberal insecurity and engagements with the replenishment of life – and power – through relationships. I follow this review with a condensed historical exploration of some of the reasons why shelter is so unaffordable and insecure in Britain, and especially London, taking stock of the complex imperialist webs with which rentier capitalism has been woven here, and then homing in on selections of policy material that evidence the deepening neoliberalisation of housing. The empirical chapters that follow focus, respectively, on experiences of 'reproductive obstruction' among millennials living in rented accommodation in London; the labours demanded of and practised by renters in order to sustain and replenish their relationships with friends, partners and family members; and the affective circulation of feeling in rented accommodation, with a focus on queer house-shares.

This book began as a doctoral research project, but before that it was a longing. I longed for the acknowledgement of my pain and that of my peers: the pain of unbelonging and transience, of ruptured, superficial or otherwise absent community; shame regarding perceived relational failures and material insecurity; the shame of participating in movements for almost 15 years but feeling hopeless, isolated and jaded. I wanted the story of my generation's dispossession to be told: how the financialisation of everyday life robbed our dreams of life-creation and love-creation by stealing the ground from under our feet, the roof from over our heads, and funnelling our declining wages into the bank accounts of the capitalist propertied classes. When I speak of generation, I want to avoid divisive homogenisations, but rather speak of my comrades, a generation that has politically resisted: those who politicised me as a 20-year-old, taught me the vocabulary and praxis of resisting neoliberalism, occupied lecture theatres during the student uprisings of 2010 and 2011. The millennial generation was the first to be flung into the private rental market saddled with tens of thousands in student debt, or to remain stuck with parents, unable to dream of what might come next. They were the first generation to graduate into the 2008 financial crisis and the subsequent intensification of rentier capitalism that has rendered Britain unliveable for a large and growing number of its population. The (re)capture of the land from the people. But without land, there is no space, and without space, there are no bodies relating. Without bodies relating, there is no love, and without love, tyranny succeeds.

Richard Gilman-Opalsky writes that 'the presence of the body – or bodies – demands a response' (2020: 27). In the crowded environments of London rental life, the spaces in which bodies relate and respond to each other are often unchosen and constrained. Is it space enough for embodied responses to be calibrated into political subjectivity, into forms of collective resistance that demand state responses? This question lingers in the background of the stories I share in this book. It is there because to speak of generation is also to engage with the verb, to generate. Generation refers to the *act* of life's reproduction, not a static moment in history. While this book focuses on the experiences of millennials as a specific age group, it engages with generation as a will to become. It is for this reason that intergenerational collaboration is so powerful. Indeed, in social housing estates, privately rented house-shares, temporary accommodation blocks and resident meetings across London, the right to greater space for becoming, relating and replenishing life is being intergenerationally demanded. The presence of the body demands a response.

And yet, for many living under the financial control of monthly debts to landlords, the cyclical trauma of housing precarity and transience obstructs and depletes the affective capacities vital for political engagement. Precarity submits dwellers to a constant state of fight–flight–freeze, where lack of stable ground seeds new traumas while amplifying those that already exist. Fracture is built into this housing landscape like embodied carbon. Traumas reverberate, too, in the housing movement's fissures: the mistrust and paranoia that separates leaseholder from tenant, private renter from temporary accommodation resident. Not only this, but the broad age-stratification of housing inequality is a barrier to intergenerational solidarities. This is a tension that is held throughout this book: systemic youth dispossession has mapped generational experience onto class, but the reiteration of generationally mediated class divisions can erase intergenerational commonalities and collaborations. Such divisions are nonetheless unsurprising amidst the everyday precarity that so many renters, largely under 40, are exposed to. In the storm of uncertainty, we grope for blame. The challenge, always, is transmuting that blame into political strategy.

Nine homes

I moved to London in 2012 as a traumatised queer 24-year-old. My renting experiences amplified my ill health and stunted my healing, because I lived in spaces shaped by insecurity, disrepair, density, unaffordability and frustration. The enforced mobility and constant impermanence of privately renting thwarted my emotional development, because it separated me from community belonging. Shifting from one street to the next every one to two years, my rootedness in Hackney was in the land rather than its people. The trees, river and marshes were anchors of home and my stable connections. I could trust the parakeets to swoop down over Leyton Marsh in the late spring dusk, grazing the tree tops, and I trusted the cygnets to grow up each year on the River Lea. I could greet the same two pigeons nesting in the footbridge. The land and its non-human inhabitants were constants, while human relatedness was in flux.

The first flat was on the corner of Urswick Road in Hackney. I shared it with my friend, a musical collaborator and comrade, and we were both in bad ways. Our home was a one-bed that we had carved into a two-bed. It cost a grand a month and the bathroom could only be accessed via my bedroom. Longing for more privacy, the following year I moved into a shared terraced house on Lea Bridge Road, via a new friend. There was a lot of fun and queer community in this house, but trauma bonding and income precarity fragmented relations. Few of us were willing to see our own faults, nor to turn inwards to solve anything. Frustrations were unaired directly, forming a tense cement. I began a romantic partnership with a new housemate, vexing existing residents who did not want to live with a couple. With limited money, we felt compelled to pool our resources to find housing, uncomfortably hastening our co-reliance. We landed in a room in a house with 11 other people on Chatsworth Road. This was a terrible place: there were at least two people in each bedroom, and rent was paid in cash, sometimes to strangers who would enter the house at night. We lasted six weeks there before finding a studio flat. It was a carpeted room with a tiny kitchen tacked on the end, but there was a communal backyard, where I sat whittling spoons. I was settled enough to adopt my cat, but the lack of space for three beings wore us down, creating and amplifying tension between us. For two years we sought more liveable environments, the rents going up and up. Eventually we split, exhausted and alienated from each other. Unable to afford the rent for our last place on my own, I was forced to move out into a room in a shared house nearby. I discovered the Middlesex filter beds, a nature reserve by the River Lea that was once a Victorian water filtration site. The marshes became my home and sanctuary.

I was 29. A year later, I married my new Canadian partner, with no other option for her to stay in the country. It was too late to do it in England, so I joined her in Toronto and we exchanged vows in a botanical garden, sweat garlanding our foreheads. After we submitted her visa papers, paying thousands to the British government's private-sector partners for the sin of foreign love, my wife sofa-surfed in Ontario for three months, waiting for the application to be processed while I was in London. Ours was the privileged experience of the 'Hostile Environment' immigration regime established in 2012. We received financial aid from my parents for the visas, and without it she would not currently live in Britain. As stories in this book similarly affirm, the financialisation of conditional forms of citizenship entrenches intrafamilial dependencies. This has relational consequences and political ones, because it ideologically consolidates the family as the arena through which subsistence and rights are financially granted.

When she finally returned to England in late October 2018, my partner was legally obliged to share my room: the visa conditions stipulated that we had to live together and all the rooms in my place were taken. Another condition was that she was not entitled to any public funds should she lose her job or fall ill, or the Home Office could sue me. The walls creaked with the weight of our combined belongings. There were seven people living in a split-level flat with one bathroom. Overcrowding and insecurity spiralled our household relations. We were a house of mainly precariously employed queer people – students, sex workers, artists, service workers – with varying degrees of substance dependency, trauma, mental illness and citizenship precarity. We muddled through the undergrowth of uneasy proximities, tending to our wounds and making new ones. Our landlord directly let the place to us, which meant we didn't have to pay any of the fees that letting agents continue to unlawfully charge private tenants. He did all his own repairs and he was quite responsive if things went wrong, which was frequently because the place was falling apart – there were beer cans wedged into the outside garden wall to stop it collapsing. He was also disrespectful of our privacy.

One morning he bounded in unannounced and sprang up the stairs to the attic room where one of my housemates was sleeping.

Eventually I managed to move with my spouse to a one-bed flat a couple of streets away. It cost about two-thirds of our combined monthly income. This time, we rented through a letting agent, but our landlord lived in the house above our basement flat. As per the tenancy agreement, we had shared access to the garden. Our landlord, an older retiree who enjoyed listening to Christian radio and tending her flowerbeds, was amicable enough at first. When the poor drainage and broken door swept hundreds of maggots from her bins into our flat, she gave us a bag of fruit to say sorry. But she also preferred to interpret my marriage as a friendship, tried to evict my cat, and repeatedly let herself into our flat while we were out to "check where we were drying our towels." The flat was dilapidated, too: there was a hole in the ceiling and we could see into her kitchen.

In the summer of 2020, the British government had ordered the public to stay at home to prevent the spread of COVID-19. We felt lucky to have access to a garden, which we hadn't used until that point owing to the generally hostile aura. Grasping the opportunity to experience sunlight, we crawled out of our dark, dusty basement and began spending more time in the garden where the landlord would also sit, looking uncomfortable. At the time, my partner was studying horticulture. With a sun-soaked garden at the back doorstep, she began growing some food in a few of her own pots. Our landlord launched an offensive, repeatedly reporting us to the letting agent for using the garden. She kicked over our garden chairs and hosed the lawn while we lay on it. Indeed, she hosed it for so many hours each day that our back step flooded and the door rotted, eventually coming off. We spent several weeks with half a door. She shouted at us through our half-door. And, soon after that, we found that our garden hose had been cut with a pair of scissors.

In August 2020 we received our Section 21 (of the 1988 Housing Act) notice to evict, at a time when evictions were legally suspended by COVID-19 legislation. This meant our landlord would have to wait a month longer to get us out. Section 21 notices allow landlords to evict tenants with no reason and with no further adjudication. Theoretically they are used when landlords want to sell their properties and need to get their tenants out to do so, or to get rid of tenants so that landlords can raise the rent. In reality, they also give landlords the power to evict tenants without any reason beyond disliking them or punishing them for repair requests. In our instance, both things were true. The date we had been given to clear out was December 2020, a horrific month for the British population. People died in droves from COVID-19, alone in their homes and in hospital corridors. We were displaced during a second national lockdown in which we weren't even legally allowed to mix with another household. I made a sign that read: 'EVICTED IN WINTER IN A NATIONAL LOCKDOWN IN A PANDEMIC BY THE LANDLORD UPSTAIRS. WHERE IS THE HUMANITY?' I stuck it on the street-facing front window of the flat.

The moment of our displacement coincided with one of the only significant deflations in the private rental market that this city has seen in recent history. When the COVID-19 pandemic hit Britain, swathes of renters retreated to their towns and villages of origin. As with all pandemics previous, the city was an epicentre of incubation and transmission. Its density, housing scarcity, deprivation and the fact that over a fifth of Londoners work in the gig economy – and therefore were not entitled to any of the government provisions to keep the workforce at home – meant that the virus was all but impossible to contain in the city. Many people fled before lockdown legislation came into force, and many more exited afterwards. Some finally used the deposit they'd been saving on a cheaper life gentrifying towns on the south coast. They popped up a few months later in *Guardian* lifestyle columns about new starts, waxing lyrical about waking to the sound of gulls and being able to grow tomatoes without ingesting fumes. The spike in out-migration left London landlords scrambling to fill suddenly vacated tenancies. For a moment, the private rental market was almost in tenants' favour. And in this window, my partner and I were able to find a one-bed flat we would never ordinarily have been able to afford.

Situated on an estate facing the canalised River Lea and, beyond it, Leyton Marsh, our flat was on the ground floor with a garden in a large shared courtyard. Opposite our back gate was a footbridge over the water that led to a willow tree. This willow, the water, the courtyard, the flat and the people on this estate finally gave me a real sense of home. For almost two years, we were able to grow, heal and ground in a flat that functioned. It cost us £1,350 per month and only had one working radiator, but it was beautiful and host to a cascade of love, pleasure, celebration and togetherness. Yet, it was only in stable housing that I was able to figure out where my heart led: not the nuclear-adjacent, assimilatory household forced upon me by state border policy, nor the rushed pooling of resources within the couple form that rentier capitalism in this city coerces people into for survival.

Thinking beyond the family

I offer this account of my relational life over the past ten years to show that it has been inextricably bound up with the assetisation of housing in London, and with the related enclosure of safety and survival within conditional forms of citizenship. All my choices to commit to, escalate, rupture or end relationships, to pool resources, move home or open out my private space have been influenced by the fact that it has been financially impossible for me or my loved ones to live on London land with real autonomy and intention. Like almost everyone else I know here, economically relying on friends, partners and family members has been the only way to survive. But was it ever thus? After all, interdependence is not only a feature of life but a necessary part of life's reproduction. It is the means through which life is made and sustained. Yet when relationships of dependency are imposed by economic structures, webs of unfreedom are woven around intimacy. We need each other more than we want each other. There is far more potential for love's promise of interdependence to remain locked, instead, in what therapeutic discourse refers to as codependency, in which people are unhealthily enmeshed, often owing to material imbalances.

A coercive regime of material imbalance is imposed upon populations by the neoliberal state, which defends and upholds the interests of capital, the ontological existence of which depends upon inequality. At the level of our close relationships, then, of course late capitalist intimacies dance in the same narrow corridors as coercion, because they so often unfold from structures and ideologies that are coercive. Marxist-feminists – and I consider myself one, broadly – have long pointed out the ways that capitalism and patriarchy are mutually constituted. Now, in this contemporary age of housing unaffordability, debt, wage decline, inflation and slashed childcare expenditure, our attention has turned to evidence of women's re/privatisation within uneven domestic labour divisions, with fewer financial and material exits from oppressive relationships and living situations. But what of the households formed through economic necessity that are not oriented around the couple form? What of the uneasy dependencies unfolding from household constellations that are accidental, unidealised, or that are placeholders for the kinship formations that people truly desire?

Thinking beyond the heteromonogamous nuclear family as the blueprint of household normality has been a central part of feminist political visioning and this remains the case. But amidst the widespread financialisation of life, thinking beyond normative family structures is not only liberatory strategy, but contemporary reality. The material resources required to establish and maintain a self-contained household with children are increasingly scarce, owing to housing and childcare costs coupled with real wage decline. In Britain, the average annual cost of childcare for under-twos is approximately £14,000, or 67 per cent of the average income (OECD 2023). There is a real crisis in reproduction, but that means there is also a real crisis in capitalism, because the social institutions through which capitalism reproduces itself have been eroded by its own logics. In modern parlance, crisis is usually equated with turmoil, havoc and suffering. However, the etymology of crisis reveals a Middle English usage of the word referring to the turning point in a disease. This book embraces this etymological ambivalence just as it embraces the contradictions baked into late capitalist absurdity. Yes, we feel afraid and yes, our suffering is very real – yes we are in crisis. But perhaps we are at the turning point of this disease, and life now beckons.

While the nuclear family is an anachronism, it remains the foundational structure through which the nation state legitimates itself and capitalism is reproduced, through uncompensated reproductive labour and intergenerational inheritance. As the state has retrenched from social welfare, the conditions of reproductive workers within family structures have worsened. In order to reclaim our right to collective social reproduction, it is therefore necessary to abolish the family as the structure through which the replenishment of society is expected to take place. When I say family abolition, I mean a political and ethical practice grounded in five things:

1. developing collective care infrastructures such that reproductive labour is not the private burden of one or two people;
2. dismantling adult supremacy and protecting the autonomy and agency of children, especially queer and gender non-conforming children;
3. exalting friendship as society's core relational foundation;
4. challenging the economic and political incentivising of marriage and the nuclear family household in policy (and, in turn, the penalisation of relationship models that are not based in these institutions such as single motherhood);
5. decriminalising all sex work.

None of this pertains to destroying existing families but allows for a praxis of defence against the ways that the family might destroy us.

This understanding of family abolition is also influenced by my personal practice of relationship anarchism. Developing the latter has involved shifting from monogamy to polyamory, in which there has been mutual commitment to embodied sovereignty between myself and partners, just as there is between myself and friends. The freedom to explore the potential of connections does not necessitate multiple sexual and romantic partners, although it can if that is where one's heart is led. Mutual commitment to freedom also does not preclude deep, authentic and long-lasting romantic partnerships. However, engaging with relational life through a relationship anarchist framework also holds space for the experience of short relationships and encounters as deeply impactful, transformative and meaningful. It holds space, too, for non-human relationships, friendships, creative partnerships, intergenerational relationships – for infinite forms of partnership – involving the same depth of commitment and importance as romantic connections. And it allows for these connections to change and end without judgement or shame. In other words, relationship anarchism decentres the monogamous couple form and its lifetime temporality as the default unit around which life, relationships and reproduction orbit.

Instead, it exalts the autonomy of individual subjects as always already relationally constituted.

This is very different from capitalist individualism – although, like any relationship model, polyamory can be practised individualistically. In its essence, however, relationship anarchism dismantles the normalised cultural legitimation of control over one's partner's thoughts, emotions, feelings and choices, freeing us to expand our relatedness beyond the couple unit. In so doing, it also has the capacity to disrupt the imbricated systems of capitalism and patriarchy. These systems both rely on logics of accumulation that are legitimated through the ideology of familial inheritance: a person accumulates wealth not simply for themselves, but for their progeny. Naturally, monogamy is required for this system to work efficiently, otherwise the benefactors of one's wealth might proliferate, undermining the very essence of accumulation. It is clear, then, that expanding our intimacies, commitments and investments beyond those that unfold from capitalism's associated relational institutions – the monogamous couple form, the blood-tie family, the nuclear household – has subversive implications for the communalising of life.

A contention of this book is that London tenants' thrown-togetherness contains openings as well as barriers to this communalising. One of these barriers is the corroding impact of rentier relations on friendship, as residents jostle for space in a housing landscape wrought by unaffordability, inequality, insecurity and poor conditions. As the empirical narratives in this book reveal, the lack of autonomy and intention with which rented household constellations are formed can feed the insecurity and transience of the renting condition, blighting the seeds of solidarity necessary for friendship and thus for strong community infrastructures. Alienated from the unworkable (and indeed undesired) nuclear family format, and alienated, too, from alternative kinship by permanent uprootedness and unchosen homes, our gardens of relatedness struggle to bloom. But bloom they must, if we are to survive this reproductive crisis, this turning point, because new infrastructures of care are urgently needed.

In *The Communism of Love*, Richard Gilman-Opalsky writes that love relations 'contain valuations that do not obey the presuppositions of capital' (2020: 53). The love of friendship cannot thrive amidst capitalistic transactions. Most obviously, it cannot thrive in transactions where a person is profiting from the labour of another. Feminists have argued that the institution of the nuclear heteromonogamous family is inextricably tied to the exploitation of women's reproductive labour, by capital and by men. For such thinkers, the nuclear family is another exploitative workplace in which the love of friendship cannot easily thrive. When we think about capitalist property and labour relations obstructing reproduction, and we understand that our species' reproduction is contingent upon interdependence and an end to unbridled accumulation, we must therefore think beyond the traditional family as the domain through which alternative care infrastructures can be visioned and born. On a political level, this might include challenging policy reform that gatekeeps economic relief within marriage. On an intellectual and scholarly level, thinking beyond the family involves decentring the couple form in our examinations of care and intimacy, and taking broader account of the diverse relationships that uphold and replenish life. This also means we must take broader account of the diverse ways in which capitalistic transactions intercede in these relationships. With this in mind, this book engages with the spaces and dynamics carved out and carved up by capital as both containing and condemning the seeds of new relatedness that we so need.

Re:generation, rent

The Freudian family romance of the nuclear family continues to shape socioeconomic policy in Britain. A premise of this book is that the political economy of this romance is key to the story of Britain's age-stratified housing inequality. It is for this reason that I focus on the experience of 'millennials' rather than a diverse range of age groups. In Britain, this generation was the first to experience the cleavage between preparation for participation in a Keynesian society – wherein employment security was achievable, public services reliable and secure housing a likely possibility for a wide section of society – and maturation into a neoliberal society, in which state retrenchment privatised welfare and subsistence within the family unit. This has bolstered the necessity of multiple lines of familial economic dependency for survival.

Many of my generation who live in southern cities have existed in a state of quasi-homelessness for our adult lives thus far. Those who haven't moved are not necessarily static through choice, but because they have never been able to move out of their origin-family homes. The only person I know in London who owns their flat is a lead actor in a hit Netflix series, and even they could barely get approved for a mortgage on a two-bed. Family wealth funds almost half of all first-time buyer home purchases in Britain (Savills 2023). The institution of the bourgeois nuclear family is therefore strengthened and legitimised through the power it has over adult children's material destinies. Yet, while millennials and younger generations dwell in the private rented sector, either awaiting financial rescue from insecurity or lacking any means to escape, they are increasingly unable to mirror and practice those same heteromonogamous relational forms. There is simply not enough money and space to do so.

The inflated cost of renting extends beyond London, but, as journalist Vicky Spratt outlines in her 2022 chronicle of the British renting landscape, it is a particular phenomenon in the south of England and its largest cities. Oxford, Brighton, Bristol, Exeter, Cambridge: all have seen such drastic house price and rent inflation over the past two decades that local populations can barely afford to live in the cities they grew up in. In these cities, it is normal for residents reliant on the private rented sector and its standard tenure, the Assured Shorthold Tenancy, to hand over more than half of their incomes to private landlords. Over years, this amounts to tens, sometimes hundreds, of thousands of pounds. Life itself has been let out: while renters work increasing hours for climbing rents, landlords count the climbing returns of passive income. Given that real wages have declined year on year for decades, there is little to work towards for many renters. What hold does the Freudian family romance have over a renting population that can barely afford to subsist themselves, let alone consider making more mouths to feed?

Beyond the south of England, house prices have generally continued to rise, but rents have not experienced the same levels of inflation as in cities closer to London. This does not, however, lessen the transience, insecurity and poor conditions that renters in these cities experience. In the autumn of 2022, mortgages also underwent aggressive inflation owing to the now infamous 'mini-budget' announced by former chancellor Kwasi Kwarteng. The mini-budget ushered in a period of unparalleled inflation and heightened interest rates in Britain. Given that mortgage lending all but ended and landlords looked for investments that would garner higher returns, the population of houseless people has grown once more: people who cannot qualify for a mortgage; people who cannot afford their existing mortgages; and people who cannot afford the increased rents charged by landlords seeking to plug profit gaps or indeed capitalise on inflation. These are the ideal conditions for a supermarket sweep of land and property by corporations, something that is already evidenced in the creation of 'investment zones' across Britain, with corporate tax incentives including 100 per cent business rate relief. Originally termed 'enterprise zones' in the chaotic mini-budget of September 2022, this is at least one of Kwarteng's ideas that remains in the policy of his successor, Jeremy Hunt, albeit without the relaxed planning regulations that Kwarteng's original initiative involved.

Obstruction from the means of stable, secure dwelling for a widening sector of British society is an age-stratified phenomenon. The 2021 national census has revealed that nearly 75 per cent of people over the age of 65 own their homes outright, while a third of 35–44-year-olds rent from a private landlord (ONS 2020a). However, the age stratification of home ownership – especially outright ownership – does not give us a full picture of wealth. Analysis conducted by the Office of National Statistics demonstrates, for example, that while a quarter of older households who own their homes outright have at least £50,000 in savings and investments, almost the same proportion of outright homeowners have no savings (ONS 2020b). Still, the proportion of renters with no savings or investments vastly outstrips these figures. In 2017, only 23 per cent of outright homeowners had no savings, contrasted with 66 per cent of private renters. These nuances are important – they guard against homogenisations that unfairly characterise entire generations as rich or poor. For example, as the ONS reports, nearly half of mortgage-paying households containing someone aged 60 or over have no savings buffer. The plight is especially clear for those who bought their council homes through Thatcher's 'Right to Buy' scheme ('leaseholders' – this is the most common type of ownership in London now, and it requires owners to pay 'ground rent' and maintenance fees to a freeholder; thus it is also technically a form of renting) but whose income remained low throughout their working lives and into their retirement. Ultimately, however, housing costs are highest for private renters. This is not only owing to unregulated, runaway rent inflation, but also because the energy efficiency of England's housing stock is dire. Energy inefficiency – old heating systems, poor insulation, single-glazed windows – already pushed almost 20 per cent of private renters into fuel poverty by 2017. The energy inefficiency of British housing stock is also one of the reasons why the 80 per cent energy price increase in October 2022 has had such devastating financial impacts on households.

If people under 40 are more likely to privately rent and people over 65 are more likely to own outright, who are the private landlords? Data collected by the English Private Landlord Survey in 2018 showed that the median age of English landlords was 57, older than the general population, and that 62 per cent of tenancies were let by landlords over the age of 55 (Ministry of Housing, Communities and Local Government 2019). Key findings from this wide-reaching national survey also demonstrate that 94 per cent of English landlords rent property out as an individual; a third of landlords are retired; and almost half of landlords let property as an investment preference (46 per cent) and/or to contribute to their pension (44 per cent) (Ministry of Housing, Communities and Local Government 2019: 6). Almost 90 per cent of landlords are White. Some smaller surveys conducted by property investment companies suggest that there has been an increase in landlords under the age of 40 in the last four years, and an increase in female landlords, but their samples are tiny and thus trends are far from conclusive. More convincing is His Majesty's Revenue and Customs data for buy-to-let investors, which demonstrate that almost half of Britain's 2.6 million buy-to-let investors are women.

What can we make of all this, and how does it map onto a conversation about reproduction, relationships and the family? First of all, we have a landlord class that is growing and diversifying in terms of age and gender, but that ultimately remains dominated by White retirees. While the age of private renters is increasing (for example, it's important to remember that the largest age group of private renters in England is aged 65 and over), this does not do away with the age stratification of ownership. As one national study shows, while there are more private renters over 65 than there are owners in the same age bracket, that proportion of outright owners is many multiple times larger than the proportion of outright owners in any age bracket up to people in their mid-50s. To me, these trends tell the story of a fascinating paradox of our contemporary economic and political system. Neoliberal orthodoxy, and the unfettered rentier capitalism that has accompanied it, has economically engineered a society that cannot reproduce the very institutions upon which the electability of the state has depended for the last 40 years. Without homeowning nuclear family households, and thus a class of people invested in property appreciation and the intergenerational transference of wealth, growing sectors of the population have no economic investment in fiscally conservative policies. Not only this, but they *must* find ways of living and relating beyond the family, if they want to survive.

So many contradictions. State policy and legislation relentlessly invokes 'family households' while paradoxically driving ecologically destructive housing construction plans that are centred around the needs of single people or couples. In his autumn statement in 2022, chancellor Jeremy Hunt addressed 'families' eight times. Meanwhile, on London housing estates, kinship networks that have grown over generations struggle against their demolition and dispersal. At its core, capital's command over reproduction is a disciplining of the very energies, substances and expressions of our desires and longings. We are torn apart from each other yet made to grip too tightly. But as birth rates fall and a demographic crisis beckons, our inability to reproduce the foundational institution of capitalism holds up a mirror to the inevitable dismantlement of this discipline. This is a mirror that the state has always attempted to shatter, by coming after those of us who threaten its false and contradictory reproductive order. Queer people are the mirror. Single mothers and sex workers are the mirror. Because these groups disproportionately practice modes of collective social reproduction, they are cast as illegitimate, often through laws that start as puerile rhetoric in papers and on parliamentary floors. But as queer people and other reproductive dissidents are scapegoated for Britain's decline in births and marriages – in other words, for the decline in nuclear family establishment – the capitalist state continues to pursue economic policies that doom the very institution it needs in order to stay in power.

This is an exhilarating prospect, but it is not that straightforward. There are plenty of ways in which the nuclear family is also strengthened by the rentier capitalist political economy. Economic ties mean that separation is often financially unviable, for example. And the age-stratified housing inequality of our current era means that younger people are more likely to pay propertied older people for insecure housing; this can create familial enmeshment throughout the life course, because growing numbers of people can't afford to move out of parental homes, are reliant on parental help to meet housing costs, or are not only faced with unaffordable rents but also need to financially support their parents. But as older generations age and pass, and the demographic impacts of unaffordable life come to bear, the same structures may not remain. The question is: what will regenerate? What will be born anew? This is a crisis brimming with emergent potential as much as it is pregnant with loss and despair. The interstices of this reproductive juncture are openings – portals to new futures. In them, precarious intimacies assemble, rupture, fruit and decompose. This book peers into these cramped spaces where intimacy and precarity entwine and disentwine, through turning to the materiality of millennial renters' lives. It considers the political potential of our collective heartbreak, and the activating capacity of feeling, as the energetic, vibrational data that assemble relationships and transform futures. It wrests the destiny of this capacity from capital's constraints, limitations and impacts, and places it in the uneasy intersubjective recognition of precarious intimacy as a discomfort that nonetheless signals the turning point in a disease.

Writing with and without the university

While I hope this book will be useful for students and academics within university settings, it is also for anyone interested and invested in the political questions, spaces and communities explored in this text. The broader purpose of this writing is for the advancement of political thought rather than the advancement of academic scholarship, because most of the ideas and experiences influencing this book do not originate in the university. Rather, they are born from a grounded, embedded politics of everyday social reproduction that I have learned about through active engagement as a bigender queer political subject, artist, teacher and playworker. I do not think it is appropriate for these ideas to undergo enclosure within the marketised industry of academia, and have written most of it without any institutional affiliation. My experience of participating in academia as an early career researcher has been alienating. By adhering to a quantity-over-quality approach to publishing 'outputs', I felt I was reproducing the conditions of my own subjugation and those of my peers. In our age of fleeting spectacle and individual competition, it is common to adulate scholarship that purports to break new ground, establish a big new idea or perform an unprecedented synthesis. I cannot worship flags arbitrarily stuck in grounds that are already home to complex, ancient ecologies of thought. I feel this book does contribute some new ideas to written conversations, but I know that many people are already having these same thoughts, because it is how I came to them myself.

Theory comes from practice. The purpose of it is therefore to refine and transform our practice so that we might have a better chance of surviving as a species. When I severed the cord between theoretical engagement and the advancement of my early academic career, my heart became hungrier for knowledge. This is because I reintegrated my intellectual curiosity with revolutionary praxis, and with prefigurative participation in popular movements. On French postmodernism, Stuart Hall wrote that the 'continuing presence' of the popular masses 'has constantly interrupted, limited and disrupted everything else. It is as if the masses have kept a secret to themselves while the intellectuals keep running around in circles trying to make out what it is, what is going on' (Hall and Grossberg 1985/2018: 52). Writing as a participant within those masses can limit the extractive flavour of academic theorising. But it is not a cure-all salve. Ultimately, I straddle both worlds: I could only write this book with integrity from beyond the university, but it would not exist without the mentorship, collaboration, training and development I received as a student, researcher and lecturer.

In this book, I therefore aim to present passages from interviews, conversations and written works without hierarchising their legitimacy according to academic proximity. I am encouraged by books such as *The Care Crisis* by Emma Dowling (2020), who weaves reflections on conversations with care professionals alongside reflections on academic and political texts, and conversations with activists and friends. Over-reliance on critique is another habit of academic scholarly practice I aim to challenge. Not everything is worth critiquing, especially when we are thinking as a movement ecology rather than as individual scholars. In the words of activist and writer Kai Cheng Thom (2017), the 'central role that criticism plays in the performance of goodness' results in 'rigid thinking that prioritises the endless reenactment of outrage and conflict while preventing us from developing strategies for reconciliation, necessary compromise and collective action'. In this book, I critically analyse texts that have been created by state policy makers. For example, I analyse welfare reform legislation, national housing policy, localism policy, border policy and urban planning programmes. At times, I critically engage with respondents' interview data. In my view, this is necessitated by the uneven socioeconomic terrain characterising the urban renter landscape I explore. I conduct this critical analysis to historically capture the political and economic frameworks through which differently situated renters traverse this terrain – not to objectify or essentialise respondents for thinking a certain way. I critique texts to make their political meanings legible, and to trace this legibility across scales of experience, from the urban built environment to the embodied matter of social reproduction – the 'messy, fleshy stuff of everyday life' (Katz 2001: 711).

This book is interdisciplinary. As a research monograph, it sits at the cross-section of feminist political economy, economic geography and urban studies.

It could also be read as a queer studies text. Within academic scholarship, I am broadly contributing to lively, heartfelt conversations about the intimate and affective dimensions of neoliberal precarity, the financialisation of the built environment and the relational impacts of housing insecurity and eviction. This book can also be read as an offering to conversations about affect and emotion in sociology, though my academic 'home' is human geography. Among feminist geographers, my work is situated within a lineage of critical theory and research on reproduction (see Katz 2001, 2008, 2011; Mitchell et al 2004; Nash 2005).

The scholarly works I am most drawn to are attractive to me because they speak to my broader anarchist political framework. This framework is state-abolitionist; concerned with the political potential of desire and affect; and concerned with collective political subjectivity as it is assembled through the cooperation, solidarity and mutual aid of people. It is a framework that has both led me to, and been constituted through, engagement with post-structuralist, anarchist, communist, queer and Black feminist thought. These theoretical strands enliven my evolving understanding of the state's composition, and the ecologies through which power can be built towards its decomposition. Crucially, they highlight the necessity of embodied feeling for the assemblage of these ecologies.

The revolution is hot. It's sensual, like spring flowers and pollen-drenched bees. It's playful, like children on roller-skates. It's destructive, like children smashing wooden pallets, and it's sad, like children tripping over pallets on roller-skates. To envision and create new futures we need desire and longing as much as we need grief and sadness, just as the cycles of natural life move in seasons. As a new wave of writing and practice on the political potential of somatics reaffirms, accessing these feelings is an embodied process that requires moving out of the mind. The written word is therefore a limited medium for understanding feeling. To really understand feeling we must feel, through art forms and practices that engage our bodily sensations.

To this end, in 2020, I supplemented the written documentation of this project with comic strip transcriptions of interview excerpts. Alongside my own vector illustrations, I also hosted a workshop at Dalston C.L.R. James library in February 2020 with local Hackney renters, in which attendees worked with comic journalist Adam Sherif to create comics depicting their experiences of renting and relationships. The subsequent collection of drawings was published with grant support from the Centre for Public Engagement at Queen Mary University of London. I have not featured these drawings in this book, but they are available to view at my website. Beyond visual art, I write and sing songs as a way of interfacing with the world. Like birdsong, our songs tell stories of love and longing, and stories of place – we sing to tell each other where we are and how to find us. Over the seven years I've been working on this project, my thoughts have always been processed through song. I have recorded, released and performed some of this work with ensembles, but most are sounds that have only been heard by me. There is occasional mention of songs in this book: my own or songs by others (I would have added more were it not for copyright issues!). This is another dimension of the book's interdisciplinarity, as well as its commitment to breaking down epistemic hierarchies. But mostly it's just that sometimes there is nothing left to do but sing.

Notes on methods

Methodologically, I sought to overcome the acquisitive nature of the ivory tower by grounding my recruitment of respondents in relational authenticity. The research I conducted for this book involved talking to some people that I already knew, and some I didn't, about renting, relationships and reproduction. These people included: the 23 millennial research participants who consented to take part in my doctoral study in 2018; four housing professionals and community members living and working in Hackney; and three further respondents who consented to take part in supplementary research about queer house-sharing in 2021. I conducted in-depth, audio-recorded interviews with 26 of these individuals, bar one who did not want to be recorded, and manually transcribed and analysed each text. The remaining four members of the original millennial cohort were interviewed in a two-hour focus group. With nine of the original millennial participant cohort, I conducted two in-depth interviews, with the second interview usually taking place in their residence. Of the resulting 26 millennial respondents interviewed from 2018 to 2021, 22 are directly cited and discussed in this book. As agreed upon in their written consent to take part in this project, I do not use any original names or identifiable information. Beyond this formal methodology, the book is influenced by: conversations with scores of residents, policy makers, campaigners, charity workers and activists I spoke to during my appointment as a researcher for the City Hall Green Group; tenant union meetings and events I have variously attended; my experiences as a playworker, both at Akwaaba, a migrant-led mutual aid organisation in North Hackney, and at an adventure playground in South Hackney; my experiences as a musician, performer and teacher in Hackney schools, homes and venues; and conversations with renting friends and peers. While my perspectives have been influenced by these encounters, I do not discuss the personal experiences of anyone who did not give explicit consent to be interviewed. However, I am an absorbent artist and political subject living in and moving through the place that is the geographical focus of this book. My life and work in Hackney constantly influence me and expand my understanding of this book's questions. At times, I therefore include broad observations from this life and work alongside the discussion of formally collected data.

Eight of the study's renting respondents lived in social housing. This meant they lived in housing that was rented from the council, a housing association or co-operative, or they lived in private sector housing that had been allocated by the council and subsidised through housing benefit/Universal Credit payments (usually termed 'temporary accommodation'). Eighteen participants were private market renters. At least two of these residents were reliant on housing benefit/Universal Credit to pay their rent (I did not ask for this information so it is possible that more were also in receipt). Three privately renting participants had previous experience of living in social housing in Hackney, and one part-owned and part-rented her flat through a shared ownership scheme.

In this book, I discuss further personal characteristics, identities and backgrounds of respondents in my descriptions of them, if these dimensions are relevant to their stories and proffered by them in interviews. This is not because I want to obscure transparency regarding the demographic composition of study participants, but because I disagree with the crude, tabular categorisation of difference that so often accompanies social science research, and that characterises neoliberal engagements with identity (and 'diversity') more broadly. I avoid racialising respondents, but I draw on language they have used in interviews to describe themselves, and I sometimes discuss their migration histories and heritages, where this does not compromise anonymity. Where I discuss these histories, it is because this information has been offered by respondents and is relevant to their experience of life. The people I interviewed had differentiated experiences of state violence. Some were at more legal risk than others simply through being or living with migrants with insecure visa statuses, or because they were engaged in forms of work that are criminalised. At times, I have therefore sought further anonymisation through limiting, for example, regional specificity or employment. I have aimed to do this without undermining respondents' autonomous self-identities. At times, I identify and discuss Whiteness, especially in relation to the focus group interview featured in Chapter 3, in which I describe one focus group member as White and the remaining three respondents as women of colour. Although I want to avoid racialisation, race is present as an axis of oppression throughout this book. It is important to note that as a White, middle-class, English and able-bodied researcher, I moved through these research encounters with social and political power that influenced their dynamics. This positionality influenced my decision to draw on extended networks for respondent recruitment, or to recruit through events where relationships could be formed, so that more organic trust and familiarity could be established.

Throughout the seven years I have been working on this research project, I have been variously embedded within and separated from the spaces and issues I examine. I was a private renter for ten years. For most of that time I had little embedded relationship to social housing tenants, beyond the people I met through my doctoral study, Akwaaba and teaching at a local primary school. My housing and planning work at the London Assembly opened up many more opportunities for me to meet and collaborate with social housing residents across the city. In 2022, I co-produced a research report with Green Assembly Member Siân Berry that gathered testimonies from numerous housing estates to challenge unfair electoral practices in the conduct of estate ballots (Berry 2022). The latter were introduced by Mayor Sadiq Khan in 2018 to give estate residents a say over demolition plans funded by the Greater London Authority. Learning from these residents pulled me towards working in a council estate community in southeast Hackney. Five days a week for six months, I helped to steward a large outdoor site where children and young people engage in free, risky play. Becoming part of this community enlivened my commitment to a playful politics of collective reproduction, and gave me more understanding of the ways that housing insecurity in the social sector obstructs reproduction, from the perspective of children. I don't kid myself that I have earned a badge of embeddedness that circumvents the extractive components of my being a middle-class researcher sometimes writing about communities I don't come from, but I do recognise that this book has more integrity for the time and labour I have given to Hackney. I hope this book can inspire other feminist researchers to reconcile their politics to their scholarship by engaging with everyday social reproduction as not only a field but a university, too.

The impossibility of financialised life

In December 2019, I drank to the possibility of a socialist Labour government, and woke to the biggest Tory majority since Thatcher. This was an electoral landslide engineered by Boris Johnson on the premise that his 'oven-ready' Brexit deal would nudge Britain over the finish line of leaving the European Union. Stopping the free movement of EU citizens into Britain was the chief premise upon which Johnson's Brexit was sold, with northern voters especially to be rewarded with geographically redistributed public investment. As the exit poll came through, we looked at the TV and said "so many people will die." We had said this, too, canvassing rainy doorsteps in swing seats that winter. By that year, over a hundred thousand people had already died at the hands of austerity policies, many of them disabled. Three months later, in March 2020, the COVID-19 pandemic began to rip through the population.

Johnson's government stalled with stay-at-home policies, subjecting England (health policy is devolved across the nations of Britain) to a series of rolling lockdowns over the course of a year, punctuated with episodes of release in which the public was actively encouraged to mix in restaurants and pubs. In the summer of 2022, some of Johnson's lies cost him his premiership. And then, for 45 days, the laissez-faire 'trickle-down' economics of his successor, Liz Truss, heightened the inflation created by Brexit and the Ukraine war oil shock. While hedge fund managers lined their pockets against the Kwarteng-crashed pound, a winter of penury began. Court-ordered mortgage repossessions increased by 134 per cent, landlord repossessions by 98 per cent (Ministry of Justice 2023). Food inflation rose to its highest level since the 1970s. As the energy price cap rose by 80 per cent, fuel companies obtained warrants to enter households and forcibly install pre-payment meters, leaving over three million people in cold and dark homes during the winter.

A crumbling empire enforcing the worship of accumulation, the destruction of the earth and mass serfdom for the profits of a handful of billionaire rulers. These are biblical times! According to scripture, however, biblical times usher in shifts in collective consciousness. Nothing does it quite like a global plague. Indeed, for many, the COVID-19 pandemic reshaped understandings of the labour required to replenish life. Subsequent industrial action in 2022 and 2023 spoke to the strengthened solidarities that the pandemic has necessitated, and waves of strikes brought railways, postal services, schools, ambulance services, border checkpoints and universities to standstills. Coinciding with this mobilisation was the emergence of a new moniker for capitalist crisis: the 'cost-of-living crisis'. Not an employment crisis, a fuel crisis, a housing crisis, or a healthcare crisis: the cost-of-living crisis describes the ontological impossibility of financialised life. In Britain, contemporary resistance against the financial cost of life has been shaped by the affective afterlife of a pandemic that has not ended. This is the emergent political potential of despair when it is collectively witnessed and held.

Collectively generated affects assemble the precarious spaces of neo-illiberal Britain. As many of the stories in this book reflect, locating the political potential of these affects is difficult in the everyday, cumulative dysregulation of racial capitalism. Terror, rage, disgust, grief. Resentment, sorrow, blame and longing. So much is broadly felt but individually contained and carried. Yet, in many of these spaces, disciplines of shame and division are gently composed. In turn, seeds of resistance are sown by the intersubjective recognition of feeling. In this book, I have tried to truthfully recount the fragmented and tense feelings circulating in London's rented accommodation, as told to me by those experiencing them. I recount these feelings not to re-establish the hopelessness of our economic landscape, but to illuminate the strength of people's desire for change, and to release the shame of our fragmentation from silent, atomised containment.

Releasing these affects through documentation is part of the decompository process required for the creation of solidarity's soils. When these affects are met, seen and mulched, seeds of commonality fertilise and grow. Through returning the state's discipline of division to this soil, we are also practising the decomposition of the state. This is especially possible because of the state decentralisation that has featured so strongly in the neoliberal project. Partially outsourced to civil society, the neoliberal state is assembled through networks of subjection that do not require governmental institutions. Private landlordism encapsulates this: the psychic life of the state plays out in its divided interests, power differentials, involuntary proximities and endemic precarity. And this decentralisation is key to our vulnerability: in the absence of formal administration, we have no protection – other than each other. So, we must assemble different networks, new soils.

2

Precarious Intimacy

Theories

To both survive and resist late capitalist economic conditions, we are dependent upon relationships. And yet, it is through relational practices that those same economic conditions can be maintained and reproduced. In British rentier capitalist society, this tension is manifest. From intergenerational property inheritance and 'friendlordism' to house-share hierarchies unfolding from 'lead tenant' designations, relationships are not only shaped by economic precarity, they can also feed it. Neoliberal orthodoxy individualises this precarity as if it is a private matter to be conducted between different stakeholders. Internalising this orthodoxy, the tenant blames themselves, their cohabitants, indeed their private landlords – for disputes with the latter are generally individualised, and while the movement for private renter rights has given a structural framing for these conflicts, neoliberal states benefit from this outsourcing of culpability. But this is not a problem of individuals.

Precarity is a discipline imposed upon populations, and its spores are in the hearts and lungs of residents across all forms of tenure. As the Care Collective (2020: 16) observes, the privatisation of space is key to precarity's corrosive effects on the tissue of our relationships, creating, in the authors' words, 'uncaring' communities where communality struggles to thrive. Subsequent chapters of this book are full of stories recounting the difficulty of creating caring communities in the uneven terrain of London's rental landscape. These stories nonetheless always demonstrate a will to care and be cared for; the desire for connection and belonging. For me, the place between this difficulty and desire is precarious intimacy.

In this place of precarious intimacy, it can be hard to plan relational futures. Questions of reproduction are troubled: what can be born? What forms of kinship are possible in unknown economic futures? Everyday practices of reproduction are also disrupted: the physical nourishment of children, for example, or the space and intentionality required to nourish and replenish social bonds. Precarious intimacies may also give rise to anxious investments in reproducing class positions: my child must get ahead, she must do well and accumulate wealth – she should go to a private tutor rather than the adventure playground. Indeed, questions of reproduction are always political. Almost by definition, Cindi Katz writes, social reproduction is 'focused on reproducing the very social relations and material forms that *are* so problematic' (2001: 718; emphasis in the original) – there is nothing intrinsically 'revolutionary' about social reproduction, 'and yet so much rests on its accomplishment'. As the stories in this book reveal, precarious intimacies are interwoven with disrupted reproductive temporalities, practices and anxieties. Indeed, neoliberal precarity is a highly temporal condition. For example, precarity invokes temporariness – short-term jobs, short-term tenancies – but it also speaks to the prolongation of this temporariness throughout the life course. Precarity also invokes the loss of a past security: an historical shifting of conditions and class positions. Sharing an emphasis on temporality, then, precarity and reproduction are satisfyingly braided concepts. They speak to everyday difficulty and long-term desire. In their interstices, precarious intimacies are assembled.

In this chapter, I outline how I am using this book's core conceptual terms: that is, precarity, intimacy and reproduction. My aim here is to demonstrate the slippages between these terms, and to explore the value of integrating them within an approach to social reproduction that is centred on the sensuous practices of making and replenishing intimate relationships. I draw on the theory and research of a range of authors to do this, tapping into currents of intellectual and political exchange that also synthesise these concepts. In doing so, I situate this book as an additional tributary to these currents.

Precarity: lost worlds, found desires

The term 'precarity' emerged at the turn of the 21st century to describe the widespread socioeconomic and environmental vulnerability associated with late capitalism, particularly the dual decline of Fordist labour relations and Keynesian welfare capitalism in the Global North. Much interdisciplinary literature on precarity has therefore concentrated on the loss of the securities accompanying organised capitalism in the 'developed' world – for example, the decline in formally contracted employment, the depression of wages, and the erosion of union power. Guy Standing's (2011) coinage of the 'precariat' as a unified class owes much to this interpretation of precarity as loss. For Standing, the 'precariat' was a new phenomenon comprising 'denizens' who occupy a shared sense that their labour is 'instrumental, opportunistic, and precarious' (2011: 6, 13–14). Such conditions can be contextualised through the onset of the 2008 financial crisis and the stringent austerity regimes states imposed in its wake. There is, therefore, considerable crossover between research on the insecurities accompanying austerity and the wider precariousness of late capitalist life. For example, in Britain, Sarah Marie Hall has researched the interface between economic crisis and personal crisis among families in Greater Manchester (2018, 2020), and Alison Stenning has explored the psychosocial experience of recession on low- to middle-income families in North Tyneside (2020). Others (Paton and Cooper 2017: 164–170; Harris et al 2019; Garthwaite et al 2020) have addressed the violent housing insecurities created by austerity policies.

Fiscal austerity in Britain has claimed hundreds of thousands of lives, and it is right and important that its devastation is documented, its undergirding ideologies exposed. However, the attention given to post-crash precarity as a recent crisis – a break from the more stable 'before-times' – can obscure longer histories of economic violence. Further, as austerity becomes entrenched as a long-term economic paradigm in Britain (albeit alongside higher levels of public taxation) we are in need of broader historical and geographical contexts to understand what precarity is and what it does. After all, poor pay, insecure employment and suppressed union power have historically characterised conditions for most workers across the globe. Several scholars indeed argue that Fordist/Keynesian employment security was ultimately a postwar exception (Neilson and Rossiter 2008: 51; Kalleberg 2009: 5; Schram 2015: 12), and Lauren Berlant famously observed that precarity became a political 'crisis' only because it hit the bourgeoisie, whereas its role in creating 'proletarian labour-related subjectivity' was long a given (2011: 105). Not only this, but as Rob Lambert and Andrew Herod remark, Fordist labour organisation itself included many aspects of precarious employment (2016: 17–18). Crucially, the racial dynamics of capital accumulation evidence the enduring nature of precarious employment for vast sections of the human population, rather than its ethnocentric containment within neoliberalism (see Hill 2017: 94–109). For example, Ruth Wilson Gilmore (2007) has shown that unfree labour continues to persist in the United States well beyond slavery's official abolition in 1866, from convict leasing to mass incarceration. Queer theorists and disability scholars have also pointed out that the precariousness of labour is mediated by structural heterosexism and ableism (Hollibaugh and Weiss 2015: 18–27; Kerschbaum et al 2017).

That precarity can confer the loss of postwar securities does not mean that it only describes middle-class downward mobility. Neoliberalism has made all lives more precarious, especially for those already experiencing systematic insecurity. For example, studies of labour flexibilisation and informality have shown how neoliberal deregulation has heightened migrant exploitation, re/creating unfreedom, transience and carceral work conditions for these workers (see Anderson 2010; Wills et al 2010; Strauss 2013; Reid-Musson 2014; Lewis et al 2015; Cassidy 2019). Housing geographers also highlight the increased im/mobility and fear imposed upon low-income and racialised city-dwellers through the dovetailing of neoliberal economic reform and anti-immigration policy (see Blunt and Sheringham 2018; Leahy et al 2018). In fact, these precarities are themselves interwoven with the widespread promulgation of contemporary insecurity as the loss of economic and political entitlements. For example, the racist propaganda accompanying the Brexit referendum and its drawn-out aftermath refined and consolidated the cultural purchase of a disenfranchised, angry 'White working class', scapegoating EU migrants for the widespread insecurity that neoliberal policy making unleashed across Britain. Prior to and during this campaign, the state's invocation of 'brokenness' and 'crisis' has legitimated its class war against low-income, racialised communities (see Slater 2014; Shilliam 2018). This has shown up in the expansion of migrant detention centres and mass deportations, as well as the systematic demolition and dispersal of urban housing estates.

The resurgence of the 'White working class' has been accompanied by the rise of another class mythology: that of the middle-class millennial stripped of their secure economic destiny by neoliberal precarity. Looming large within this mythology is the figure of the child. Sought but unreachable, the middle-class family cannot be re/established: the 'good-life' fantasy is in disarray. Lauren Berlant describes post-Fordist affect as a 'scene of constant bargaining with normalcy in the face of conditions that can barely support even the memory of the fantasy' (2011: 278). Amidst precarity's erosion of reproduction, this bargaining can be located in the psychic pull of the middle-class nuclear family. In the same way that engaging with precarity as lost security has discursively constructed a White working class invested in 'taking back' these entitlements, so too has a middle-class millennial subjectivity formed around the retrieval of lost destinies. However, psychic identification with these lost destinies can manifest regressive politics – traditional institutions of marriage and family, for example, may be fetishised. As Kathleen Millar (2017) points out, the discourse of precarity as derogatory has the potential to maintain 'normative forms of work and life' (see also Nancy Ettlinger [2007] on the reproduction of precarious conditions via attempts to gain certainty through classification, homogenisation and legitimisation).

To make such observations is not to exculpate the state discipline of precarity as a source of profound suffering for populations across the globe, nor is it to ignore the real pain of lost pathways to self-actualisation. Rather, it is to explore the politics of social and cultural *responses* to imposed, systematic uncertainty. Do we reach for the classificatory strategies of capital and state, damming the fluid movement of our interconnected lives – banning gender recognition reform, banning small boats of asylum-seekers, enclosing the wellbeing and safety of city-dwellers within gentrified enclaves – or can we formulate something liberatory from the revelation that we are on our own: *we* are on *our* own. For Judith Butler, precarious life is an ethics of cohabitation – the involuntary interdependence that all human beings are subject to. While states politically manage populations through the strategic distribution of this dependency according to individual lives' 'grievability', human interdependence remains unchangeable. Our vulnerability remains unchangeable; it is our ontological truth, our *dharma*. This concept of course precedes Butler and Western philosophical tradition by several millennia. Most indigenous American epistemologies, for example, are grounded in reciprocity and interdependence (see Grande 2004: 149; Coulthard 2014; Barker 2018) and challenge the existence of fixed categories. For example, sociologist Silvia Rivera Cusicanqui (2012, 2023) uses the Aymaran geologic concept of *ch'ixi*, the unification of opposites, to construct a prefigurative politics of decolonisation centred on cultural hybridity. Such work presents a theoretical alternative to urges for certainty and classification that thrive amidst the widespread precarity of our current age. Indeed, this precarity *reveals* networked life: its necessity, but also its immanence.

Remembering our always-already interconnectedness is a soothing thought in frightening times, but the networked life of neoliberalism is concerned with connecting individual consumers, customers, producers and sellers, not building collective solidarity. In this landscape, the camps of identity and ideology are appealing pseudo-communities, walled in by fear, grievance and co-opted desire. As carla bergman and Nick Montgomery write, surveillance and control are 'increasingly participatory' through digital technology, yet these forms of subjection are felt 'as *desires*, like a warm embrace or an insistent tug' (2017: 55; emphasis in the original). Neoliberal networked existence presents us with a simulacrum of participation, interconnection and desire, feeding on our hearts without replenishing them. Our affective engagement *is* the commodity: the pile-ons, the denigration, the arousal, the nostalgia, the trauma. Beyond our prescribed roles in this affective supply-chain, however, the precariousness of interconnection is humming with liberatory potential as much as it is unease. An infinite rhizome, each point connected to any other point, our interdependence, when animated, can dislodge the insecurity and terror (see Deleuze and Guattari 1987: 21). But this animation must be desired.

Desire has an ambivalent rap in left thinking. For Richard Gilman-Opalsky, it is antithetical to communist love. Desire, he writes, it 'not itself a practice'. I disagree. Marx himself was not anti-desire but concerned with its alienation. If desire is alienated through exchange value, it is surely something worth reclaiming. In Bradley Macdonald's reading (1999), Marx's conceptualisation of money represents the reification of human potentialities into 'inhuman, refined, unnatural and imaginary appetites' and the engendering of desire as an egotistical, restricted '*sense of having*' (1999: 25; emphasis in the original).

While Marx prefers to talk positively about humans' 'passion', 'drives' and 'sensuousness' rather than their 'desiring' capacities, communist practice clearly involves the recalibration of desire. When understood and experienced as the loss of Keynesian securities, precarity's desires may be longings for institutions and entitlements that are relics of a bygone stability. Such desires can be politically mobilising, especially when they promise the fulfilment of a nostalgic longing, but they tend to speak to the restitution of piecemeal economic and political entitlements rather than social transformation. In this way, nostalgic desire can be politically harnessed for the consolidation of capitalist class relations rather than their dismantlement.

For example, in a housing context, systemic precarity has animated both needs and desires for more 'affordable housing'. On the face of it, this is an essential demand for the human right to shelter. 'Affordable housing' connotes habitable space, capped rents, the ability to put down roots and achieve more financial security. But it is never so simple. Wound around this call for housing affordability is a competing nostalgic desire for a different version of affordability in the form of accessible mortgages. These visions of affordability are irrevocably in tension, and the fulfilment of the latter deepens the urgency of the former. For those longing for the lost promise of home ownership, desires for 'affordable housing' tend to lead to demands for higher construction quotas. When these quotas are fulfilled through the development of new-build apartments, built on demolished estates or imposed on existing ones, and sold through 'shared ownership' schemes, we see how the desire for escape from precarity – and the restitution of a nostalgic entitlement to owner-occupancy – can be the harbinger of insecurity for working-class tenants. Such is the power of desire, then, to transform the built environment and material conditions.

Understanding the political power of desire is helped by engaging with the concept of affect. Broadly, affect is a way of understanding feeling as the embodied capacity to affect and to be affected, rather than as the active expression of an interior, individually boundaried emotion (see Anderson 2006: 735). With affect, Melissa Gregg and Gregory Seigworth observe, a body is 'as much outside itself as in itself – webbed in relations – until ultimately such firm distinctions cease to matter' (2010: 3). Its relational and embodied composition means that affect is generally rendered 'pre-cognitive' by scholars (see Lorimer 2008; Pile 2010), after Brian Massumi's reading of Deleuze (in turn reading Spinoza!). In this theorisation, affects are not reducible to ideas, but are *emergent in their relation* to ideas (see Deleuze 1978); affects are the coming-together of multiple intensities, produced by actual *and* potential relations (Massumi 1995: 93). This potentiality speaks to the immanent quality of affect. When we conceptualise desire as affective, we similarly transmute an individually held and expressed fetishisation – 'I desire this type of house for me and my wife and children' – into a relationally mediated, embodied and collective *will* – 'we desire housing'.

bergman and Montgomery write that tuning in to affect is about 'learning to participate more actively in the forces that compose the world and oneself' (2017: 65). These forces are assembled through affective attachments; they are not merely imposed by some monolithic and distant power. For example, Shona Hunter (2015: 30) shows how 'love' for Britain's National Health Service (NHS) is circulated by its 'movement through objects' – nurses, doctors, service users, politicians. This love has been instrumentalised by the state for the advancement of nationalism in Britain. In 2016, emblazoned on the side of Boris Johnson's 'Leave Campaign' tour bus, the NHS was falsely promised £350 million a week if Britain left the European Union. And, in 2020, rainbow flags traditionally associated with LGBTQIA+ pride became synonymous instead with gratitude for NHS staff treating COVID-19 patients – or 'battling' the virus, as militaristic language routinely proclaimed, on the 'frontline' of an epidemiological war for the nation. Clearly, our affective attachments and investments – especially to institutions – are valuable political currency. But this should only remind us that affect is agential; our collective feeling is not destined for co-optation by the nation state. It is co-opted precisely because it is politically threatening.

We acquiesce through feeling just as we resist through feeling. Filling streets and waving Union Flags, we collectively rejoice in the crowning of a billionaire hereditary monarch. Marching in silence and holding green hearts, we collectively mourn the 72 lives extinguished in the 2017 Grenfell Tower fire and express disgust at the treatment of this atrocity's survivors. Grief is politically threatening, because through honouring lost lives, we challenge racial capitalist doctrines of disposability and worthlessness. These doctrines are integral to a system of accumulation that relies on the sacrifice of 'surplus' populations. Britain's political regime therefore sanctions the collective expression of grief only within the parameters of the nation state: an annual day of remembrance and military fanfare for men slain in the Great War. A national mourning period of ten days for the Queen. No bell has tolled for the 225,000 people who died of COVID-19. No public events were cancelled in their honour. Nor for Aberfan, Ronan Point, Hillsborough, Grenfell. In the silence and censorship, the wound perdures and the violence is re-enacted.

Made legible through expression, grief is an alchemist, transmuting dense affects of bitterness, fear, shame and despair into love. The British government's criminalisation of protest is an attempted removal of our right to grief, amidst other collectively generated affects. This evidences the politically threatening nature of mourning. Indeed, grief and mourning have been instrumentalised by some of the most transformative political and social movements. In the 1980s and 1990s, AIDS Coalition to Unleash Power (ACT UP) engaged directly in the generative power of grief and despair. As Deborah Gould (2012: 107–108) has documented, mounting AIDS deaths and government indifference created a vacuum of despondency from which confrontational direct action was unleashed. Sometimes this action involved using lifelessness itself. For example, on Freedom Plaza in 1998, the dead body of Steve Michael was displayed in a political funeral – one final act of dissidence by the deceased founder of ACT UP Washington, DC. Standing next to her son's casket, Steve's mother remarked that he "took a person like me and showed me that I was powerful" (see Gaines 1998). Grief propelled this demonstration and activation of power. Buried in the stiff silence of shame or stoicism, or lost in the frantic churn of our over-complicated and alienated daily lives, when we turn away from our pain, compartmentalise our losses, and refuse the stillness of reverence, we reject our own power to feel. In doing so, we limit our capacity to relate, and thus to transform our conditions through the intersubjective articulation of desire. From grief, then, desire.

Capital's wastage of life engenders so much grief. In this book, much of this grief relates to the loss of home, kinship, parenthood, community, belonging, health and self-actualisation. There are stories of death, estrangement, violence and forced displacement. There are griefs that are culturally minimised – the loss of friendship, for example – and there are griefs that are intergenerationally carried, from Empire's warzones to council battlements under developers' hoardings. With this book, my intention has been to create a space for this grief to be uttered. Precarity as a neoliberal discipline relies upon the individual internalisation of pain. In gathering and expressing these seemingly individual griefs, however, that discipline is made brittle. And as it softens and crumbles, we are left in the soil of our vulnerability – an immanent precariousness that is, conversely, the very means through which the terror of precarity is resisted. Gathering these griefs has involved attending to the 'odd moments' of precarity – the affects and intensities of 'crisis ordinariness' (Stewart 2007: 128; see also Berlant 2011) that, in their iteration, can produce household atmospheres thick with resentment, or prickling with anxiety, or radiating, too, with the love of shared struggle. In this way, this book dovetails with a surge in geographical work focusing on the affective and embodied life of economic precarity (see Wilkinson and Ortega-Alcázar 2018), including the ways that precariously situated people undertake 'calculative practices' and attune (Newhouse 2017) to the financial disciplines and logics that increasingly organise their lives. Such practices also offer insight into the methods undertaken to manage the grief of stolen presents and lost futures.

Investigating these affective methods brings us into closer contact with the aforementioned 'classificatory strategies' that, while undergirded by grief, can maintain the violence of systemic precarity. In this book, I frequently conceptualise these strategies as examples of alienated labour, and I note their appearance in circumstances of housing uncertainty and relational fragility among cohabitants and neighbours. Why alienated labour? Surviving the informality of neoliberal labour relations requires affective work – hyperactivity, simultaneity, restlessness and cunning, in the words of Tsianos and Papadopoulos (2006) – that is extracted from bodies, heart and minds in the service of profit. Digital knowledge and service economies are indeed founded on the 'creation and manipulation of affects', as Michael Hardt famously observed, producing 'social networks, forms of community, biopower' (1999: 94–96). In this way, neoliberal precarity is an affective condition that we tend to work feverishly to maintain because of the social networks it generates. In this book, I consider housing precarity to engender affective labours that are similarly alienated by the exigencies of landlords' profits. Amidst informalised routes to housing access, unaffordable rents, and dilapidated, overcrowded living environments, affective strategies are undertaken to create relationships that will help people survive. These are not always relationships of mutuality, solidarity or collaboration; they may be hierarchical and exploitative. They may unfold from a desire to classify and categorise, to control or leverage. They may *beget* precarity.

The task of workers' liberation is to reclaim our labour from exploitation. Affective labour is not bound to capitalism; the work of generating and circulating affect is vital for the replenishment of life's integral relationships. Reclaiming our labour requires us to understand the ways that it is alienated. This alienation is not only enacted through top-down forces, it is sustained through our own participation. To really see this, we must bring the 'ugly stuff' to the surface without stigma or shame – our chances of effective resistance depend on it. As Carolyn Veldstra indicates in her research (2018) on the suppression of 'bad feelings' in precarious working conditions, burying these affects complicates efforts to 'read a straightforward politics of resistance' among workers. Visibilising the affective coping mechanisms employed to navigate precarity equips us with opportunities to alchemise them (see also Gorman-Murray [2015: 66–69] on 'inertial heteronormativity' in the wake of the 2008 crisis). This is not an individualised, therapeutic practice. It is the collective political work of intercepting our labour's alienation.

Intimacy: feeling work

I have suggested that affective labour – the work of shared feeling – is alienated by the profit relation, and that rented accommodation is a space in which this plays out. Precarious intimacies dwell in this space. Critically engaging with intimacy indeed requires spatial thinking, because intimacy is about closeness of different kinds. The stories in this book illustrate intimate relational dynamics that are shaped by capital. They also show how rentier capitalism is upheld by and thrives on specific intimate structures: short-term social relationships, for example, or the couple form. This approach to intimacy and space situates this book within a lineage of Marxist-feminist geographical thinking that began in the 1960s, when feminist explorations of intimacy began deconstructing spatial boundaries to uncover the politics of categorical essentialism. For example, the deconstruction of the family as the naturalised domain of domestic womanhood prompted the scrutiny of wider traits attributed to female subjectivity. This book contributes to this lineage because it similarly dismantles the gendered privatisation of intimacy within a sealed-off domestic container (see Pratt and Rosner 2012). I consider intimacy to be politically powerful; a power that is threatening to capital. As such, I engage with the rentier capitalist economy as a disciplining force attempting, on the one hand, to corrode closeness between people while forcing unwanted proximities, and on the other hand, potentially dooming its own dominion by necessitating the communalising of life for survival.

In the early 2000s, feminist research across the humanities used spatial deconstruction to explore cultural phenomena, political systems and embodied experience, leading to an 'intimate' turn in scholarship (see Price 2013; Moss and Donovan 2017). As Geraldine Pratt and Victoria Rosner (2012: 18) observe, this attention to spatial deconstruction extended long-standing feminist engagements with intimacy as closely related to the global. To study the intimate, in the words of Ann Laura Stoler, 'is not to turn away from structures of dominance but to relocate their conditions of possibility and relations and forces of production' (2006: 13): it is so often *through* intimacy – through closeness, relating, familiar knowing, embodied exchange – that structures of dominance are made possible. Such is the power of reclaiming and reshaping intimacy, and such, in turn, is the incentive for its western liberal construction as interiority: a 'fiction', according to Lisa Lowe (2015), that is grounded in the erasure of 'the circuits, connections, associations, and mixings of differentially labouring peoples'. Attending to these connections and mixings can shine a more expansive light on the extractive intimacies necessitated by capital. For example, Pavithra Vasudevan (2019) investigates North Carolina residents' 'comfortable intimacy' with landfills as a facet of the complex violence of everyday racial capitalism (see also Price 2013). Although I predominantly focus on interpersonal relationships between people, this book approaches intimacy with a similar expansiveness. There are stories of children's embodied relationships to leaky ceilings; tales of ill-fated intimate investments in friends–cum–landlords; there are fantasies of the intimacies that could have been, were it not financially impossible to leave parental homes or have more than a single bed.

Intimacy and affect are conceptual bedfellows in this book, especially where political economy is concerned: the *work* of intimacy can be usefully understood through the concept of affective labour, for example. Existing discussions of work, intimacy and affect among scholars have tended towards theorising the 'presence bleed' (Gregg 2011) between personal and professional identities precipitated by the technologies, infrastructures and governance practices of financialised capitalism (see also Wilson 2015: 250; Cockayne 2016; Lai 2017: 916; Richardson 2018). In these studies, the work centred is often professional and waged. By contrast, this book focuses on the ways that the affective and material work of reproducing intimate relationships is shaped by the precarity of financialised rentier capitalism. I do not ignore waged work, but I tend to engage with it in its contingent relation to the 'sensuous labour' of social reproduction (Katz et al 2015) and the making of cohabiting relationships.

This book therefore also contributes to a rich seam of feminist scholarship on the politics of home. These politics are ambivalent – while second wave feminists tended to conceptualise the domestic sphere as a site of unanimous reproductive oppression for women (see Mitchell 1971; Federici 1975; Rich 1976; Chodorow 1978), post-colonial feminists and Black feminists have sought to defend the home – with or without its internal hierarchies – against the incursions of colonialism and White supremacy. These are incursions that 'whitestream feminism' (Grande 2004) also enacts through its homogenisation of the domestic unit as universally oppressive (see also Mohanty 1991: 20). The colonial underpinnings of this characterisation are evidenced, not least, by their historical appearance in urban regeneration schemes that have sought to 'sanitise' city regions of poor migrant communities through stigmatising their family and household dynamics (see Saberi 2019). It is of no surprise, then, when racialised communities guard their doorsteps closely against the unwanted guest of Whiteness. 'Tell those kind of folks that you will meet them in a luncheonette or a bar', culinary anthropologist Vertamae Smart-Grosvenor wrote (1970: 154), observing the 'bad vibrations' that White capitalist modes of consumption brought to kitchens in Black households.

Understanding the home as a site of intimate oppression therefore cannot be limited to the boundaried container of the family, because these relationships are never contained or boundaried. They are situated within legacies of intergenerational trauma and intergenerational wealth; they are assembled through contingencies of policy, ideology, cultural and economic production. And, they are generative of these realms. Intimacies between cohabiting people are therefore thick with the affective residues of systems and structures that frame differentiated lives. For example, the home may be a locus for the 'small felt places of ongoing colonialism' (see Sarah de Leeuw [2016: 20] on indigenous communities in British Columbia), or the 'affective registers' of dispossession at the 'community, family, and individual level' (see Brickell [2017: 12] on forced eviction). But the home is not only a receptacle for these residues; it is also a place to foment resistance through intimate solidarities. To this end, for example, Chris Harker's writing (2009: 329) on Palestinian domestic life centres intimacy as politically generative, countering geographies of Palestinian homes that focus solely on the violence of the Occupation.

Like intimacy, 'home' is a nebulous concept, transcending shelter, household and cohabitation. Homelands, feeling at home, homecomings, homing in: to speak of home is so often to speak of a return to something immanent to ourselves, something inalienable that roots us in place – a place beyond the material household. Home is, in Alison Blunt's and Robyn Dowling's words, a 'spatial imaginary' (2006), an assemblage of spatial feelings and practices related to belonging, safety and sovereignty. There are politics to this assemblage, sharpened amidst the endemic precarity characterising access to dwindling land and deepened social inequality: exclusions, enclosures, borders. In this context, imagined territories of conditional citizenship are guarded increasingly closely along racial, gendered and sexual lines (see Fortier 2003: 115–135; Waitt and Gorman-Murray 2011). On a national scale, a revived isolationism saw a duped population 'take back control' of their sense of national home in 2016, excluding perceived outsiders. At the level of the London rented household, feelings of safety, sovereignty and belonging are rarely guaranteed for long, and there are politics to their affective distribution (see also Blunt and Sheringham [2018] on 'home-city' geographies). As this book explores, residents may similarly grasp for certainty through geopolitical claims and divergent perspectives of safety and belonging. These perspectives are often gendered, racialised and classed: distanciation from 'unsafe' neighbours on mixed tenure housing estates, for example. Such politics may be local and intimate, but they are vertices of much wider power geometries. An inter-scalar approach to home illuminates these geometries. This is apparent, for example, in Rachel Pain's (2015) work on the 'continua of violence' between war and domestic abuse, and Ella Harris et al (2019: 161) on pop-up housing in Lewisham, where intimate 'on-edge' anxieties are entangled with the 'spectral presence' of gentrification.

Engaging with the materiality of home – the materials and objects that assemble home space – is also an inter-scalar business, opening out questions of intimate attachment to belonging/s. Among many of this book's respondents, the spectre of displacement looms psychically large, bringing with it a precarious attachment to the 'things' of home: a parent's painstakingly installed bathroom sink; shoeboxes of photographs carried from one rental to the next. In this way, I hope this book will also contribute to a growing body of geographical work on the material-object intimacies of home. Adriana Mihaela Soaita and Kim McKee (2019), for example, explore the intimate dimensions of destabilised attachments to home through processes of assembling, de-assembling and re-assembling dwelling space in Britain's private rented sector. Similarly, Adam Elliott-Cooper et al explore 'un-homing' as the removal of a sense of belonging to community or home-space (2019).

The inter-scalar nature of intimate attachments to material home is made more apparent by considering migration and diaspora (see Tolia-Kelly 2004). London is extremely diverse and Hackney, the borough I chiefly focus on in this book, is particularly rich in difference (Hackney Council 2019). Experiences of 'home' and its intimacies are therefore plural and often ambiguous. The largest Charedi Jewish community after New York and Israel resides in Stamford Hill, following immigration that began in the 1920s. A diverse Caribbean population has populated Hackney since the 1960s; Vietnamese migrants have settled there since the 1970s. Throughout the second half of the 20th century, waves of Turkish and Kurdish immigration built robust communities in the south and east and central parts of Hackney. In the 1960s then 1980s, migrants from sub-Saharan African countries began to settle in Dalston, and South Asians – especially Bangladeshi and Pakistani communities – have established roots in Hackney since the 1950s. There are Irish Traveller sites, mosques, Buddhist monasteries, synagogues. Walk from Bradbury Street in Dalston to Hackney Downs and you can taste Ethiopian yemiser wot at Kaffa, hear Pentecostal preachers outside Dalston Kingsland station, smell Turkish gözleme on the high street, Jamaican ackee and saltfish down Ridley Road Market.

A sense of home and belonging in Hackney is made through this multiplicity of home intimacies, expressed in vivid fabric patterns, scotch bonnets and ginger, fresh challah, dancehall. For some of the respondents in this book, a strong relationship to cultural heritage was a core mode of familial belonging, especially for those cohabiting with their families of origin. However, this was sometimes a fragmented belonging – for example, where relational and intimate choices clashed with familial expectations. As Chapter 5 explores, a fragmented sense of belonging was also evident in queer shared households, where experiences of exclusion from origin-families could be echoed, rather than healed, by class and racial politics among cohabitants. Queer renters with diasporic heritage can therefore experience home intimacies as especially precarious. This may amplify the significance of attachments to material anchors of belonging – I am reminded here of Chinese-Canadian trans artist and story-teller Kai Cheng Thom (2019), who describes her embrace of the *cheongsam* dress to ground both her womanhood and Canton roots.

Queer and diasporic relationships to home un/belonging reflect the ongoing containment of cultural, social and economic resources within state-sanctioned household structures, and therefore within state-sanctioned practices of intimacy. As Catherine Nash (2005: 453) notes, blood-tie kinship 'underpins ideas of the natural order of social life within the state'. It is the 'foundation of the social'. Through delegitimising alternative structures – queer kinship, single motherhood and collective parenting among others – the state stratifies access to intimacy, affection and care. It pushes queer children out of families, for example, and it polices the spaces where queer affection and sexuality can be expressed (see Ingram 1997; Hubbard 2001; Nash and Bain 2007; Oswin 2008). While the incorporation of queer intimacy into the sanctioned institutions of heteromonogamy has afforded rights to those who can assimilate, it once again borders those rights within the parameters of the nation state. Let us not forget that rainbow conservatism legalised gay marriage in Britain in 2014, a year after the Tory–Liberal Democrat coalition government imposed a benefit cap overwhelmingly affecting single mothers. Marriage equality has been wielded by western imperialist regimes as a cultural weapon; a legitimising device for invasion, occupation and 'development' (see Puar 2007; Conrad 2014; Hubbard and Wilkinson 2015; Ritchie 2015). A queer and multiamorous critique of the nuclear family household is therefore an anti-colonial critique. There are contours of commonality between the state's discipline of queer intimacy and the state's racialised policing of migrant kinships: both are concerned with bordering.

Some stories in this book demonstrate the impact of border policy on familial intimacies among renters, framed especially by the 'Hostile Environment' model of immigration control ushered in by Theresa May in 2012. There are also stories of the various ways that economic policy – welfare reform, for example, including cuts to social security benefits – erects borders and barriers around intimacy among low-income renters: containing them, for example, in overcrowded, multigenerational households they cannot afford to leave, or obstructing them from friends and family through atomised, transient lives in temporary accommodation. And, there is the physical, in-your-face bordering of local planning policy at the city-wide and borough level, where speculative construction schemes result in gaping residential inequalities: different doors and gates for social housing tenants on mixed tenure new-build estates; locked away playgrounds earmarked for demolition. These borderings are woven in with state models of legitimate relatedness and intimacy. From the intimacies of the multigenerational migrant household to the intimacies of the housing estate playground, racial capitalist logics obstruct, contain, disperse and fray relational bonds.

Again, however, in so doing, the state reveals the political power of intimacy, and thereby the political power of pleasure, love and desire. Emancipatory projects are increasingly foregrounding these elements for transformative change, reflecting a shift towards somatic healing as an abolitionist strategy, often with spiritual or transpersonal overtones. In her hugely influential 2019 book *Pleasure Activism*, for example, adrienne maree brown uses somatics – 'mind/body/spirit' integration – to ground holistic healing of individuals within mass movements for change. *Pleasure Activism* is a manifesto for the power of intimate, embodied practice for radical collective transformation. For brown, somatic 'longing and pleasure' can be a source of power that results in 'abundant justice'. As such, her work reflects a shift in therapeutic practice away from 'talking' therapy or therapy aimed at 'cognitive behaviour', thus bridging it to the affective turn in interdisciplinary scholarship. Like somatics, affect is concerned with 'pre-cognitive', non-representational feeling. In both a political and therapeutic context, engaging with somatics and with affect decentres the continual 'representation' of harm and injustice as the primary route to alleviate their impacts.

Embodied epistemologies are ancient, and the contemporary shift towards centring the body as a source of knowing reflects a return to these epistemologies rather than the invention of a new paradigm. This return is connected to the politics of indigenous resurgence, whereby the immanent, emergent knowings of the body are the interface through which communities relate and cohere. Edna Manitowabi, head woman for the Eastern Doorway of the Three Fires Midewewin Lodge, describes the Nishnaabeg theory of creation as centring the personal in the original: the 'first person' created is inseparable from 'me, or you'. This relational subjectivity means that community responsibilities are assumed according to one's own 'gifts, abilities, and affiliations', and Nishnaabeg theory is lived through spiritual, physical, emotional, and intellectual engagement in the context of community members' own personal lives (Manitowabi 2011: 75–76). One's own personal divinity is conferred and understood through embodied knowledge, and relationally practised for the benefit of the community. Although affect theory has a comparatively modern western philosophical lineage – for many scholars it can be traced back to the 17th-century philosophy of Baruch Spinoza – there is much in common between some of its political applications and those of indigenous resurgence. This is especially true of the role of affect theory in anarchist strategising for political change. For example, in *Joyful Militancy* by carla bergman and Nick Montgomery, the authors engage with a range of affect theory, anarchist thought and indigenous theory to suggest that the 'rigid radicalism' holding back movements in Turtle Island/North America must make room for the 'subtle work of learning to love places, families, friends, and parts of ourselves in new ways' (bergman and Montgomery 2017: 67). This subtle work involves engaging with activating capacities – the capacity to affect and to be affected. It is the body – of which the mind is part – that is the interface through which this affective activation takes place (see also *Touching Feeling* [2003] by Eve Kosofsky-Sedgwick).

Through this activation, the work of collective political change can be consciously animated. Describing the power of embodied feeling, Audre Lorde writes that the erotic is:

> not a question only of what we do; it is a question of how acutely and fully we can feel in the doing. Once we know the extent to which

we are capable of feeling that sense of satisfaction and completion, we can then observe which of our various life endeavours bring us closest to that fullness. ... Within the celebration of the erotic in all our endeavours, my work becomes a conscious decision – a longed-for bed which I enter gratefully and from which I rise up empowered. (Lorde 1978: 42)

In this book, my emphasis on the political potentiality of intimacy is inspired by these ideas and their lineage. My engagement with embodied experience situates the book within vibrant conversations among feminist geographers about intimate scales of experience, wherein boundaries between mind and body are, in the words of Liz Bondi and Joyce Davidson, 'surely meant to be messed with' (2011: 597) (see also Hutcheson and Longhurst 2017: 46; Salih 2017: 744). But this is not just a book about intimate experience, it is an exploration of practice – of the work of intimacy. It is a documentation of the ways in which capital alienates this work through rent-seeking, and an observation, in turn, of the liberatory potential of reclaiming this labour. Intimacy, like love, is productive – we must study what it 'does' (Morrison et al 2013: 516).

Understanding the precarious intimacies assembling relational life in late capitalism means engaging with love and intimacy as a set of affective practices that are longed for but estranged from hearts by the 'poverty of exchange value' (Gilman-Opalsky 2020). All beings love; all beings are love. There is plenty going on in the world that would convince you otherwise. This is why our collective pursuit of liberation from capitalism is inextricably tied to our collective manifestation of loving awareness. Capital has, as Gilman-Opalsky puts it, 'long sought total autonomy from the real needs of human community' (2020: 45). Indeed, capital is an attractive placeholder for vulnerability – money protects you from needing people. But the 'dead labour' comprising capital, to use Marx's term, incorporates the work of love. A theme running throughout the stories of this book is the siphoning of this work into the bank accounts of landlords and letting agents; the six figure pay-cheques of corporatised housing associations; the dividends of multinational construction giants.

Reproduction: the politics of remaking relationships

The work of intimacy and love looms large in feminist conceptualisations of social reproduction. Over 20 years after British feminist campaigner Eleanor Rathbone won 'family allowances' for mothers in 1945 (Pedersen 1995), socialist feminists expanded Marx's concept of 'social reproduction' as the unpaid labour done by women to reproduce the lives and bodies of the (male) waged worker in capitalist society (see Benston 1969; Federici

1975; Vogel 1983; Fortunati 1995). In these texts, social reproduction is a framework through which patriarchy and capitalism can be co-theorised through an historical materialist analysis – that is to say, an analysis that acknowledges the changing conditions of oppression over time (see Ferguson 2017). From this perspective, social reproduction comprises the practices and labours undertaken to maintain and replenish capitalist relations and gendered hierarchies at a given point in history. As such, Cindi Katz posits that social reproduction should be considered something that both precedes and exceeds production.

Still, not everything that we produce and reproduce in a capitalist society is reducible to tradeable commodities. Social reproduction is necessary for the replenishment of life, and life is much more than capitalism. A contemporary renaissance in writing on social reproduction thus focuses, largely, on the neoliberal depletion of care capacities required for life's maintenance (see Gill and Bakker 2003; Bezanson and Luxton 2006; Katz 2011; Bhattacharya 2017; Bhattacharyya 2018; Gimenez 2018). Life is 'increasingly on edge' (Meehan and Strauss 2015: 2), with implications for the labours that support it. In the words of Nancy Fraser, the intensification of financialised capitalism has drained society of 'the very social capacities on which it depends' (2016). Much contemporary literature on social reproduction thus focuses on the neoliberal depletion of care capacities. For example, Gillespie et al's research (2018) on the Focus E15 mums' campaign in Newham – an ongoing fight by largely single mothers collectively organising against forced displacement from social housing – evidences the drainage of care created by local government disinvestment (see also Fernandez 2018; Luke and Kaika 2019). The transference of national 'deficits' to individual homes has also generated increasing interest in the debt industry and its relationship to household social reproduction. Studies of microfinance, for instance, have shown how social reproduction is 'spatially stretched' through migration and distant labour markets (see Johnson and Woodhouse 2018; Green and Estes 2019). The unaffordability and insecurity of renting in London is similarly depleting of residents' capacities to perform the 'sensuous labour' of everyday life – the intimate work of social reproduction that holds relationships together and enables survival.

Yet, it is important to resist the depoliticisation of social reproduction, and to avoid its characterisation as the innocuous work of caring. The romanticisation of care is braided with its feminisation. This is oppressive to women, but it also obscures the role of reproductive work in maintaining systemic oppression. In reality, the labours and practices we undertake in relationships are often re/productive of power differentials as well as connection, care, love. In this book, I expand social reproduction to include the work of inter-relating among friends, housemates, family members, partners. Through exploring the politics of this social reproduction, I observe some of the ways that precarity is remade by relational practices, rather than relieved. My attention to this is influenced by theories of the neoliberal state that note the decentralisation of public services to local 'empowered' communities as an immersion of non-state actors in the language and practices of governance (Sharma and Gupta 2006). This decentralisation has solidified civil society as an annexe of state authority, revealing the capacity of populations to discipline themselves and each other (see Aretxaga 2003). Power, in the words of Judith Butler (1997), is not only an object of opposition but what we 'preserve in the beings that we are'. In the context of urban housing inequality, this discipline bleeds into the ways that space, shelter and safety are bordered through relational practices – for example, monitoring co-tenants who may lack citizenship status giving them the 'right to rent' (Home Office 2015, 2016); or exploiting quasi-hierarchical roles in shared homes (such as 'lead tenant') for material betterment. As stories in this book reveal, these interactions are often experienced – by all parties – as emotional work. Engaging with relational practice as the work of social reproduction is not to insist on its burdensomeness. Rather, locating the place of this work in the reproduction of power illuminates the liberatory potential of its reclamation.

This is because power is not only power 'over': dominion, coercive authority, exploitation, control. Power is also our collective affective capacity; how 'fully we can feel in the doing', as Lorde writes. This collective power can seem elusive in racial capitalism, as an economic and social system that relies on the differentiated value of life – on 'power over' – to produce capital (see Robinson 1983). Enforcing this system of differentiated value requires state violence, enacted by an assemblage of actors – institutions of government, like the police, but also 'ordinary people'. I think here of the enraged motorists leaping out of their cars and physically dragging elderly climate protestors out of the road. And I think of private landlords, gatekeeping shelter behind extortionate rents, discriminating against racialised and poor residents. It is possible and necessary to conceptualise state violence as incorporating these ordinary transgressions because they, too, uphold and preserve systems of differentiated value. In doing so, they diminish collective power.

Gargi Bhattacharyya writes that ours is a capitalism that can 'extract additional value from people who are deemed to be lesser' (2018: 22). In this system, devalued human beings are shifted to the 'edge' lands of the labour market, or excluded completely from wage relations – they are expelled from the means of their own subsistence, in the service of surplus value (see also Sassen 2014: 29). This additional value is not only extracted through uncompensated labour, it is also generated through the inflated price of subsistence. Rented accommodation is a key example of this. The financialisation of shelter in turn feeds back into the devaluation of labour, because amidst real wage decline, longer hours are required of the worker to make rent. The worker becomes more desperate for work, diminishing their power, and increasing that of their boss and landlord. These conditions, together with the digitalisation of labour – from an app-based gig economy to the acceleration of artificial intelligence – are fertile ground for the rendering of human labour as increasingly disposable, redundant and surplus to capitalists. At the same time, the accumulation of capital relies on human consumption. There is a contradiction, therefore, in the redundancy of the worker but the necessity of the consumer.

This contradiction is resolved by the racialised delineation of human society into different classes: those who have value to capital as consumers, and those rendered surplus and 'ungrievable', to use Butler's term. The COVID-19 pandemic amplified and exposed these social fault lines. In 2021 it was reported that in England, six out of ten people who had died thus far from COVID-19 were disabled (Health Foundation 2021). Across Britain, the discharging of patients from hospitals to care homes without testing them for COVID-19 – a policy ruled unlawful in 2022 – meant that there were over 40,000 COVID-19 deaths among care home residents (Disability Rights UK 2022). Death from COVID-19 has been significantly more likely among Black and Asian communities (Perkin et al 2020), largely owing to economic vulnerabilities. For example, among these communities there is a high proportion of healthcare workers, transport workers and couriers; their jobs required them to remain at workplaces with higher risks of transmission. A higher prevalence of zero-hours contracts among these workers meant no coverage by government financial support schemes and thus no capacity to stop working to protect oneself from the virus. Poor housing and environmental inequality also increased COVID-19 vulnerability for racialised workers, who disproportionately live in overcrowded, multigenerational housing in densely populated urban areas. Then there is the mass disablement of two million people in Britain living with post-COVID-19 symptoms, collectively coined 'Long Covid'. Long Covid sufferers often endure many months, or even years, of crushing exhaustion, pain and dysautonomia, among a swathe of other symptoms affecting several different organs of the body. Throughout this ongoing pandemic, Britain's political and economic regime has thus shifted more racialised and disabled people to the 'edge lands' of subsistence – places abstracted from real livelihood, where precarity is complete and encompassing.

The key 'success' policies of the COVID-19 pandemic's first year were indeed those that solidified racial capitalist logics of differentiated value through singularly protecting a consumer class. These policies were: the furlough scheme for salaried workers, whereby the government gave financial assistance to companies so that employees could stay at home and isolate; and the 'Eat Out To Help Out' scheme to 'boost' the British economy by financially incentivising consumers to go to restaurants through government-subsidised discounts. While the pandemic amplified this differentiation of life, it has been an enduring feature of Britain's political and economic regime – within and beyond the nation's constructed borders – for centuries. A system that extracts value from those 'deemed to be lesser' requires a symbolic modality for this deeming. In a neoliberal society, individual, private wealth ultimately determines one's social destiny. While the liberal ruse purports that this is up for anyone's grab, financial security is largely accessed through symbolic currencies that exceed the money relation. At the sharp edges of precarity, this differentiation is more pronounced. For example, in documenting the struggle for sex workers' rights, Molly Smith and Juno Mac (2018) highlight how possession of a British passport, cis-genderedness and Whiteness are key currencies in sex workers' capacity to achieve subsistence, as well as relative safety and security at work.

This system of value differentiation has exhaustive implications for the work of social reproduction. In essence, the work of life's replenishment is harder and denser for those shifted to the market's edge-lands and wastelands. This book therefore joins a chorus of different conversations seeking to redress the ways that social reproduction is theorised beyond its original conceptualisation as the unpaid work of predominantly White, heterosexual, married women with children. After all, in a middle-class context, there is a history of these women and their husbands actually relying on racialised labour for social reproduction. Slavery, Alys Weinbaum (2019) writes, has a 'specifically reproductive afterlife' (see also Cooke 1950; Lorde 1981; Roberts 1997; hooks 2000a; West and Knight 2017). Expanding social reproduction theory to include the breadth of differentiation separating and hierarchising workers – people engaged in the labour of sustaining life – demonstrates the enduring political potentiality of this framework for conceptualising the relationship between exploitation and oppression, and for exploring the role of 'extramarket' currencies in determining the 'market' valuation of human lives (Bhattacharya 2017).

One of the strategies for making this differentiation legible is thus attending to labour that is extramarket, invisibilised, immaterial or disregarded – the 'everyday and sometimes everynight' experiences of work, in the words of Kathi Weeks (2011: 18). Discerning invisibilised labour can reveal suppressed subjectivities. This, in turn, awakens us to the ways in which our joyful alterity is abused through the division of our worth. And in this awakening, we find a transmutation of power from hierarchy and authority to collective desire and will. In this book, I identify labour in unexpected places, times and encounters: the tender work of mending familial estrangement; the mental and emotional labour of educating parents about the housing market; the de-escalation of twilight conflicts. In revealing the political economy of these labours – their relationship to the production of surplus value, their necessitation by urban inequality – I aim to offer richer and deeper renderings of respondents' lives and identities.

Identifying such practices as work is nonetheless contentious, owing to the 'concept creep' of emotional labour as a term (see Beck 2018). Arlie Hochschild, who coined the phrase 'emotional labour' in 1983 to describe the expressive and gestural work required of air stewards, has critiqued the term's recent 'domestication'. Indeed, with growing awareness of especially gendered disparities in listening, support-giving, encouragement and other forms of emotional care, there has been an increase in online discourse critiquing embedded expectations of emotional labour in relationships. While the politics of emotional labour are highly pertinent, such critiques often dovetail with neoliberal frameworks of healing that are centred on private individual therapy, self-improvement, and an embedded stigmatisation of inter-relational, community responsibility. An individualised therapeutic solution to emotional labour guarantees that this labour will remain alienated.

Through discerning modes of emotional, affective and intimate labour in this book, I am not seeking to illuminate metabolic practices that should be abolished, or that could be 'resolved' with a wage, a fee or an outsourced worker. Rather, I am concerned with the alienation of the necessary work of life's replenishment. Marx describes the labour process as involving the realisation of something that 'already existed in the imagination of the labourer at its commencement' (1967/1887: 127). Alienated labour involves the subsuming of this imagination – the original vision is changed or lost through the extractive relations of capital. I apply this idea to the affective labours discussed in this book by focusing on their alienation by rentier capitalism. Who, or what, is commercially benefiting from these labours and their geographical and temporal organisation (Gillian Welch sings: 'Never minded working hard, it's who I'm working for')? What are the conditions within which these labours are carried out? How do these relations shape the sovereignty of hearts?

If alienated labour involves the distortion and extraction of the labourer's creative imagination, then alienated emotional labours involve the work of remaking fantasy as much as reproducing material life. Many of the stories in this book speak to the significance of fantasy – of hopes, aspirations, expectations and 'anxious strivings' (see Katz 2017) – in the mediation of intimate relationships: a mother's fantasy of her son earning enough to buy a house in cash, for example; a millennial renter's fantasy of being asked to live in his girlfriend's parents' house; desires for distance from mythological, racialised urban danger. As respondents' accounts attest, such fantasies engender affective work so that they are integrated – or dispersed – within relationships. Attending to this imaginative plane brings us back to the psychic dimensions of neoliberal precarity, where nostalgic longings for a lost economic era drive practices that are both symptomatic and productive of precarious conditions. Engaging with these psychic dimensions thus reconciles alienated affective labour to the reproduction of precarity, and subsequently to the reproduction of differentiated value. In other words, through exploring the affective labours undertaken to reproduce relationships, we can also identify the social reproduction of structural advantage, as 'other people's children' (Katz 2017) or friends, lovers, dependents, cohabitants are seen as a threat to the sustenance of this advantage (see Kaufman 2005; Holloway and Pimlott-Wilson 2016).

Like an ocean current, an historical materialist approach to social reproduction thus flows through this book, carrying the role of relational labour in the recreation of class society as well as the necessity of this same labour in the replenishment – and liberation – of life. The contradictions of this current sometimes buffet and pull the text into rock pools that appear politically stagnant, as we come up against the enmeshment of life's work with the reproduction and advancement of precarity across generations. But it is precisely in these ostensibly stuck places, these rock pools, that unexpected ecosystems form – new ways of life. In the context of London's housing crisis, new ways of life are necessitated by these contradictory politics of social reproduction, not only because of intensified imperatives to care and depend in the absence of state investment, but also because the metabolic means of class reproduction are so eroded. In *The Logic of Practice*, Bourdieu's conceptualisation of social reproduction rests on the 'economy of material and symbolic exchanges between the generations' that leads to the reproduction of class (1980: 167). This is often described as social 'mobility', in popular commentary. As we know, in Britain, neoliberal precarity is entwined with the dismantlement of this mobility; the children of generations who benefited from the postwar welfare state have been stripped of the same reproductive means. This includes their capacity to biologically reproduce: to produce new generations.

While lamentations about being 'priced out of parenthood' (Cosslett 2018) have tended to emanate from White, middle-class commentators, demographic shifts evidence widening economic infertility across British society, largely as a result of the cost of housing. These are nevertheless fertile grounds for the recalibration – and retrieval – of reproduction as a site for imagining, in the words of Ginsburg and Rapp (1995), 'new cultural futures and transformations, through personal struggle, generational mobility, social movements, and the contested claims of powerful religious and political ideologies' (see also Anagnost 1995; Strathern 1995; Franklin & Ragoné 1998). Through capturing the precarious intimacies assembling the everyday lives and envisioned futures of millennial renters in London, this book contributes to the ongoing expansion of reproduction as a site of social and political reimagination. My focus on a specific generational experience reflects this troubling of reproduction, as millennials' capacity to remake their parents' kinship models eludes economically, and as the waning cultural appeal of the nuclear family butts against nostalgia for tradition, security and certainty in a precarious world. In the cramped spaces of London's rented homes, reproductive practices and desires respond to the shifting sands of precarity. Longed-for kinship futures ebb from probability, replaced with the more immediate reproductive imperative of remaking everyday life in nebulous, fluctuating constellations of uneasy dependency. The precarious intimacies assembled in response to this imperative are filled with ambivalence, as the grief of lost futures and stressful presents entangles with affective strategies to assert control, as well as affective labours to care, interdepend and provide safety. But by reaching into these rock pools, where the water of time appears stuck, we touch the remaking of temporality itself. The stories and discussions in this book speak to a remaking of reproductive temporality, through highlighting the futures that are etched out through the uneasy necessity of prolonged house-sharing and multigenerational dependency. And, these stories speak to the animating power of intimate experience in articulating alienation. Through identifying and expressing the alienation of affective labour by rentier capitalism, I hope that this book can contribute to building affective capacities and thus to building collective power.

Histories

A brief history of housing and empire

The roots of housing inequality in Britain are in the unequal ownership of land. Activist and writer Guy Shrubsole (2019) has revealed, for example, that half of England's land is owned by 1 per cent of the population, a number that mainly comprises corporations and aristocrats. Similar circumstances characterise land ownership in Wales, Scotland and Northern Ireland (see also Wightman 1996; Cahill 2002). The origins of this inequality can be found in the mutual development of private property and agriculture from the early Middle Ages, when throughout Europe, ancient rights of common use were replaced by the institutionalised right to enclose and cultivate privately owned land (Mazoyer and Roudart 2006: 335). In England, this process formally began with the Norman invasion, with William the Conqueror parcelling land and granting estates to 'land-lords'. Enclosure movements subsequently dominated land legislation from the 12th to 19th centuries, mainly focused on the privatisation of open fields and 'waste' lands used by commoners for gathering and grazing (Christophers 2018: 167–176). Land that had provided for thousands of people through a rich diversity of wildlife, fuel and crops was bordered by fences, ditches and hedges for commercial farming. Mass evictions of agricultural labourers from their plots were often violent. In *Capital Volume One* (1967/1887: 682), Marx describes the 'systematic rooting out' of 3,000 in Sutherland, their homes 'destroyed and burnt, all their fields turned into pasturage'. While centuries of enclosure were met with centuries of resistance (see Wood 2007; Linebaugh 2014), many ancient rights of common have been effectively extinguished in England and Wales (Foundation for Common Land 2019).

Emerging from these developments in landownership was England's urban property market, where throughout the Middle Ages, large-scale non-occupying ownership intersected with single-occupier ownership of burgage plots or dwellings. By the early 1300s, London was divided into units comparable to contemporary freeholds (Harding 2002: 552). Historian Vanessa Harding has shown that, much like the housing sector now, the medieval urban property market involved multiple tenurial interests: rents could be owed to a landlord for properties owned through burgage tenure or quit-rents could be owed by multiple units to a central institution – usually ecclesiastical – that had granted properties to individual occupiers (2002: 553–554). Indeed, by the early modern period, the overwhelming majority of households in London were rented, incorporating a varied landscape of landlord–tenant relations that was not always grounded in socioeconomic class. For example, William C. Baer (2011) has highlighted that landlords, who comprised the working class and gentry, could simultaneously be tenants and vice versa, and landlordism was often used as a source of independent income for women and supplementary income for struggling households.

Early modern landlords were nonetheless unregulated and lacked formal organisation, and amidst London's population boom in the 17th century, this contributed to increasing divides in living standards. With a steady in-migration of young, poor workers, London's population more than doubled over the course of the 17th century, creating the demographic conditions for a housing shortage. In the absence of sufficient housing infrastructure, rising socioeconomic inequality resulted, with poorer tenants in less stable employment paying higher premiums for leases with shorter durations, often in overcrowded and cramped conditions. The current unaffordability and disrepair crisis in London's housing maps onto this history, and it is driven by the same issues.

The intensified urbanisation that accompanied industrialisation between the mid-18th century and the First World War transformed the demographic landscape of Britain and increased socioeconomic inequality (Law 1967). In a historical echo of neoliberal Britain, increasingly disparate urban living standards in the 19th century were largely attributable to the deregulation of the construction industry and the financialisation of housing. As systematised production increasingly dictated the temporal and geographical life of labour, the broader working-class experience was characterised by housing and labour markets that were unhindered by legislation or union power (see Rodger 1987: 112). By 1881, the number of people living in a London house averaged just under eight. Overcrowding brought higher levels of alcoholism, violence, stunted growth, mental illness and infectious disease. Life expectancies declined in England's biggest cities, reaching lows of 30 and 31 years that had only occasionally been observed throughout the entire early modern period (see Szreter and Mooney 1998: 89). The prevailing liberal ideology, encapsulated by the New Poor Law 1834, meant that requirements for residential building were minimal. Supervisory powers of building agencies were curbed, and the transferral of housing responsibilities to local councils resulted in any residual obligations being largely ignored. Moreover, the longevity of Victorian housing meant that unregulated building standards had ramifications for subsequent generations – adjustments to existing stock could not fix more integral problems. Coupled with over-speculation and over-expansion, most homes for urban workers were built shoddily and in hurried bursts (Rodger 1987: 120–123). Remembering Grenfell and the cheap cladding hastily wrapped around that tower, we recognise that we still live in this history.

Nonetheless, as the second half of the 19th century progressed, criticism of the living standards of the urban poor swelled in cultural commentary, and as the injustices of housing exploitation received greater attention, accompanying movements in science and culture threw the issue of working-class housing to the political fore. Discoveries in bacteriology and increasing emphases on middle-class respectability foregrounded the home as the locus of temperance and morality (Steinbach 2016). And in the wake of Chartism, fears of revolution intermingled with fears of the spread of infectious disease to social and political elites. These developments, together with the purchase of philanthropy and liberal reform, resulted in the housing conditions of the urban poor being taken up by parliament in the 1860s, where attention was centred on the slum dwellings of inner London. Responsibility for sanitation and inhabitability was assigned to property owners via Torrens' Act 1868, and in 1875, the demolition of slums with high mortality rates was made law through Cross' Act. In practice, however, many people displaced through slum demolition were not rehoused – the idea that the 'pigs created the sty' endured (Rodger 1987: 126–129; see also Yelling 1982). The vast majority of low-income housing remained in the private sector, and middle-class suburbanisation increasingly meant that urban poverty was out-of-sight, out-of-mind (Rodger 1987: 129). John Boughton (2018) has also highlighted that, since philanthropic housing solutions were profit-based – a 5 per cent rate of return was guaranteed on building investments – private financial gain continued to drive housing construction, with steep rents locking out those most in need.

Late 19th-century and early 20th-century criticism of the conditions of the urban poor often focused on overcrowding, with representation of overcrowded slums drawing heavily on colonial imagery, from Middle

Passage slave ships to the 'immoral' dwellings of indigenous communities (Swanson 1977). These images fed into the cultural decline of laissez-faire in the 1880s, with liberal reformers increasingly linking the conditions of the urban poor to a loss of White Christian piety (see Mearns' *The Bitter Cry of Outcast London*, published in 1883). Together with the growing influence of Marxism and Fabianism, these cultural shifts materialised in policies such as the Housing of the Working Classes Act 1890, which allowed local councils to build their own housing stock. From Garden Cities to cottage suburbs, ambitious architectural schemes were specifically designed to provide decent and attractive housing for the working class. But as Brian Lund's work (2016: 67) has highlighted, rents were still unaffordable for the poorest – the latter were 'filtered' out of the system. In fact, without affordable replacement housing, overcrowding was often intensified by slum clearances. By the time the First World War broke out, council homes numbered only 24,000.

Colonial tropes of density, proximity and dirt became co-constitutive with ideas of genetic superiority in the housing initiatives of the interwar era (Olechnowicz 1997). This period oversaw the construction of over a million council homes, initially as a result of Lloyd George's placatory 'homes for heroes' electoral campaign. In this campaign, the deepening cultural associations of slum-dwelling with genetic inferiority formed part of a discourse of physical pedigree that crystallised around eugenics and the vindication of war (see Lund 2016: 69; Boughton 2018). The historical backdrop to Labour's Housing Act 1930 was therefore the integration of genetic advancement and economic 'mass upliftment'. This act attempted to eradicate slums by incentivising their clearance and enforcing rehousing. After the Second World War's destruction of half a million homes, Labour's victory in 1945 ushered in a period of housing reform wherein local authorities were the main providers (Holmes 2003: 3). However, as Beverley Mullings (1991) has shown, while 'respectable' White working-class families were invited into the fold of national betterment, Black families were largely excluded owing to an exclusionary five-year residential condition embedded in immigration policies on housing.

Postwar housing discrimination against Black communities was also connected to Britain's shifting race relations during the Second World War. While the fall of Nazism eroded the acceptability of 'scientific' racism, efforts by campaigners like George Padmore to criminalise racial discrimination were met with disinterest from the Labour government, who discouraged Black Caribbean immigration as a solution to postwar labour shortages (Olusoga 2016; Gopal 2019). News of British recruitment drives nonetheless spread across the West Indies, particularly among those who had already served in the British military during the war, and the subsequent arrival of the *Empire Windrush* to Britain in 1948 saw the in-migration of almost 500 Caribbean workers – all of them obviously British passport-holders, as

British colonialism had forced them to be crown subjects. It was subsequently in *spite* of the British government's opposition that Caribbean migration to Britain increased in the early 1950s, and it should be noted, therefore, that Nye Bevan's construction of townships for a 'mix' of social groups was manifestly not with a view to multicultural public housing provision.

Taking office in 1951, after local authorities struggled to meet building targets, the Conservative Party entrenched the racialised dynamics of postwar reconstruction. Although the Tory government oversaw the construction of 229,000 dwellings by 1953, standards declined and the concept of council homes as 'poor' housing was re-established (Holmes 2003; Boughton 2018). For example, as Mullings highlights, local authorities were made to specialise in slum clearances and rehousing initiatives while the government concurrently encouraged owner occupation and landlordism (this was echoed in the Localism Act 2011). A shift towards funding high-rise blocks of flats came to characterise council housing provision, and this was continued by the Labour government's mass building initiatives in the 1970s. Enduring emphases on owner-occupier benefits nonetheless stymied building plans, and in the wake of the racist Immigration Acts of 1968 and 1971, increasing numbers of racialised communities were not rehoused. Coupled with the government's shift in focus to housing improvement rather than construction, and the tightening of public spending on housing amidst high interest and inflation, Black and Brown populations bore the brunt of homelessness.

So then, as now. Tightened public spending, high interest and inflation: these are three core economic characteristics of Britain in 2023. While they are always presented as inexorable by our political regime, these conditions have been manufactured through the growth of the financial industry as a successor to the British Empire. The built-in racism of unequal housing provision is part of this imperialist-financial legacy, whereby the wealth of colonised populations has been stolen, hidden and used for the continued inflation and enclosure of land. For example, the 1925 Trust Act legalised the storing untraced offshore funds, creating a loophole for foreign-based companies that effectively made Britain a tax haven (Palan 2003; see also Guex 2000). This loophole was expanded in the wake of Suez Crisis in the 1950s (see Harvey 2003). As a result of the crisis, increased speculation against the pound rendered the dollar/sterling parity decreasingly feasible (Boughton 2018). Seeking to manage this, the Bank of England sold off its dollar reserves to maintain the same exchange rate, restricting the use of the pound for trade in non-sterling areas. However, in response, overseas banks sought out different forms of finance in the form of non-resident US dollars (Burn 2006: 230). The Bank of England did not prevent this, automatically creating a market where specific transactions in foreign currencies between non-resident parties were treated as if they were not occurring in Britain – or indeed anywhere. The so-called 'Euromarket' was born in London (Palan et al 2009), becoming a crucial vehicle for circumventing international fiscal regulations and propelling the creation of more offshore markets throughout the 1960s. A cannibalising meta-economy was born, one that did not play by the rules of ordinary tax-payers, and that ultimately took over the organs of parliamentary democracy.

Despite the growth of this cannibalising financial system, postwar inflation in Britain was generally blamed on the international price of oil and on British workers. In the 2020s, we remain caught in this same rhetorical web. In the 1960s, for example, Britain's cheap access to oil was hindered by transnational cooperation in the Middle East, especially the newly established Organization of the Petroleum Exporting Countries (OPEC) (Garavini 2011: 475). OPEC's leverage increased revenues for governments in oil-producing regions throughout the 1960s, posing further political challenges to oil-consumer regions and multinationals through the accession of radical governments across some OPEC member states – Libya, most notably. This threatened Britain's oil supply, crystallising in the late 1960s and early 1970s with the Six-Day War and Yom Kippur War, both instigated as a result of Israel's imperialist occupation of Gaza, the Sinai Peninsula and the West Bank in Palestine (see Bichler and Nitzan 1996; Harvey 2003; Judt 2008). Members of OPEC threatened to cut production by 5 per cent and to post monthly price increases until Israel withdrew. They also launched a complete embargo on oil to nations that supported Israel. Between 1970 and 1973, oil prices increased by 300 per cent (Schumacher 1985; Garavini 2011). This impacted on British oil consumption, which declined by 11 per cent by the mid-1970s.

Just as we have been forced to listen to Liz Truss and Rishi Sunak blame contemporary inflation on Putin's war in Ukraine, the OPEC oil shock is widely considered to have been the main source of British inflation in the 1970s. But it is not the whole story. The oil shock in the 1970s coincided with government attempts to engineer rapid growth through reducing interest rates, deregulating bank lending and cutting taxes, causing industrial wages to lag. Wage demands – culminating in the 1972 and 1973/1974 miners' strikes – became another of the government's scapegoats for both inflation and fuel scarcity, engendering even further decline (see Beckett 2009; Medhurst 2014; Hellema 2018). By the summer of 1975, inflation had reached almost 27 per cent. Together with the virtually non-existent taxation of oil companies as North Sea oil extraction began, an ensuing fiscal crisis forced Britain to take a US$4 billion loan from the International Monetary Fund. Yet, amidst the primacy of a right-wing media machine, the subsequent 'winter of discontent' paved the way for Margaret Thatcher's electoral success (see López 2014; Shepherd 2015). This history teaches us to suspect and pick apart invocations of 'inflation' as uncontrollable responses to global market movements. Those markets have been formed in the image of our own crumbling empire. And they are the matrices within which the renters in this book are caught. Building a contextual understanding of rentier capitalism in London therefore requires looking outwards geographically, far beyond the city and far beyond Britain's domestic borders, because Britain's economy has never been domestic.

As we have seen, the imperialist activities of Britain in the Middle East were crucial in the establishment of a deregulated financial industry and, in turn, the overseeing of inflation in the British economy. Britain's continued close ties to violent imperialist administrations in the Middle Eastern region (and of course beyond) have co-produced decades of war, forcing millions from their home countries, many of whom have settled in London. The logic behind this 'vested interest in regional instability' is capital accumulation: as Middle Eastern oil production decreased in the 1970s, the United States stoked conflict between Iraq and Iran, as well as in Libya and Kuwait, increasing demand for weapons (Bichler and Nitzan 1996). In 1988 the British state subsequently won a US$25 billion weapons deal to supply Saudi Arabia. Despite Britain's sale of weapons to Saudi Arabia being ruled unlawful by national courts in 2019, arms exports to the regime have continued year on year (Sabbagh and McKernan 2019). This embedded financial relationship between Britain and imperialist, militarily aggressive regimes like Saudi Arabia is monumentalised in London's built environment, which is increasingly characterised by foreign direct investment (FDI) from oil-rich regions. For example, in 2020 it was revealed that the President of the United Arab Emirates, Sheikh Khalifa, has a London property portfolio worth £5 billion, generating hundreds of millions in rental income annually (Davies 2020). With a Brexiteer government keen to establish a trade deal with the six-country Gulf Cooperation Trading Council bloc, this kind of FDI is on track to expand.

Through the racialised demonisation of poor dwellings in slum clearances; through immigration legislation with five-year residential conditions for Black families; through the selling-off of the city to geopolitical accomplices in war and ecological destruction: Empire is ever-present in London's built environment, and the residents whose stories narrate this book are variously entangled in its web. This is a reflection of the migratory flows that compose London's diversity. In this book, there are stories of diaspora directly caused by British imperialism; journeys to London necessitated by war and regional impoverishment. And, there is the ongoing experience of this diaspora in urban neighbourhoods, where migrant populations are squeezed out through the same processes: the enclosure and financialisation of land and space.

The precarity characterising renters' lives in London must be understood through these legacies and the differentially situated subjectivities they produce. In turn, so must renters' practices and perspectives of reproduction. While a sense of reproductive obstruction for middle-class millennial renters may relate more strongly to the incapacity to own a home and create a family household, reproductive obstruction for poor tenants, especially in racialised migrant communities, may involve more expansive and more immediate hindrances to the replenishment of kin relations: the obstruction of existing children's lives through the robbery of their clean air; the eradication of their green and recreational spaces to grow, play, connect and create; their displacement and exposure to eviction and homelessness; their policing rather than nurturing through youth services. All renters, including those with middle-class backgrounds, jobs or bank accounts, are exposed to different dimensions of this precarity, whether they have dependents or not. But to rigorously understand the imperialist systems undergirding that precarity, we must recognise the presence of differentiated value – of inequality – in mediating the sharpness and depth of its impacts on renters' lives.

Capital city

The precarity renters encounter in London is the result of deliberately manufactured unaffordability. This unaffordability can be traced back to speculative property investment, and this, in turn, unfolds from financial deregulation. A deregulated financial system means that governments are no longer able to control the amount of money that is in circulation, guaranteeing inflation. In the late 20th century, this was not only a result of inadequate taxation, but because most money began to originate in private banks, since weakened regulations allowed them to print it (see Harvey 2007; Pettifor 2018). Weak regulations also meant no criteria as to what credit could be loaned for. Private banks wanted to grant loans at the highest rates of return, and an explosion in speculation resulted. With ever-increasing credit generated through speculative finance, inflation escalated once more (Pettifor 2018: 48–49). In her book *Big Capital*, Anna Minton observes that high levels of inflation and high rates of interest are appealing conditions for speculative investors, who are attracted to rising prices that 'exclude users' (2017: 36). With its high rates of rental return and value appreciation, property became an optimal location for private business to store surplus value.

In the 1980s, this process was accelerated by the orthodoxy of privatisation and deregulation at the heart of Thatcherism. While tackling inflation was a central feature of Thatcher's monetarist rhetoric, her continued deregulation of the financial system and fixation on home ownership guaranteed its continuation (Tomlinson 2012: 75). Not only did more credit flood the system, but unregulated private banks also acquired the power to increase interest rates throughout the 1980s. This meant that money was more easily available but more expensive. Meanwhile, the British economy was reshaped around the artificial inflation of owner-occupied private property. First, the

Housing Act 1980 passed legislation to realise the 'Right to Buy' scheme, mandating local authorities to sell council homes to tenants for sometimes nearly half of what they were worth. Constituting the biggest privatisation in Britain to date, this sell-off was worth £40 billion in its first two-and-a-half decades (Meek 2014: 414–416). In 1982, the subsidising of housing for low-income residents was also transferred to local authorities in the form of housing benefit, which has ploughed so much public money into the private rented sector that Vicky Spratt describes it as a 'state subsidy to private landlords' (2022: 35). While council stock was being gutted, however, the construction of private homes fell. This created the conditions for acute house price inflation. Thatcher's privatisation of public land – through targeting its 'underuse' – further accelerated the impact of land prices on property inflation (see Curwen 1994: 59; Minton 2017: 31–33; Christophers 2018: 357).

Property inflation created financial incentives for the expansion of private landlordism, encouraged by the 1988 Housing Act's creation of the Assured Shorthold Tenancy (AST). The AST allowed landlords to carry out 'no-fault' evictions at two months' notice. The 1988 Act also signalled a return to social housing provision without public expenditure through housing associations (non-profit organisations that emerged from Victorian philanthropic trusts) in partnership with private finance. With the introduction of the 'buy to let' mortgage in 1996 and New Labour's extension of 'Right to Buy' to assured tenants in council housing and housing associations, the growth of the private rented sector was hastened as social housing stock shrank (see Walker and Jeraj 2016). By the last years of New Labour under Gordon Brown, 'social housing' was no longer even defined in terms of public investment (see Housing and Regeneration Act 2008).

The socioeconomic and cultural impact of Right to Buy was extremely significant. It solidified a culture in which policies to address economic marginalisation and need were considered impingements upon private property rights. These rights were increasingly aligned with an ethno-centric nation of modern consumers, freed from the fetters of the miners' union 'ransom' and imbued with a renewed imperial pride following the Falklands War (Jackson and Saunders 2012). Through her construction of a 'deserving' people, racism was a key tool in Thatcher's neoliberalism. Racism was not a departure from the previous Labour government (let's not forget that 'rivers of blood' Enoch Powell actually joined Wilson's Labour in the mid-1970s). However, the 'anti-asylum' character of Thatcherite racism was new, because it exploited the rise in refugees fleeing war in the Middle East. Racist oratory became policies (Cole 2017: 38): the British Nationality Act 1981 introduced three new types of citizenship to differentiate between White 'patrials' that were 'closely connected' to Britain, and those deemed less desirable. Police violence against Black communities escalated (see

Dixon 1983: 162–171; Panayi 2010: 42; Eddo-Lodge 2018: 149). Thatcher's affiliation between Whiteness and self-sufficiency ensured that much of the new middle class supported her neoliberal economic policies. Inflation was blamed on the poor, fiscal consolidation heralded as the solution, and the price of assets steadily increased. In this way, citizenship became ideologically tied to market participation, since only those with purchasing power were deemed as valuable to the economy.

In the wake of Right to Buy, the key market enfranchising citizens was the housing market. A language integrating affordability with consumption subsequently began appearing in policy discourse on housing. Blair's New Labour government from 1997 and the Conservative/Liberal Democrat coalition that came to power in 2010 both couched housing provision entirely in the language of market 'affordability', prompting the proliferation of new sub-markets within the private rented sector. Landlordism was further encouraged through the 2011 Localism Act, which devolved housing responsibilities to local housing authorities, obliging them to address them through the private sector. The transition to private rental investment was lubricated yet further by changes in 2011 to Stamp Duty Land Tax, making it cheaper for large-scale investors to purchase rented property. Stamp Duty has remained lower for buy-to-let investors than for people seeking to buy their first home to live in: another tax break for landlords. Real Estate Investment Trusts also encouraged investors to increase their property portfolios, through extending large-scale property investment capabilities to individual 'residential' investors (HM Treasury 2012). As detailed in the 2011 Housing Strategy for England, for institutional investors, 'Build to Let' funds allowed the large-scale buying up of property for letting. Build to Rent, as it is now known, has become a distinct asset class of the British private rented sector, mainly cashing in on the long-term renting needs of affluent young professionals priced out of ownership, although 'affordable' stock quotas are minimal and generally unenforced (White 2018).

As London's housing crisis deepened in the early 2010s and greater numbers of young urban professionals were consigned to long-term private renting, the government awoke to the political benefits of engaging with this new class of downwardly mobile, frustrated tenants. National and local policy began to respond to those 'locked out of home ownership' or 'forced to flat-share' (Mayor of London 2014: 38) by paying lip-service to private rental oversight and expanding an 'affordable' intermediate housing market, often through private-sector partnerships with housing associations. The Housing and Planning Act 2016, for example, provided for a database of 'rogue landlords and property agents', and extended Right to Buy to housing association tenants. In the social sector, fixed-term tenancies were ruled as mandatory over secure tenancies. Housing associations have indeed become vehicles for stealthy privatisation through 'affordability', driving the superficially appealing construction of affordable homes while often displacing council estate tenants in order to do so. In 2018, Theresa May announced a grandiose £2 billion fund for housing associations to build low-cost homes, while reinforcing her 'personal mission to get more people onto the housing ladder' (HM Government 2018).

So, while a new language of housing affordability addressed a broadly millennial demographic of 'locked-out' private renters, 'social' became a moniker for market non-participation. The entanglement of affordability with market participation has been especially salient in city-level planning policy. For example, as Mayor of London, Boris Johnson declared aims of delivering 42,000 homes per year, with 15,000 earmarked as affordable. Of these, 40 per cent were 'low cost' home ownership and 'Affordable Rent for working Londoners' through the provision of mixed products to attract new providers and forms of private finance (Mayor of London 2014). One of these products was the now-ended 'Help to Buy' scheme for homes with values up to £600,000, with no income limit for eligibility. Schemes such as Help to Buy fall under the broad remit of the 'intermediate housing market', a touted solution to the housing crisis that generally relies on private-sector partnerships with large-scale housing associations to meet housing need while delivering high returns. 'Shared Ownership' is another such scheme: residents purchase a share of a leasehold property but pay an additional monthly rent to the housing provider. Through such schemes, the nebulous definition of affordability has been used by councils and developers to ostensibly meet social housing need, while actually diversifying profit streams for private developers and corporate landlords.

This has been advanced by Mayor Sadiq Khan. In his first term, the Affordable Homes Programme saw the dispensation of £3.15 billion of central government funding for the creation of 90,000 new homes, with 58,500 of these homes earmarked for either shared ownership or London Living Rent, and 29,000 set at Affordable Rent. London Living Rent was pegged at a third of the average household income for the specific borough, and Affordable Rent was allocated according to eligibility. Both London Living Rent and shared ownership were targeted at middle-income households. Affordable Rent, although targeted at lower-income households, was also set at up to 80 per cent of local market rates – hardly affordable if taken to its limit (Hill 2016). To accelerate the delivery of the programme, the 2017 draft London Plan included a 'threshold approach to viability'. This meant that development schemes could fast-track building if they met an 'affordability' threshold without public subsidies, functioning as an incentive for developers to increase affordable housing stock (Mayor of London 2017a, 2017b, 2017c). However, in practice this has propelled urban regeneration schemes that have ridden roughshod over the desires, bonds and needs of existing communities, largely comprising social housing tenants. Owing to the opacity of affordability, then, housing associations have cashed in on the viability threshold through developments that enhance their rental revenue. Britain's 13 biggest housing associations paid their executives £22 million in the 2022–2023 financial year (Kersley 2023).

I spent 2022 in the Green Group office of London's City Hall, trawling through policy documents, communicating with residents and housing campaigners, and helping to facilitate the committee work of Green Assembly Members. In my role, I discovered that the policy-driven fragmentation of tenants into varying degrees of worth, according to their market participation, has etched a landscape in which the delivery of 'affordable housing' is displacing vast numbers of people and driving gentrification processes that literally do the opposite of increasing affordability. This fragmentation is felt within the housing movement, too, because the interests and demands of private market renters – often summarised as 'more affordable housing' – is often at odds with the interests of social housing campaigners, whose homes on estates are threatened with the wrecking ball on the premise that 'more affordable housing' must be built on their bulldozed remains.

During the pre-election period prior to council elections in May 2022, there were many calls from local tenant unions for councillors – predominantly Labour councillors – to pledge support for 'affordable housing' construction quotas. Councillors' promises to advocate for the delivery affordable housing were chalked up as wins. I wanted to celebrate too, and to support the efforts of my friends in the movement for private renter rights. But my enthusiasm was dampened by the knowledge that councillors have political and even financial interests in regeneration schemes that are legitimated on the basis of affordable housing quotas, and these schemes drive the racialised and classed displacement of social renters out of the city. Southwark's Leo Pollak, for example, was forced to quit his council role after it was discovered that he was using a fictional Twitter account to pressure residents to vote for infill development schemes. Beyond such murky dealings, the environmental implications of mass building programmes fundamentally contradict central government climate goals. England's entire net zero carbon budget would be spent by its current house-building target. Why, as so many of the residents I have connected with asked, is retrofitting and refurbishment not an option? Why must 'affordable housing' be constructed from scratch, on ground zero of existing, well-designed postwar housing stock? If the regeneration of estates truly is for the meeting of the affordable housing needs of poor and vulnerable families, why are most of these homes so small, and designed for single dwellers or couples?

This book challenges the hierarchisation of private and social tenant that has come to characterise policy responses to growing housing need. By examining the experiences of both private and social tenants, I also want to trouble the class politics of reproduction; to think beyond reproduction as a future-oriented set of desires for an idealised familial kinship, and to consider the ways that the daily reproduction of lives, bodies and relationships is shaped by a market that trades on these very longings. This market compensates middle-class millennial renters with sub-market schemes promising piecemeal foots on property ladders, and appeases private tenant grievances with affordable housing construction schemes. But these very same compensations and appeasements are so often obstructions for millennials living in socially rented accommodation: residents with children living in overcrowded homes rented from housing associations or councils, watching mature trees uprooted from their communal gardens, watching new-builds go up, and watching young private renter couples move in, their hearts full of tentative hopes of settling down and building something.

It shouldn't be obvious

In Hackney, urban regeneration has not always been in the service of profit. In the 1890s, on the initiative of the Reverend Evelyn Gardiner, the graveyard at St John's Church in Hackney underwent regeneration for public use. With designs drawn up by Bloomsbury architect Fanny Wilkinson, the burial ground was refurbished, and paths, plants, grass and seating were created. All of it was funded by London County Council, the Board of Works and the Metropolitan Public Gardens Association (London Gardens 2014). When I first began this book, the same area was blocked off by huge screens. Behind them, cranes, scaffolding and construction workers developed 58 luxury apartments on top of the old cemetery, with asking prices starting from £575,000 (Hackney Gardens 2019). Now, in 2023, the apartments are a year old. A sterile gated enclave is carved into this formerly public park. Such images have become routine in Hackney.

New housing developments in the borough can also contain and conceal older council blocks. At the Pembury Estate, I saw this process with my own eyes. Situated near Hackney Downs park, Pembury has been portrayed as violent and disorderly for decades. Estate residents' have been historically involved in local uprisings and subcultures, from resistance to the council's anti-squatting policy in 1993 to anti-police unrest during the 2011 riots. And, Pembury has been afflicted by 'postcode' gang violence unfolding from criminalised survival work (Hackney History 2011; see also Phoenix and Phoenix 2012). Regeneration began in 2016, with the construction of several new buildings and blocks of flats, including a street-facing community centre, Co-operative supermarket, café and restaurant. Of the 268 new homes built by Peabody Housing Association, 149 were for private ownership, 40 for shared ownership and 79 for rent. The new street façade is literally built in front of the older council housing blocks and community centre, which at the time of writing is earmarked for demolition.

I spoke to Catherine, an older leaseholder who owned her council flat through Right to Buy. She had raised her son on the estate, witnessing the ebb and flow of resident demographics and police presence. For Catherine, there had been a decline in Pembury's community cohesion as a result of 'mixed tenure'. She mentioned that the community centre was due to be demolished without residents' consultation. Peabody had constructed a new community centre in 2016, but it was not as open nor accessible, and the 'cook-up' barbecues that Catherine used to organise with her son were now impossible. She had challenged Peabody personnel about it, but was frustrated by the minimal response. I managed to talk to a Peabody employee about it too: Jackie, a support worker for residents at the Pembury. Jackie said that the new community centre did offer activities for local residents, but there was never any mixing between social tenants and private market residents. Her job involved visiting tenants who had families on the estate. She described very poor living conditions in some households, and deliberate segregation of social housing tenants from private renters and leaseholders:

'There are quite a few families on this estate who live in flats that have been bought but then the owner rents them out, and the condition's just disgusting. You've got how many families living in a three-bedroom flat, but the living room's turned into a bedroom so that's four. And it's just overcrowded. But then that can stem into things like immigration status. It's because people shouldn't be here, or they're doing it legally and it's the landlords of the property. The one I went into today I just thought, "How do they get away with this? What are they getting away with?" It's absolutely disgusting. ... You can always tell the difference (between social and private tenants). Social are light bricks. Leaseholds are the dark bricks. There's a gym for the private but not for the social. Because they didn't buy their properties, they don't have access to the gym. But actually I suppose sometimes, I think maybe that's how they want it. Or actually they don't mind it, you never know. But it shouldn't be like that, it shouldn't be obvious.'

It shouldn't be obvious – and yet, financialised regeneration speaks to, and constructs, the differentiated value of residents with an increasingly normalised salience. And many would argue it always was obvious: the enclosures, clearances, displacements, containments, curtailments. The wars fought over money and dominance that now scrape London's skies, and the diasporic peoples that live in that shadow, in borrowed time and space. How does love grow in the dwindling, stolen timespace of precarity? In this book, I wonder about the intimate practices that propel life's reproduction amidst it. I explore the affective work of making, and letting go of, familial futures. I look at the resentment and the dead-ends, the embarrassment and the reaching for control. I seek to honour the grief and love in all of it, without muting the ugliness. Through visibilising the discomfort, I also want to document the effort. This effort, the work of precarious intimacy, is ours to reclaim – a struggle that begins with recognising differentiated experiences of the same system.

3

Obstructing Reproduction

Having a child

"One day I want more kids," Penny said. "Finance holds me back. You know, money is an issue. In a two-bed flat we could have a baby here, but I wouldn't want two bigger kids." Penny and I were seated at a table in a new café on Hackney's Pembury Estate, where she lived with her husband and toddler. Originally from northern England, she had moved to London over ten years ago. At the time of our discussions, she was 36 and worked for a prison reform charity. She had noticed and responded to one of my study advertisements online, in a Facebook group. The next time we met, Penny and I chatted at her dining table in the recently built flat that she part-rented and part-owned. The small living room where we spoke was filled with toys and playmats – the ephemera of a cosy chaos that goes hand-in-hand with living with children. Penny pointed across the playscape to a mahogany sideboard, a gift from her grandmother. It was large, imposing for the size of the room we were in. But it had found its use, displaying PlayDough sculptures and renderings of Peppa Pig. "It's worth a fortune," Penny said, "and it looks ridiculous in this flat. But what am I meant to do with it? Who has a house big enough these days to have room for a sideboard?"

For Penny, reproductive obstruction was entangled with the spatial constraints of life as part-renter, part-leaseholder of a shared ownership new-build on the Pembury Estate. These sentiments were broadly shared by the privately renting millennials I interviewed from 2018 to 2019, regardless of whether they already had children. Of these 23–36-year-olds, most were resigned to leaving London to have a family, bar a few who had direct or indirect access to inherited wealth. Priced out of home ownership and stuck in the private rented sector, economic obstruction and thwarted kinship were lived in synergy. It was beginning to dawn on Penny that the promise of security through shared ownership was unrealistic; she still felt like a renter, and the double payments were a struggle to meet. She wanted a place that would sustain a growing family without so much hardship, and this new-build on the Pembury wasn't it.

These renters' stories echo a recent swell in commentary emphasising British millennials' waning financial capacity to reproduce. Journalist Rhiannon Lucy Cosslett, for example, has lamented that rising house prices have led to declining birth rates in Britain (2018), and more recent reports from Gateway Women, a support organisation for women who are involuntarily childless, indicate that 20 per cent of women do not have children by midlife, with 80 per cent of these 'due to circumstance, not infertility' (Kalia 2021). Journalistic pieces on the subject suggest that Generation Z is even more certain that the cost of living – and especially the cost of housing – prohibits them from having children (Coombe-Whitlock 2022).

The broad statistical picture is that there has been a decline in national birth rates since the last peak in 2012. The Office for National Statistics reports that in 2019, there were 640,370 live births in England and Wales. In the same year, fertility rates – measured fairly crudely by the 'number of children per woman' – for women in age groups under 30 were at the lowest level since records started in 1938. However, fertility rates increased among women over 40 (ONS 2020c), and in fact, the overall fertility rate rose in 2021 – but again, only within older age brackets (Thomas 2022). Having children therefore appears to have been delayed rather than cancelled. Property inflation and attendant real wage decline are part of this picture. While caution must be exercised around inferring statistical causality (lower birth rates have been reported at times of real wage growth too, for example in the late 1990s [Chartered Institute of Housing 2019; ONS 2019]), there is a growing cultural discourse linking barriers to reproduction with the economic plight of younger generations, owing to the cost of housing. And while this discourse stems from lived reality, it is also politically and culturally productive of reproduction itself: it tells kinship-stories about what must be acquired and achieved for the tenable replenishment of families.

I am interested in the ways that such reproductive imaginaries are imbricated with economic life for millennial renters. In this chapter, I draw out the politics of these imaginaries, and how they speak to the different lives that can be made and remade amidst precarity. First, I explore the assumed dependentlessness embedded in the transient temporalities of London renting, and I dig into the ways that the reproductive mandates of this system are reflected in the imaginaries of private renters. Second, I think about the ways that social tenants' access to the urban means of social reproduction is eroded by the consolidation of a rented sector in London that is oriented around transience, density and childlessness. I explore narratives of 'escape' from Hackney's private rented sector that locate reproduction beyond the city, and, resonating with Cindi Katz's concept of 'social childhood', I consider the ways that this placement aligns with the erosion of city infrastructures that reproduce the lives of the children that depend on them. The final section of this chapter shifts focus from the reproduction of families to the reproduction of romantic relationships: I explore economic obstructions to the formation of intimate relationships and, in turn, the realisation of familial dreams.

Gentrification scholarship has often focused on the ways that new urban residents drive unequal urban processes. This is easier to gauge among private homeowners, less so with private renters. Middle-class millennial renters are not to blame for the insecurity they are subjected to: they are not their own landlords, and rarely policy makers. Yet, it is important to look at the places where renters' economic consciousness and policy narratives converge, because they uphold each other. The bridge between them remains the family, which legitimates policies that construct renting as a stop-gap experience before a striven-for ownership endpoint, and, paradoxically, reform private renting so that it is culturally solidified as a workable, long-term solution for meeting family housing need, which it is not.

Consuming kinship

Children take up space, and they generally don't pay rent. This makes children unattractive to private landlords, who have the power to discriminate against tenants with dependents. As private renter and parent Alice told me, searching for a new flat with a new-born felt "incredibly hopeless." "Everywhere that we were looking," Alice said, "nobody would rent a place to us because we had a baby." A new White Paper published by the Department for Levelling Up, Housing and Communities in June 2022 outlined that intended legislation will stop private landlords issuing blanket bans on children. The new Renters Reform Bill, the paper details, will also abolish Section 21 evictions so that renters can 'confidently settle down and make their house a home' (DLUHC 2022: 7). On the front of the White Paper, a young, attractive heterosexual couple embrace, smiling with contentment. They look peaceful. Next to them is a sign, indicating that the terraced house behind them had been 'LET'. The paper defines private tenants as customers – Annex C of the document gives a grid of information entitled 'customer experience'. It is a list of things that tenants might want to know about their current rights, and what would change if new legislation were passed. The smiling new residents of this privately rented home are peaceful: theirs is a world in which private renters are finally furnished with the possibility of having a family if their landlord is nice, in a rented that home that they at least can't be evicted from for no reason – except, as the White Paper details, if the landlord wants to sell up or move any family members in.

The reality is that being evicted at a whim owing to the privileging of property rights over human life is not sufficient security for children: the White Paper is inadequate, as is the Renters Reform Bill. As the paper sets out, private renters are not currently able to 'make their house a home'. Other than this paltry set of proposed reforms, the sector's insecurity has been capitalised upon by a nebulous 'affordable' housing market, promising a solution while perpetuating the overall problem. This harks back to Mike Davis' analysis of neoliberal housing solutions in the majority world, where schemes supposedly aimed at poor people have effectively been co-opted by and for the middle class (2007: 63–65). In a London context, the impermanence of the rental market has been solidified through the integration of affordable housing products for middle-class consumers with short-term attachments to urban space and community, not least through the demolition of long-standing, intergenerational communities on housing estates. These products – like Penny's shared ownership flat – can fulfil residents' longings to settle down and have a family in a self-contained home, but they remain susceptible to both rent and mortgage inflation and are small, owing to the latest London Plan's emphasis on densification. As a result, they are often not sustainable solutions for long-term stability in the city, even for the minority of renters financially able to access them. For many of the private market renters I talked to, then, visions of self-contained family futures were located beyond the city, which was seen as offering an unaffordable, interstitial mode of relational life.

This was especially true of the many private renters who lived with multiple people in order to pool housing costs. Melissa, a 26-year-old Chicagoan charity worker, saw renting in London as only "good for now" – something that suited her life currently but was never going to be long-term, because it was incompatible with her future family plans. She lived in a two-bedroom apartment in a tower block with her boyfriend, Matthew, and their mutual friend, Tom. "The housing market here is just very different to where I'm from," she said in our first interview together. Seated at a table in a pub overlooking Hackney Downs, we were discussing her desires to potentially have children with Matthew. "It's much more expensive, everything is smaller," she said, "I think that owning a house is seen as a step you take towards your future." Another private renter, Clare, lacked the concrete, coupled exit plan that Melissa was mapping out, but was no less solid in her beliefs that having children was a galaxy away from her shared housing circumstances. Clare was 34 when I interviewed her in 2018, and lived in a privately rented home with multiple people she didn't know. "Something that's come out of living in London," she said, was "as I get older I worry that, what if I change my mind in ten years when it's too late? At the start of the year I saw an ad on Facebook for egg donors. And I thought 700 pounds would be useful." Clare donated her eggs through the advertised company and, in the process, was able to store some for free, should she be in a different economic situation a decade in the future.

Both conversations reflected the impact of dwindling home space on shaping private renters' lives as dependentless (see Harris and Nowicki 2020). This was echoed by Melissa's boyfriend Matthew, a 29-year-old marketing professional at the time of our discussions. Matthew similarly envisioned family formation as conditional upon escape from London, and even escape from England. "If I was staying in England, I've made my bed" Matthew stated bluntly in our first meeting at his workplace. "I'm probably just never going to own a house. I'm just that generation – I can't imagine having kids and a flatmate. I'd probably have to move out, especially when kids are the ultimate thing." Matthew and Melissa's joint understanding of reproduction as incongruous with London life was framed by the constraints of private renting, but it was also influenced by their perception of a family home as a self-contained space oriented around their partnership. I read their association between urban escape and child-rearing as speaking not only to the life-limiting material conditions of London's housing crisis, but also to the 'economic and psychic investment' represented by children (Katz 2008). Embedded within these discussions of the future is the naturalisation of renting as something that people with children do not do. This is a product of rentier capitalism. And, on a broad cultural level, it feeds back into upholding rentier capitalist logics, deepening the wastage of urban childhoods through 'landscapes of neglect', including underfunded housing and infrastructure (see Katz 2001: 715).

This detriment was more directly alluded to by several private tenants over the course of this project, as they contemplated familial futures. Twenty-eight-year-old construction worker Leon had lived in the same flat for four years but did not consider it his long-term home, citing a lack of sovereignty. As we discussed the possibility of Leon having children in the future, he explained that new pathways were presented by his girlfriend's house, which her parents owned:

> 'I don't see my flat as "home." I just see it as a means to an end. That's the core thing about renting, right? It's not really your place, you feel the impermanence keenly. The thing is with Laura, I know that it's there, it's not something hypothetical. It's funny how many problems that solves. You know our kid would have a decent chance and also some sort of security.'

The possibility of a stable, self-contained space that also doubled as an asset compounded Leon's sense of renting as impermanent and thus irreconcilable with reproduction. The fact that his girlfriend had access to this security was already woven in with his hopes for a future child's "decent chance," because his current home was not a place where that could ever be realised.

For Jonathan, a 29-year-old charity worker privately renting a one-bed flat with his girlfriend, housing instability had fostered feelings of immaturity regarding reproduction. Reflecting on his former aspirations to have kids, Jonathan cited a trade-off between wanting a family and needing to be near London for his career:

'Ten years ago I thought of course by the time I'm 29 I'll want kids. The main factor would be feeling like I've only been an adult for the last two years because it's very difficult. If you have that fairly bourgeois luxury of doing something that you love, then actually it starts really late.'

Through noting that his sense of reproductive possibility had been recalibrated owing to "bourgeois" career choices, Jonathan sketched out a delayed ascent into something akin to full adulthood. He went on, however, to emphasise that the constraints of London renting obstructed family formation: "If it was possible for me to be here but also have more space and greater economic stability, would that mean that I would have started a family earlier? I think it's certainly that question of the margins of what you can earn and what you can afford." Again, reproduction is weighed up in an economic equation.

For the private market renters I interviewed, then, the route to having children in London was largely paved with bricks that were owned. This could involve inventive financial workarounds, exemplified by 24-year-old private renter Nasra, who shared a flat in London Fields with her boyfriend and two housemates. Having grown up in Hackney, Nasra's long-term attachment to the area made her reluctant to leave London to have children. She mentioned that both she and her boyfriend would "like to be able to raise children" in the city, but housing unaffordability was in the way. Nasra's proposed solution to this was to work and save money in Dubai. Elaborating on possible plans, she said it would be a "fun way to make some easy money" and that the income tax relief offered by Dubai's fiscal regime would mean she could make enough to "bring money back home and put down a deposit." This interest in a kind of micro foreign investment reflects Hackney's growing unaffordability, but echoes, too, the deferred aspirations and suspended relational dreams embedded within the rented sector overall. In contrast to Jonathan, Nasra described a shift from reproductive consignment to creative strategies of transnational accumulation, ensuring home ownership – and thus secure familial kinship – in the neighbourhood she grew up in, and in proximity to her mother, who lived in Tottenham.

In David Harvey's *Seventeen Contradictions*, the author writes that opening up social reproduction to the realm of monetisation leads, in the long run, to (marginalised people's) dispossession and eviction (2014: 198). In the absence of social mobility, Harvey writes, a 'highly unequal and tightly channelled' process of social reproduction is the automatic stand-in (2014: 196). The assetisation of housing can be read through this analysis: where capacities to create and reproduce family households are gatekept by extortionate house prices and climbing rents, individual financial workarounds can improve an individual's circumstances. On a large scale, these strategies continue to lock marginalised people, including their dependents, out of local urban subsistence. These are the reproductive bounds of the financialised city; to locate and envision a future family life within it, it can appear that the only route is to spread the same smoke that is driving you out.

Remaking a child

My discussions with social tenants reflected, in turn, a sense of their family households living on borrowed time: that there were too many children, or too many adults, and not enough room or resources, because the state did not want them there. The latter is true: the political regime in Britain has constricted working-class reproduction predominantly through economic coercion. Austerity policies and regeneration frameworks communicate reproductive imperatives, especially for social housing tenants in London. For example, introduced in 2017, the child benefit cap is an austerity policy that altered entitlement to Universal Credit on the basis of a family's size, cutting the limit to two children. Another austerity policy, the 'Bedroom Tax', is not as on-the-nose, although its reproductive messaging is clear. Introduced with the 2012 Welfare Reform Act, the tax financially punishes social housing tenants who have a spare room and are in receipt of benefits, deeming them to be 'under-occupiers'. Regardless of whether this is due to an adult child leaving home, the death of a family member, or because of the needs of a disabled resident, social tenants face reduced benefits if they have space that the state deems superfluous. Given the yawning gap between incomes and rents in Hackney, this financial hit can result in rent arrears that lead to eviction. This problematises reproduction for renters in social housing in several ways: young adults risk plunging their families into homelessness if they leave home; children with different needs are forced to live in potentially crowded housing; extended family members, should they need a place to stay, are also forced to live in crowded space. Both the benefit cap and the Bedroom Tax speak to the entrenchment of the market as the arbiter of whose life can be cultivated and reproduced in a given place. The reproductive desires and kinships of those reliant on public welfare funds or subsidised housing are subsequently constrained.

In my time working at the London Assembly with Assembly Member Siân Berry, I visited several social housing estates throughout the city, including Broadwater Farm, Achilles Street, Kilburn Square, Carpenters and Wornington Green. At these estates, I spoke to residents who were campaigning against development schemes that would demolish their homes and/or significantly reduce their green spaces and amenities. One of the research projects I conducted with estate residents was about their experiences of estate ballots, which were brought in by the Mayor of London in July 2018 to give estate residents a yes/no choice over demolition, if the development was funded by a Greater London Authority (GLA) grant. While the ballot policy was a positive development, all of the residents I spoke to felt pressured to vote 'yes' to demolition. They reported intimidation, bribery and manufactured consent through superficial consultations, and anti-demolition campaigners felt censored and surveilled. Why did their homes need to be torn down? The housing stock of these estates was often a lot more structurally sound than the freezing, poorly ventilated Victorian terraces let to private renters. The sturdy red bricks of 1960s estate design were not wrapped in the cheap, new flammable cladding that lit up Grenfell Tower in 2017. Flats in these estates are often more spacious, with broad walkways and communal gardens. People who were already struggling with overcrowding told me that their situation was about to get worse – smaller floor plans had been circulated for the new-builds they were being forced to move into. They had been promised flats and were getting maisonettes. The trees were being cut down and the children's play area built on. Long-standing infrastructures of intergenerational, collective and social care were at risk of demolition too. On top of the debris, 'affordable housing' was going to be built.

Next, I recount a focus group interview with four millennial parents renting in Hackney across a range of tenure. Their stories proffer examples of how enfranchisement within the private rental market mediates tenants' abilities to imagine, plan and create idealised familial lives. What is the right to reproduction if not the right to the future? As the discussion reveals, dreams of an idealised familial future beyond the insecurity of London renting were in tension with the social-reproductive needs of participants bound to the city's cultural and community infrastructures, and its casual labour markets, for their families' survival. As I analyse the focus group text, I argue that the placing of idealised family life beyond Hackney speaks to a deepening geographical inequality in social reproduction whereby, as Katz writes, disjunctures are as 'likely to draw upon sedimented inequalities in social relations as to provoke new ones' (2001: 716).

The focus group assembled in the nursery playroom of a Hackney Children's Centre on a cold February morning in 2018. At the start there were three participants, all of whom lived in accommodation rented from a social landlord: Mariam, who lived with her two children and husband in a council flat; Chandice, who lived with her partner and three children in a flat she rented from a large housing association; and Anzuli, who lived in temporary accommodation with her three daughters, in a flat allocated by Hackney Council but owned by a private landlord. Anzuli's rent was capped at 'social' rates and subsidised through Universal Credit/housing benefit. The diversity in tenure among participants was indicative of the increasingly convoluted terrain of Britain's social housing sector, where private-sector landlords are often relied upon for housing provision and large housing associations progressively operate similarly to large-scale property developers. The array of different stakeholders and organisations involved in letting and managing socially rented properties therefore means that accountability for repair is often diluted and distant. In keeping with this, almost everyone at the start of the focus group interview had experienced difficulties with holding their landlords accountable and had felt the effects of it in the practical, psychological and emotional aspects of maintaining their families.

The practical, psychological and visceral effects of this obstructed everyday reproductive work and created barriers to envisioned family futures. Anzuli, for example, described a leak in her kitchen that remained unaddressed, mentioning the ways it had negatively impacted her daughter:

'We found out that the water that's leaking is from the toilet. The flats above us, every time they go to the toilet and flush it, I'm getting it and I've emailed them, I've called them, I've written a letter and nothing's been done. They acknowledged my letter eventually, so they have come once to rip out the whole ceiling and put in a new one. And then it's been three weeks, the same problem. Obviously they haven't sorted out the cause of the problem so it's gonna continue. And now it's affecting the walls – there's a split in the middle.'

Continuing with her story, Anzuli described the ways that the physiological effects of disrepair were written on her child's body, impeding reproduction and her ability to care for her family:

'My eldest child is a clean freak. Every little thing that happens to her now is because of this leak, because now she knows that the water's actually from the toilet. So, she thinks they're trying to kill her because she can't clean, and she's mopping the kitchen floor every two hours. As soon as she sees the liquid, she's getting the mop. She's got a belly-ache – it's because of that. You know just last night I made dinner, I was so proud of myself trying a new recipe. That took a whole day, you know, to make this recipe for my girls. Laid the table, turned around to get a spoon, and all I can hear is, "Drip! Drip! Drip!" I had to throw the whole lot in the bin! I spent all that money to prepare that meal and we couldn't even try it.'

Preceding the moment that Anzuli discarded her meal were cumulative degrees of obstruction: the worsening leak, the indifference of her landlord, her daughter's spiralling paranoia. Life's work was interceded by a proliferating assemblage of substances, anxieties and wasted practices, and the leaky soundscape was a reminder. Similarly, Chandice described the difficulty of managing her daughter's health in overcrowded living space, and the obstacles she faced in trying to find alternative housing. In a discussion about access to outdoor space, Chandice mentioned that she wanted move to a less crowded home, but had so far received no response from her landlord, Sanctuary Housing Association:

'They say in the class [my daughter] has a disability, but even though I've done all my paperwork, sent it off to the housing, still waiting, nothing's happened yet. All of them in the little room is cramped. And they're sharing a bed, only the big ones sleep up top. I know, what can I do? You have to make ends meet, you just have to put up with it.'

Like Anzuli, the present was obstructed for Chandice, leaving the future even further from reach. This was echoed further in Chandice's description of leaks in her ground-floor flat, which were hard to manage in her crowded home:

'At times I do get flooded out and this is to do with the draining. For some reason, the water is bubbling from my kitchen sink – it comes up, floods up. Most times it's either the washing machine or it's someone's water we always see come bubbling up and flood out the whole of my kitchen. And there's five of us. Dad, me, three children, two bedrooms.'

Mariam, too, described the impact of limited space and disrepair on her children, whose desires for a future outdoor space were obstructed by present uncertainties. "When I moved, I had two children, now I have four," Mariam explained. "That's why my daughter wants outdoor space. But I don't like ground floors, I just don't feel safe. Lots of people I know, when they live on ground floor, they have flooding problems – damp, moisture problems."

Despite the shared theme of disrepair obstructing everyday family life, there was a sense of solidarity between Mariam, Chandice and Anzuli, discernible in soft murmurs of agreement and knowing laughter. A fourth group member, Rachel, joined half an hour in, and introduced herself as a single parent to one child and a private renter reliant on Universal Credit/housing benefit. Rachel lamented the expense of renting, but she mentioned that she had a good rapport with her landlord owing to her efforts in maintaining the property. "As landlords go," Rachel said, "I'm really fortunate. But then I'm also quite up on what my rights are – and he knows that. I pay my rent on time, I look after the flat. I keep it really nicely. When you've got children, you can't just let things go by the wayside."

In the room, there was a drop-off in murmurs of shared understanding, and this persisted as Rachel outlined her desire to leave London. "I've earned a big chunk of money so I can then move out of London," Rachel explained. "I want to move to the Kent coast. I'm paying through the nose for what? To go to the park and go home, go to the park and go home." As she continued, Rachel's focus on re-establishing family life on the south coast of England became braided with her divergent perception of urban community as a resource for familial reproduction. Indeed, Rachel described at different points how wearied she was by the sensory intensity of Hackney, linking this to an excessive presence of other people. She mentioned that she wanted to live "in the middle of nowhere where I haven't got any neighbours. No dog poo when I step outside of my house, no sirens. I just think you get an even tighter sense of community when there's people few and far between."

Her association between coastal living, lower population density and a higher quality of family life contrasted with the thoughts of others in the group. Anzuli, for example, recalled her unhappiness when the council briefly reallocated her to housing in Essex. In her four years of living in Essex, Anzuli said she was "so miserable." "I didn't like it," Anzuli said, "it was too quiet. I'm a loud chick. It was me that was miserable because there was no one to talk to." Mariam agreed, stating that she was similarly positive about neighbourly community as a source of support, particularly while she was at home looking after her baby. "I like living in places where there are lots of people to chat and talk to and say 'Hello there!'," Mariam shared, "and if you just look out your window you can see people going, coming."

Rachel's antipathy towards populous urban life also appeared to be interwoven with mistrust of people as the potential source of accidents or violence. Embedded within the former were memories of the Grenfell Tower fire, which had occurred six months prior to the focus group discussion. Resonating with observations made by Harris et al (2019) in their work on PLACE/Ladywell, the horror of Grenfell affectively clung to all of the group members' concerns, particularly those living in tower blocks. Chandice, for example, mentioned that she sometimes had to wake her neighbour when he did not hear his fire alarm. Citing a sense of responsibility, Chandice said:

'After Grenfell you feel frightened of living on the second floor. Sometimes I can hear my neighbour's alarm going off and I have to go knocking. He just says he puts the power on to cook and he forgets it and fell asleep. Sometimes he can't find the strength to stand up, he's not getting the help.'

Rachel responded to this, flagging the risk that the neighbour posed to Chandice and her family. "You're relying on all those other people in that building to be safe and careful and to not fall asleep with a fag in their hand," she said. Rachel's mistrust in the safety of neighbours unfolded, too, into a discussion of her fears of London's population more broadly. She cited terrorism: "If I left London, I wouldn't have to go anywhere that I'm gonna get blown up or run over by a van," Rachel explained. "Since having my little boy, I stand on the Euston Road and I think, 'Any one of these cars could just do that'. There are that many crazy people and they are saturated in these busy areas." Rachel's anxious imaginings of unknown assailants and her fears of a "saturated" population conveyed a belief that densities of people obstructed the secure replenishment of her family's life. This loudly contrasted with the experiences of Chandice, Mariam and Anzuli, for whom proximity to community was essential for wellbeing and safety – be it through the everyday interactions with neighbours or through making sure elderly residents were looked in on and considered.

Beyond the focus group, Penny similarly idealised a more rural existence and mentioned that her desire to have more children was contingent upon leaving Hackney in the future. Like Rachel, she also voiced concern around raising a family amidst a sense of rising urban violence:

> 'We're having massive discussions about moving out of London. I grew up on a farm in Yorkshire and I think I'm just missing that. Finance holds me back but also you know, it's just harder than I thought, money is an issue. You know, in a two-bed flat we could have a baby here, but I wouldn't want two bigger kids. The increasing violence, like London in general, gun, knife crime in general, it just seems to be a bit more prevalent than in previous years. In this area, especially as she's growing up, I don't really want her involved in that. I'm fed up of being in a block on an estate.'

Penny's association between violence and "this area" reflected her concerns about the actions and behaviour of her neighbours. While her fears were not grounded in material experience of violence, she affiliated the capacity to expand and maintain her family with rural life and its implied safety. Both Rachel and Penny's perspectives highlight the socioeconomic contingency of reproduction both in terms of everyday labour and the fulfilment of ideal lives. For Chandice, Mariam and Anzuli, proximity to community was preferable, and often essential, for the social reproduction of familial life. For Penny and Rachel, this same proximity was a source of fear and familial obstruction. From my perspective, these disparities were framed by racialised experiences of the city – I read Penny and Rachel as White, and the remaining focus group participants were of Afro-Caribbean and South

Asian heritage. For the former, the promise of coastal or rural life appeared to be at least partially entangled with self-containment and distance from the racialised unknown, and from the spectre, rather than reality, of violence.

Similarly, another individual respondent, Alice, who lived in a privately rented one-bedroom flat in Clapton with her two-year-old child and partner, said that she had never thought of London as suitable for raising a family and was looking for an "escape plan." Alice, who was also White, was originally from the north of England. She dreamt of returning:

> 'I think growing up in East London would be the greatest gift we could give Sam but I just don't think it's gonna be feasible. I think she could really learn just to be incredibly expressive without fear of judgment. I think maybe just after Sam was born it was fine, but once she started to be able to move about, so maybe for the past year, we've been on the look-out, like what's our escape plan, what are we gonna do. I always said that London was really good for when you were young but I would never have children here.'

The focus group's divergent experiences thus distilled themes that emerged across the study more broadly, wherein the promise of reproductive security beyond Hackney was entangled with the inherent incompatibility of renting with familial reproduction and also with a sense that concentrated urban populations – sometimes coded as people of colour – were themselves obstructive to familial reproduction. It is within such divergences that we can see how 'vexed and slippery' social reproduction is (Katz 2001: 717), especially in the context of the racial-capitalist city, where eroded capacities to reproduce daily life can give rise to desires for a geographical and social mobility that is class exclusive. Mapping contours between these disparately (yet proximately) situated subjects reveals the political economy of reproductive temporality. The future may be a sea breeze, isolation, an appreciating asset, a safe child, an expanding family: a reward for enduring density, risk, the unfairness of high prices. The future may also be tomorrow's dinner, another letter written to the council, another concerned knock on the door of a neighbour. This is not to say that the everyday challenges of social reproduction in unaffordable and insecure accommodation eluded the private renters cited here. Rather, it is to observe the politics framing their imaginative capacity to place reproduction beyond this city, and beyond this time.

Economic intimacies, nuclear dreams

The COVID-19 pandemic has been a revelator of late capitalist society's deep injustices. Indeed, some of the themes emerging from my research in 2019 have been loudly affirmed by these more recent revelations. The unaffordability of solitude and autonomy, and the precarious intimacies unfolding from this, is one of them. In 2022, with the cost-of-living crisis taking centre stage in Britain, this theme gathered more attention. 'Cost of loathing crisis', the *Daily Star* splashed across its front page on 13 October 2022:

1 in 3 who split up still living in the same house.
1 in 8 of them are still sharing the same BED.
And 15% even allow new lover to stay the night.

Economic obstruction from making informed, intentional decisions regarding one's intimate life has been a central battle line for anti-austerity feminist activism in Britain since 2010. Feminist action group Sisters Uncut formed explicitly around this issue, targeting the defunding and closure of domestic violence refuges as indicative of the coalition government's direct attack on women. As rents, mortgages, food prices and fuel costs spiralled in 2022, the cost of leaving a partner became out of reach for a widening number of people. Yet, for others, unaffordable housing costs have meant that even the first steps towards romantic relationships are denied. Several of my conversations with millennial renters in 2017 and 2018 spoke to this phenomenon – to another form of reproductive obstruction that is sparsely raised in discussions about 'generation rent': the unaffordability of intentional intimacy, owing to a lack of autonomy in limited space.

In conversations about plans for the future, relational aspirations and desires for kinship or family, it was not always possible for respondents to get past the first roadblock: having the money, time, space or even permission to date anyone. Faiz, for example, was a 25-year-old actor and delivery courier living in Dalston when I met him first in 2018. He told me at length about the breakdown of a relationship, which he felt had become untenable because of his unreliable income and a lack of private space. Faiz lived with his sister and parents in the same council-rented house that had been his home since he was 14. Spiralling private rents in Hackney had made it impossible for Faiz to move out of the house, exacerbated by his sporadic income and insecure work conditions. Another set of difficulties had flourished around legal changes to social housing brought by government welfare reform. Owing to the Bedroom Tax, Faiz was bound by the financial consequences his parents would face if he moved out of the family home – the rent would go up and, if his parents couldn't pay it, they would be evicted.

Conflicted by feelings of filial duty and a strong desire for escape, Faiz described the difficulties of living in an oppressive home environment and its impact on establishing and maintaining intimate relationships:

'My dad can't work as much as he could, and every week he comes back like, "I'm so stressed out, the rent's gone up, they're not counting you as a minor anymore." And actually one big stress for me is that if I move out, I have to move out privately without declaring it because otherwise that room's empty, so either the rent goes up a disgusting amount and my dad can't afford to stay there anymore, right, because he loses some benefits or something, or he has an extra room, and the council's like you've got an extra room, you have to move, and he gets kicked out of the house. ... Six months ago, I really, really liked this girl, and I could see myself being with her for a long time, but she knew I could never introduce her to my parents, at least not until things were super serious. That's kind of a big burden, isn't it? So, she could never come round to my house, just to chill out. It was always on her to host me. Conversations, phone conversations were really, really muted or I had to go out to take the call, which meant you can't really relax. It fell apart.'

Faiz felt that his intimate life was on hold. In an anxious and strained atmosphere at home, his romantic life was conducted in secret. As our discussions progressed, he continued to pinpoint his economic situation as the main obstacle to a fulfilling intimate life. The second time we met was in the foyer of Dalston's Premier Inn. Faiz said that he liked hanging out here because it was a warm and free place to learn lines, although there had been a recent altercation with someone working there who had told him to leave. We sat in armchairs near the elevator, framed by a rainy dusk backdrop of traffic and busy footfall on Dalston Lane outside. The conversation returned to his break-up, and specifically to his ex-girlfriend's new partner. He was bothered by this development, and it seemed to bring up feelings of shame about what he hadn't been able to offer her. He blamed himself and his material situation:

'It was someone she was going out with before and I know about him and he's got this big job in an accounting firm, and I know what it's like, this used to bug me in the relationship. Now they can go have fancy tea somewhere. Or go to a menu and order the bottom half of the menu and not go (sharp inhale), "Mhm, seven pounds, yep..." My relationship with money was so different to her relationship with money and it felt like I couldn't keep up. Not in a way that I can't keep up with what you're doing, but I don't feel like we're fulfilling everything that you *could* be doing. Because of me.'

Faiz drew a clear economic distinction between himself and his ex-partner. He saw himself as a hindrance to her economic destiny, a destiny in which costly activities could be enjoyed and expensive food could be ordered, in the company of a romantic partner who was able to financially keep up. The embarrassment Faiz expressed at being unable to express "chivalrous" gestures caused him real anguish, and his sense of economic exclusion from a middle-class dating pool was compounded by his desire to form intimate relationships beyond the Bangladeshi community his parents expected him to marry within. He wearily outlined the irony of being too poor for success in arranged marriages but too poor to exploit the freedoms of his failures:

> 'I think my parents have given up. If I had a job, there'd be more pressure, it'd just be, "Give us your CV, what's going on?" Right now, they don't actually have a leg to stand on because like, what am I doing? In a way that's my get-out clause. If I was dating an Asian girl she'd get it, the whole situation that I'm in, and we'd work through it. But it's a bit different trying to explain that to someone who's not from our culture.'

Faiz was enmeshed with a particularly tight matrix of different pressures and policy impacts: desiring a dating life beyond his parent's values while navigating housing immobility in their council-rented home, a stuckness that, resonating Blunt and Sheringham's 'home-city' geographies (2018), spoke to the interlocking of welfare reform and the rising unaffordability of the local private rented sector. Exacerbated by an unreliable income stream, Faiz appeared tired of the shame of precarity and its effect on his dating opportunities. He was sustained by his art, and prioritised it by stealing away to spend evenings in hotel foyers, receptions and friends' houses to run lines and find respite. But these moments were inadequate compensation for an independent life he did not have the resources to create.

Faiz's longings for intimacy and love were shared by private renters who were similarly dating 'outside' of their class habitus. While these renters generally had fewer barriers in terms of policy and parental pressures, they felt financial disparities keenly in their romantic lives, especially where home ownership was a feature. These disparities fed a fragile and tentative approach to reproductive aspirations because renters without parental safety nets or inherited resources were not clear where they stood with their partners. This was the case for Leon, whose girlfriend, as we know from earlier discussions in this chapter, lived alone in a house owned by her parents. Leon was ambivalent about her comparative wealth and her upper-middle-class background. There was curiosity, but there was also alienation. Leon had a prestigious degree in English literature from a famous, wealthy university. He was the first in his Polish family to access higher education. But his economic trajectory since completing it was one of struggle – he had watched more middle-class peers follow their creative passions, gilded by parental wealth and achieving success that Leon had once dreamt of. Leon was an accomplished musician and songwriter, but he couldn't afford to work in the arts. He had even been forced to quit a desk job in media because it paid him too little to survive. As a teenager, he had worked alongside relatives in the building trade, so he was able to instrumentalise that experience and go into construction. He said he was still somewhat bitter about it all, but that the resentment faded when he found out how little people were earning in the environments he had once pedestaled.

Leon and I first met up at a café in Haggerston, on Kingsland Road. It was a tiny, lively place, and the heart of his neighbourhood world: the people who worked there had become good friends to him. He told me about the discomfort of broaching future plans with a partner who had more wealth and security than him:

> 'If we were both renting a place, I probably would've said to her now, "Shall we just get a place where we both live?" But because she's in a place where, essentially, it's her house already, and I'm just in a house that I rent, I can't really say, "Can I move into your house?" Do you know what I mean? The thing is, I wouldn't want to pay her rent anyway. I think that'd be really weird and really power imbalanced.'

Leon was reluctant to enter into a transactional rentier relationship with his girlfriend, but the discrepancy in their living circumstances was frustrating the process of settling down with her, which is what he really desired. He was nonetheless keen to express that her family was financially generous and that he was grateful:

> 'Even though they're very well off, they're not dickheads. They're very generous, very welcoming. They're not greedy people, do you know what I mean? They've done a lot, quite a lot of nice things for me already. They're very generous. I could imagine coming to some kind of arrangement with them. But ultimately it's her decision, my girlfriend, it's up to her really.'

Lacking his own means of escaping the private rented sector, Leon was compelled to make an "arrangement" with the parents of his romantic partner: the reproduction of his romantic relationship was braided with the class reproduction of her family, and his potential role was to convince them of his place in it. Recalling Bourdieu (1980: 167), Leon's capacity to establish a nuclear family household with his wealthier partner required him to negotiate a role in an 'economy of material and symbolic exchanges' between generations.

Nasra, also a private renter living in De Beauvoir, a ward in the south of Hackney, was similarly ambivalent about her boyfriend's class background. She had grown up in social housing in Hackney, and as her aforementioned saving plans spoke to, she was not interested in living anywhere else. Like

Leon, Nasra also wanted to create a future with her boyfriend that included a self-contained household and kids. At the time of our discussions, the couple shared a bedroom in a house she shared with two other housemates. She had regular, securely contracted work at a big museum in Central London, but the pay was poor, and she disliked the idea of her boyfriend paying for things that she couldn't afford. In fact, the wealth disparity had nearly put her off:

'His salary kind of put me off a bit because I don't like feeling like I'm dependent, like somebody's looking after me in that way. I'm very independent with my own finances and I never ask for money and I never borrow money or he never pays extra for things for me in that kind of way. We tend to just live at my level of being able to spend, rather than living at his level. … I thought that with him earning so much more than me that it was gonna be an issue and I didn't want to fight about money, and I didn't want to have to say no to things if he wanted to do them because he did have money.'

The place of money in the mediation of Nasra's romantic life was clear. What's more, it played on her mind when she thought about a family future with her boyfriend. She felt self-conscious in front of his family, and she wondered what their future kids would be like. Nasra's childhood had been framed by the sharp edges of racial capitalism. Her dad had been incarcerated and her mum had struggled to feed her and her sibling. Nasra left home as a teenager and even though she was only 24 when I first interviewed her, she was already thinking about the kinds of precarity she was desperate for her future kids to avoid. "I want a completely different life for my children," she said. "My mum did an amazing job, she's a very strong woman, but there's so many things I'd do differently. And none of that's her fault, she couldn't have changed any of that, but now I have the opportunity to." Like Leon, Nasra tentatively saw her boyfriend's background as one of these opportunities: a route out of the private rented sector and a pathway towards a family life in which her future children were secure. "Money is fucking great," Nasra told me. "That kind of security, not having to worry about going hungry – I've been there and it's not fun. I would hate for my children to have to go through what I did, not being able to eat properly at the weekend. That is pure motivation for me." But the thought of rearing middle-class children was also a source of ambivalence. She already felt she had to perform a different identity with her boyfriend's family, "to be a bit more middle class" and "tone down the council estate accent." She was perturbed, nonetheless, by the idea of raising children with class entitlement:

'On the one hand it'd be nice to have middle-class children in the sense that they wouldn't have to worry about the things that I did, but also at the same time I don't want them to be brats and I don't want them to grow up spoilt. I want them to understand struggle. I see my boyfriend's nephews, they're really spoilt, and it drives me crazy. I look at them and I'm like, "Oh my god, if my kids end up like this, I'm gonna scream!"'

For Nasra, the prospect of escaping precarity via the cultural and class capital of her boyfriend seemed to amplify the importance she placed on her own financial independence, with ambivalence about social difference solidifying a desire to preserve her identity.

Among some of the renters I spoke to, these circumstances were flipped: they were financially supporting or putting up partners who had less money than them. There was Maja, for example, who was a 28-year-old Scandinavian photographer and bartender living in a shared live/work warehouse in Hackney Wick. Maja had inherited money from her mother, who had died six years before. As a result, she was able to sporadically support her boyfriend, Brandon, who stayed with her on-and-off. Maja envisaged a future in which the balance would eventually be reset. "Eventually I just assume that we will be in opposite situations," she said, "because he knows I have this money and I'm also working, so I don't really need it right now. I just want to him sort himself out – I trust the universe to balance itself out eventually."

Elaborating on their entangled lives, Maja explained that her boyfriend struggled with sharing a room with her but his employment precarity meant he was caught in a cycle of moving back into whatever space she was currently renting, and he came from a low-income background where there was no space to go back to. The unfolding codependency sometimes caused conflict, and Brandon would accuse her of enabling him. "Whenever he's stressed and we start to have an argument, it always about how he doesn't want to share a room," she said, "and sometimes he gets angry at me for – this is a bit backwards – letting him take up so much space." Tensions in their relationship were therefore generated by an unavoidable disparity in their economic circumstances. The difficulty of this inequality was amplified by Maja's limited space; while she felt compelled to support Brandon and share her resources, they were still confined to one privately rented room. Like all of the respondents cited in this chapter, the lack of space and expense shaped their present relational dynamics as well as their sense of what came in the future.

By opening out obstructed reproduction to consider the politics of envisioning familial futures, the politics of life's everyday replenishment, and the economic barriers millennial renters face to maintaining romantic relationships, I have sought to construct a more expansive understanding of the ways that London's housing insecurity stems intentional relatedness.

In doing so, I also aimed to draw attention to the racial and class politics surrounding market dis/enfranchisement, and the different ways that reproduction is imagined from within and outside of the private market. The accounts I share reflect shifts in policy towards the consumption of interstitial modes of kinship within the rented city, rather than the genuine provision of long-term housing for families and kinship constellations of diverse kinds. In this sense, the rental market's hostility to dependency, care and social infrastructure is materially imprinted in dwindling floor space, prohibitive rents and the managed degeneration of social housing, with a view to the construction of yet more small new-build flats – flats that residents like Penny still felt trapped within. Regardless of their tenure and backgrounds, however, all the residents cited here shared longings for connection, nurture and intimacy. These longings often stemmed from the grief of wasted nurture: spoilt meals, leaky toilets, unaffordable dating lives, memories of childhood poverty. And, these longings sometimes stemmed from a desire for distance from these griefs: a place for nurturance that was removed from the slow violence of London's precarity.

4

Labours

Capital is an act: the act of extracting uncompensated labour to accumulate wealth and power. The systems of value and currency upon which capitalism relies are therefore interwoven with institutions of oppression, which legitimate the stratified devaluation of labouring populations. In the words of Lucí Cavallero and Verónica Gago (2021: 3), 'currency expresses social relations, that is, relations of force'. Capital needs to know who to pay the least, or not at all. So, looking at the places where capital is accumulated through unwaged labour can help us to understand the ways that it disciplines and enforces different labouring subjectivities. In the words of Tithi Bhattacharya (2017: 92), understanding that the 'relationship between wage labour and capital is sustained in all sorts of unwaged ways and in all kind of social spaces' is vital to the project of dismantling capitalism. In this chapter, I thus turn my attention to affective labours carried out by millennial respondents living in rented accommodation, with a view to understanding the ways that this labour is exploited and alienated by rentier capitalist accumulation.

One of the reasons that solidarity can feel so hard is that the systems of devaluation that are baked into racial capitalism generate different types of currency and leverage for subjects across society, not just at the very top. It is little wonder, then, that the electability of neoliberal regimes has relied upon the intensified demonisation of 'difference' to legitimate a system where people vote for whatever piecemeal privileges they hold. Housing has featured strongly in such campaigns. For example, throughout the 2010s, Tory electioneering often contained references to immigration diminishing the availability of housing for British voters, or decreasing house values. Throughout this era, successive Conservative governments have also demonised disabled people, engineering their intensified socioeconomic devaluation through defunded services, benefit cuts, fitness-to-work tests and discriminatory rhetoric (see Pring 2017). This has increased the work it takes for many disabled people to carry out their everyday lives. In her book *Crippled*, journalist and writer Frances

Ryan describes the experiences of Philomena, who had been waiting for an NHS wheelchair for four years:

> Without a wheelchair, she had to walk with crutches, a portable nebulizer sitting in her handbag for when she got out of breath. She was soon paying for it: as she got home, she put her crutches down and sat on the stairs, and her husband had to help her straight to bed. (Ryan 2019: 171)

Amidst the retrenchment of the state from welfare, both Philomena and her husband pay with their bodies, through increased strain, pain and care labour. Capitalist systems of value live in our bodies and mediate our relational interactions. Within and between differentially embodied subjects, labour is demanded, practised and exchanged through these systems of value.

In relationships, these politics are rife, and interrogating them has always occupied a central place in feminist organising. But remaining singularly focused on gendered imbalances risks reiterating women's work as taking place within the 'white bourgeois heterosexual notion of the private' (Rose 1993: 131). As we know, women are not universally devalued. They are also participants in systems of valuation, producing economic and social meanings that render some people's work well compensated and others uncompensated. But compensation is not the ultimate objective: our creative and reproductive labour can never be truly compensated by a wage. Love relations, Gilman-Opalsky (2020: 53) writes, 'contain valuations that do not obey the presuppositions of capital'. Love slips through capital's nets. In her quasi-autobiographical book *Love's Work*, the late philosopher Gillian Rose wrote that work is the 'third partner' in relationships between women and men. It 'equalises the emotions' – love's work is 'the constant carnival; words, the rhythm and pace of two, who mine undeveloped seams of the earth and share the treasure' (Rose 1995: 131). I read this as a celebration of the devotional work experienced in partnership. Partnership does not require monogamy, heterosexuality or even humans. Partnership involves the work of symbiosis. In the words of Octavia Butler, partnership is 'giving, taking, learning, teaching, offering the greatest possible benefit while doing the least possible harm' (1998: 145). The work that love calls us to do is alienated by capitalist modes of value, but the work itself is not the problem – the work is everything.

Living in the precarity of advanced capitalism involves negotiating different configurations of dependency that can amplify systems of differentiated value. In the words of Kendra Strauss, precarity encompasses 'both "labour" and "life"' (2018: 625). Perhaps most obviously, patriarchal power – and violence – is strengthened by the erosion of state-funded childcare. As Lucí Cavallero and Verónica Gago (2021) write of Latin America, precarity 'constitutes a specific economy of violence in which femicide and travesticides are its culminating scene'. In Britain, campaign group Pregnant then Screwed organised an 11-city-wide protest in October 2022. Their protest highlighted that chronic underfunding has rendered Britain's childcare system the second most expensive in the world, and that mothers are penalised with 45 per cent lower earnings in the six years after giving birth. The campaign's key objective is the greater inclusion of women in the formal labour market. This is an important goal, but it also reflects a classed ideal of labour formality that has imploded for many sections of society. It speaks to a desired return to a Keynesian economic regime, rather than the transformation of the way that reproductive work is valued – with greater childcare provision, employers will no longer 'miss out on a pool of brilliant, talented mothers like us', the website reads.

When we widen out our understanding of reproductive work so that we are not solely focused on mothering subjectivities, we find that systems of differentiated value create higher burdens of social reproduction for all sorts of people, all sorts of networks, households, communities and groups. When we expand our understanding of reproduction beyond the figure of the child, to consider the replenishment of all relationships required for survival, we arrive at a more nuanced perspective of the ways that racial capitalism alienates differentially valued reproductive workers from their labours of love. Making this alienation legible also helps to reveal the systems, structures, power relations and hierarchies that are socially reproduced through relationships. In the precariously shared spaces of London's rented accommodation, the transmutation of people into secure returns on assets enmeshes them within extractive, transactional economic relations that can subsume life's relational work within the production of rent. In this chapter, I explore some of the ways that this relational work is experienced and practised.

The work of cumulative precarity

As we have seen, the idea of collective obstruction from anticipated entitlements has always driven the racial ordering of Britain's political economy. A tension in this book is that discussions of millennial precariousness can similarly augment an image of White detriment. It is vital to challenge this construction by carving out room for axes of racialised and classed oppression within conceptualisations of millennial insecurity. In doing so, we can retain the significance of generational inequality, while acknowledging that many millennials are dealing with precarity on a range of temporal and geographical fronts, including intergenerationally – since, in the words of Saidiya Hartman, the legacies of empire are 'yet to end' (2002: 761). One way is considering the cumulative aspects of precarity. Thinking about precarity as cumulative accounts for the everyday negotiation of insecurity across multiple temporal scales: the mediation of present policies, the navigation of historical state violence and engagements with a broader sense of generational obstruction.

Cumulative precarity requires intensified burdens of affective and relational work. This conceptualisation reflects burgeoning syntheses between three strands of geography: research on the political economy of generational subjectivity (see Moos et al 2018; Tomaszczyk and Worth 2018; Taylor 2021a); studies of the everyday negotiation of government policies on welfare, housing and immigration; and scholarship examining the spaces and politics of precarious labour. By bringing these areas of study in deeper conversation with each other, we can expand geographical understandings of precarity to engage with historically sedimented insecurities that are both intergenerationally reproduced and generationally distinct. Uncovering the work of cumulative precarity especially visibilises the forms of labour required to mediate stacked insecurities and traumas within familial relationships. As the narratives in this section show, this labour can incorporate the work of preserving generationally divergent fantasies of future advancement as well as the work of mediating state violence across timelines. This points to an expansion of 'generational' experience to include multigenerational transmission.

I focus next on stories shared by three millennials living with members of their origin families in social housing in the London Borough of Hackney. Framing their stories is an increasingly 'neo-illiberal' (Hendrickse 2020) policy paradigm that has accelerated the dispossession of low-income households in Britain while ramping up the detention and deportation of migrants, in particular migrants of colour. As ever, subsistence in Britain is historically bordered along lines of ethnicity and racialised citizenship (see Benson and Lewis 2019; El-Enany 2020). Reflecting this, the stories I discuss reflect experiences of millennial precarity that are racialised, not only through contemporary policies but also through longer histories of British state violence targeting poor people of colour. These institutional legacies, on a global and local scale, are the fabric through which contemporary policies are woven. It is in this way that cumulative precarity is so binding. Where precarity is intergenerationally mediated, multiple temporalities make the webbing of everyday life's relationships; future dreams of advancement must be reconfigured, present realities both hidden and managed, memories and lasting impacts negotiated. In concentrated, shared space, this is intense reproductive work.

Demonstrating that the 'monstrous intimacies' of slavery's legacies are the 'original trauma and the subsequent repetitions', Christina Sharpe's attention to the imbrication of intimacy with 'spaces for witnessing' speaks to the deep ambivalence of kinship as a domain within which the affective work of negotiating trauma is done (2010: 65). Attention to such ambivalence – particularly with its emphasis on the tense relationship between temporal and spatial scales of experience – is crucial for geographical research on familial relations more broadly. To make sense of familial care and love as a site of affective ambivalence, bell hooks' work on love (2000b) is also a key reference. In particular, hooks' distinction between love and care makes room for the laborious impositions of familial relationships alongside the revolutionary joys of defending and sustaining them. Perhaps the liberatory potential of affective labour in relationships is rooted in engagement with history and memory as temporal scales of experience. As Sharpe's work demonstrates, memory is relational. In this way, precarious subjectivities are constituted by the work of relating to what was, what is, what could be, what might have been. The affective labour of *relating* across scales is a key foundation of cumulative precarity as it is mediated and lived.

Legacies

I have been acquainted with Themba since 2014, when we met through music. At the time of our interviews in 2018, she was 26. Themba had lived in Hackney virtually all her life. Her mum moved from southern Africa to Britain in the 1980s where she met her dad. Themba still lived with her dad in a council-rented house, along with her three sisters, one of whom she shared a bedroom with. The inflated cost of private renting in the area meant she couldn't move out, and she didn't have a clear idea of when that would ever be possible. But she was close to her room-mate sibling and for now she managed.

We were already on familiar terms, so when I first interviewed Themba, she came round to my shared house. I managed to find a time that no one was using the kitchen so we could chat in private. It was February and apocalyptically warm for winter. 'Early evening, February summer, my painting taken off the wall', one of my songs from that time starts, documenting the breakdown in housemate relationships that would shortly motivate my departure. Themba was working in education at the time, having just finished a degree. She was deeply dedicated to her church community and the ensemble she played in. She wanted to work in education with young people caught in the criminal justice system, and as our conversation got underway, she explained that she had also experienced the trauma of state violence at a young age. These experiences still reverberated in her family relationships, and they interlocked with different forms of housing and income precarity. When she was 11, she and two of her sisters were removed from the home they shared with their mum and put into foster care in South London. They didn't move back to Hackney until Themba was 16, when they went to live with their dad. Most of the siblings were still estranged from their mum, and her housing insecurity made it even harder to keep in contact – she had been evicted via Section 21 multiple times.

Themba described her ongoing anger towards the actions of Hackney children's services. As a child, SWAT teams had broken into her home to take her little sister and the council had told the siblings that they could only stay in Hackney if they were willing to split up:

> 'We were like, "Why did it have to be like that?" You know? I think we were really angry at social services because we were like, they ruined our family. Especially our older sister. She said, "They've ruined our family, basically, there's nothing that can be said that is great about Hackney Social Services." But she, that's how she felt, and I think we all would agree because I think there was a better way to go around it. … And we were just angry, like you know they never let us find out what was going on. They never let us go to – we kept asking if we could go to the family court to hear the decisions they're making on our life. So they didn't let us do that, even.'

Themba's experiences echo many of those documented in scholarship illuminating the institutional racism of state child removal (see Bywaters et al 2017). While much of this literature is focused on US child welfare systems, the same structural inequalities exist in Britain and were expanded under New Labour (see also Neale & Lopez 2017; Support Not Separation campaign). Themba described how trampled agency and concealment continued to reverberate in her familial relationships. She had taken over the delicate role of interceding from her older sister, but lines of communication were made more fragile by her mum's housing issues:

> 'I think our sister was really just tired of passing on messages, so she was like, "It's your choice." And since then, we've had some contact with her, but it's kind of hard to maintain a relationship with her, because she goes up and down, here there and everywhere, I know she's having problems with her housing as well. She was in a house that – well for one, wasn't really in a great condition anyway, and then she got evicted. I don't really know why, she showed us the letter and the letter didn't really specify why they were evicting. It looked like a normal house, but it was like a normal house with all the different rooms, but they were renting all the rooms out to different people. … It did put us off visiting and then sometimes she didn't want us to come to see her in that environment. So the last time we heard she was evicted and she was living somewhere else, I don't know where.'

In the same interview, Themba went on to explain that the pressure of being a relational intermediary was complicated by legacies of omission that surrounded their removal as children. Themba stated repeatedly that her youngest sister didn't "know anything" about their childhood experiences: the burden of memory and communication was carried by the eldest daughters.

'Our little sister has not known anything about what's going on with our mum because we thought it wouldn't help her. We said it wouldn't help her to get better if she knew what was going on with our mum and we're like, if they see each other, it's just gonna set off some kind of weird reaction or something, and it will just make them both worse. It's just been trying to find a way to introduce that a little bit. Because she doesn't know anything. And if our mum sees her how she is now, she's gonna be like, "Why did you let her get like this"?'

Themba's capacity to hold a relationship together between her mum, her sister and herself required different types of affective work: managing communications, visits in sporadic locations, protecting her mum and sister from realities. This work was not created but intensified by the contemporary housing insecurity that made eviction a repeated occurrence in Themba's mum's life. Constraints were cumulatively transferred across generations, augmenting the labour of managing present relationships. At the same time, this labour was compassionately carried out, driven by empathic considerations and what bell hooks describes as 'mindful remembering' on behalf of her siblings (hooks 2000b: 209). As she attempts to find ways to heal the estrangement between her sister and mother, Themba's emotional work recalls 'the space of possibility' that hooks assigns to re-engaging with spaces of 'lack' in earlier life (hooks 2000b: 221). To valorise this work risks reifying Themba's position as family mediator and romanticising state violence as somehow 'useful or instructive', in the words of Saidya Hartman (2008: 14). But to make this work legible is a necessary part of understanding the ways that precarity can be cumulatively experienced. In mainstream narratives of millennial insecurity, this work is largely unseen.

Nouman's story similarly shows us the work of cumulative precarity. I got to know Nouman because we both attending the same political meeting in late 2017. He was a 24-year-old postgraduate student at the time, and bartending locally. Nouman lived in a house rented from a housing association in east-central Hackney, with his parents, two of his siblings, his sister-in-law and her two children. Nouman's bedroom was in the attic. It was rough and ready up there: a mattress, a Playstation 4 and a bucket under a leaky Velux window, but it was his safe haven of quietude and independence: a place to get away from the density of living with so many family members. Like Themba, privately renting in the area was off limits for Nouman. He dreamed of running away to Berlin and participating in trade union movements there – it would be more affordable than trying to live independently in his own neighbourhood.

London had been Nouman's home city since the 1990s, when his family left Afghanistan as refugees. His older brother had arrived unaccompanied before them and Nouman's dad joined nearly three years afterwards. "By the time my dad saw me, I think I was about three years old," Nouman told me. "Two-and-a-half years passed and he saw me again when he came back here – he managed to actually successfully legally emigrate here." The varied legal circumstances of his cohabiting family were a source of stress and anxiety for Nouman. When he first got residency in England, Nouman's father was allocated council housing outside of London, and although his dad now lived with the rest of his family, Nouman was fearful about any potentially compromised legalities to do with this. These fears were heightened by rising Islamophobia and crackdowns on social housing tenants, fuelled by scapegoating that is peddled by most British newspapers. "I have no fucking clue why they do this," Nouman told me, voicing concerns that "technically he's not supposed to be living with us." He was concerned, too, about his sister-in-law living in the house, since the 'Right to Rent' policy enforces passport checks for social housing occupants, and Nouman's brother was still trying to reach the Minimum Income Requirement to sponsor her visa (HM Government 2019a). He had taken on extra work to not only pay for the spouse visa but to prove to the Home Office that he met the minimum annual salary of £18,600 required for his wife to live with him. Nouman's sister-in-law could thus neither safely stay nor leave during the process: she didn't have the right to live there, but she didn't have anywhere else to go.

Such are the ontological absurdities that have been created by the 'hostile environment' framework of immigration policy. Amidst the material and legal threats posed by both of these situations, it was hard affective work for Nouman to relate to his dad and brother. He argued with his dad about the original council flat and the potential legal dangers he feared, trying to encourage his dad to think about it differently. "I feel really fucked," he said, "I am genuinely scared because it won't just look bad on him, it'll look bad on all of us, you know what I mean?" Nouman was keenly aware of the media sensationalism that families like his could become the target of: "Any random guy they find, they'll just report it: 'This guy, he's got all this' – you know what I'm trying to say. Sensationalist headlines." Precarious futures met with precarious pasts, and Nouman was in the middle of it all.

His relationship with his older brother similarly involved mediating precarious experience across multiple temporalities. First, there were the contemporary insecurities unfolding from the confusing legalities of living with his brother:

'My elder brother, he's not really supposed to be living with us. He's not supposed to be living with us, but he's got nowhere else to go. Basically, he got married to someone who wasn't from this country, but as a result – you know how the rules are, you have to put your wages and your salary, they have to be a certain amount. And then after he married, he was in a less financially secure situation, so he had to live with us with his wife and kids. And now he's trying to get his wife's visa, he's having to work a lot more hours than he should, and it's not good for the mental health of my family. Everyone's just shouting and arguing with each other, stuff like that. Money. My parents are always like, "Why did you have all these kids, why did you get married?" It just gets personal sometimes. It's just family life. If you go back 10, 20, 30 years ago, people like my elder brother could afford to move out, live in a flat and just kind of have their families but in this generation we just can't. We have to stay, we're so vulnerable. I mean I guess we're lucky that our parents live here, and they have a big house. And you know, these arguments would've happened 30 years ago. But thing is, we could afford to go away.'

For Nouman, then, an overarching sense of generational obstruction – a collective sense of vulnerability – was associated with the legal and emotional precarity of living with his brother. Decades ago, he and his brother might have been able to live apart and have some distance from the tension. But in 2018, he was unable to opt out of his family's stacked predicaments. As a result, he was also unable to take space and distance from their traumas. This was part of Nouman's affective workload, and he was deeply aware of that.

'It just gets very personal, like my brother did go through a lot. He grew up during the war. So he was born in 1984, the war in Afghanistan was from '79 to '89. And then there was a civil war which we lived through. We had a sibling who died before I was born in Afghanistan so he would have been aware of that, present when that happened. He came to this country undocumented, on his own, as a refugee, before all of us. But my parents have kind of always been hard on him and I think it's psychologically affected him.'

From his brother's traumatic childhood experiences to the interlocking insecurities of cohabiting in a crowded home amidst hostile border enforcement, precarity was mediated through relational histories and closely shared space. Within this space, Nouman practised forms of affective mediation to sustain familial relationships, caring for his brother's children and de-escalating conflict. He noted and appreciated the affective work that the children did, too. He loved living with his niece and nephew, commenting on their happiness:

'There's just something about kids, they've got a very unique viewpoint of the world. They're very naïve but innocent, and it refreshes you.

I could be the most depressed person one day and I'll just see my niece and nephew and they'll be watching cartoons and they'll come up to me and I'll be like – hey, I feel better now!'

Cheering each other up was a two-way street. Nouman explained that he had strategies for keeping them content and distracted when tensions flared:

'My niece is three and my nephew is five months. Sometimes I take my niece to the nursery, sometimes I babysit them when they're out. Sometimes when my sister-in-law and my brother get into arguments, I take them into the other room and put some cartoons on for them, for them not to see that.'

Such relational work was necessitated by cumulative insecurities circulating in shared space, a space in which, in Nouman's own words, several family members were "not supposed to be living." Against this enduring state directive, Nouman worked to rationalise, relate and repair. Doing so required, in Christina Sharpe's words, the reformulation of intimate spaces produced by the 'psychic and material reach' of Empire (2010: 4). Nouman's story is grounded in distinctly different histories of that Empire – Sharpe is explicitly referring to transatlantic slavery – yet, the combined psychical and material reach of war, undocumented migration and contemporary state violence created burdens of intimate re-engagement that he was keenly aware of. Sedimented insecurities were managed with everyday strategies of de-escalation and care. Nouman was glad to have the attic to retreat to.

Fantasies

Nouman was a political activist and he rejected his family's meritocratic value systems. At the same time, he felt he had to suppress his real life from his parents to protect their fantasies of advancement. Sarah Marie Hall's emphasis (2020: 178) on the 'temporalities of crisis and conjuncture' within austerity's everyday relationships resonates here, whereby the ways people 'image themselves' are knitted together with previous experiences of hardship as well as future imaginaries. In a similar vein, Nouman's efforts to protect these fantasies were rooted in his father's earlier experiences as much as the material pressures of the present, and intensified by cohabitation:

'I've had quite a few discussions and arguments with my dad like, "You've got this degree, why are you doing all these shit jobs?" Obviously, my dad's gone through a lot. He fought in the war, he was a soldier during the Russian occupation, he was a soldier during the Afghan civil war, he was in jail. So his constant reasoning is, "I've gone through all this struggle, so there has to be some fruit to it, you have to become an office man, and you have to buy a house." They do have expectations of me to become some kind of dude, some salary man, but that's not what I want to be. And it would help if I could live away from them and just get on with my life, but because I'm there all the time, these conversations always pop up, over breakfast or lunch. Constant, constant, constant.'

Nouman also mentioned that he felt compelled to construct a false narrative of social mobility to preserve these aspirations. He expressed hurt, for example, that his parents hid his job from extended family members:

'I want them to be happy, I want them to not worry. Whenever they go to family meetings, whenever someone asks "What does your son do?", they're always like "Oh, our son works in an office!" They make up some bullshit. It makes me feel really bad, I feel really shit! I'm like, why did you have to tell them that?!'

Nouman was bruised by his parent's shame, and had learned to pre-empt it by coming up with alternative stories of his working life in conversations with relatives:

'They were asking what I was doing and I thought for a second and was like, "Yeah the bar is great!" and then was like aaaahhh! So I just played up more of my studies part. Because if I'm not working, if I don't talk about – I can basically just go on about my studies and shit. That'll just put them off what I'm doing work-wise. And my activism stuff came up and I basically gassed myself up.'

Through talking about his political work with relatives, Nouman gamed the meritocratic imperative, finding a conversational hack for the pressures of carrying the projected aspirations of a family that had gone through so much trauma. In doing so, he preserved his integrity but also carved an image of attainment. While his boundaries were so compromised by his living situation, he showed up for himself and the people who relied on him. But in his own words, the communicative and affective work of negotiating cumulative precarity was "constant, constant, constant."

Like Nouman, Faiz was militant in his dedication to art over financial aspiration. But like Nouman, that didn't stop it hurting when his parents expressed their dismay that he had not achieved the middle-class security they had assumed would unfold from a university degree. "I've had to like, take materialism out of my dreams," Faiz told me in one of our interviews. Part of a large British-Bangladeshi network, Faiz's family had lived in East

London for generations. Members of his wider family had been homeowners for decades, but Faiz's parents had refused to get a mortgage for religious reasons. Both his parents and his sister were religious, but Faiz said he was no longer a practising Muslim. He described the ways that this bifurcation had intensified disparities in economic understanding. As discussed in the previous chapter, Faiz was also unable to leave the family household, not just because he couldn't afford to, but because he wanted to protect his parents from underoccupancy penalties. He had also witnessed how much work his mum had put into their council-rented flat. As well as the personal value of this work, his mother's investments had increased the financial value of the house, entrenching Faiz's sense of stuckness. He felt that he risked squandering his mother's invested labours in the home, if he asked the council for help with his own housing situation.

> 'They've literally done things like change the sink themselves because the council won't do it. It's a small, tiny sink. And my mum's really house proud, she's like, "No, I want a nice sink." The council wouldn't do it so she went and bought a nice sink for herself. And like, there were two lamps in the living room and the council wouldn't turn it into one big lamp because it was nicer to look at, so she did it herself. She really has increased the property's value, and it means that I can't go to the council for help.'

On top of this sense of filial duty was the additional frustration of unaffordable private rents and the impossibility of ownership. This bind of immobility created burdens of communicative work. Amidst divergent economic understandings and beliefs, Faiz felt compelled to educate, explain, justify and rationalise his own precarity. He detailed how he had tried to convince his mother of the impossibility of buying a house in London in cash:

> 'My mum is completely deluded! So I had to have this conversation like, "Let's just work this out, OK. So you think I'm gonna make what, 50 thousand pounds a year, and I'm not gonna spend a single penny of it." She's like, "Yeah just give it all to us, we'll help you live." OK because you know, we're doing so well now, but anyway. ... So we just counted out 50, 100, 150, 200 – we're talking about 15, 20 years of not spending a single penny. To eventually buy a house in cash. Do you realise – and then I spoke her through what inflation means and I spoke her through taxes and how the way the economy works is set up so you can't just save it.'

The work undertaken by Faiz to highlight economic realities was embedded with the reproduction of everyday life in the household he shared with his parents. This labour was affective: entwined with the relational production of atmosphere and feeling in the home. For this atmosphere to be tolerable, these thoughts and conversations had to be fielded. Without the means to rent independently, Faiz had no choice but to participate, and no choice but to fray his boundaries. If biopolitical production involves labour that 'works directly on the affects' (Hardt 1999: 99), we should note these forms of affective work – the immaterial labours of social reproduction – as one of the central means through which the surplus value of the built environment is extracted. Faiz's involuntary living situation obstructed intentionality around communicative labour with his parents. Like Nouman, he felt dragged into their projections and felt like he couldn't get through to them. Again, the precarity accumulated across generations interlocked with contemporary insecurities that his parents struggled to accept as reality. Faiz's mum clung to imaginary pathways to security:

'I remember my mum telling my dad off like, "Why didn't you look at this five years earlier? Now the prices have gone up so much!" So I had to have this conversation and my mum's trying to convince me to give acting up and I was like, "Look, what do you expect me to do?" She's just like, "Get a normal job, they start you on 30k, you work up to 50k and then 60k and then you just buy a house." But in my religion you're not allowed to take a mortgage because it's got interest. A lot of my other family members who aren't as zealous, they bought houses in Stoke Newington, sold it off six, seven years ago and then moved out to Redbridge. ... You know, there's just something there. Anything they're building now is additional. I feel like we are still kind of in the pits.'

Explaining realities and justifying choices were part of Faiz's role as an intermediary between multiple temporalities. Alongside managing his mum's anxiety for the future as well as her financial regret, Faiz nonetheless defended his own dreams and identity. This work was relational, then, but inclusive of the self: it involved going back repeatedly to the same issues, helping his parents to reframe their aspirations in light of economic realities, but it was also reflective and solitary – learning methods of detachment from materialism, weighing up how best to protect himself as well as his family, figuring out the future while mediating the past.

Such accounts reflect generational disjunctures unfolding from the neoliberalisation of housing, wherein pressures to play into aspirational fantasies of a forgone middle-class security are amplified by multigenerational cohabitation – a cohabitation that is in itself economically indicative of late capitalist precarity. For the privately renting millennials I spoke to over the course of this project, these generational disjunctures were still a feature of life, but the pressure to educate, legitimate and justify was lessened through geographical distance: boundaries between family members could be more easily established and held.

Laborious conversations were not entirely unavoidable, however. Jonathan, for example, was a 29-year-old private renter at the time of our discussions in 2018. We were loosely acquainted, having originally met through the anti-war movement. Jonathan, who was originally from East Anglia, worked for a non-governmental organisation. It had been an uphill struggle to get a secure job in the third sector, and he described a trajectory towards this destination that had been laden with student debt, multiple service sector jobs, and highly insecure rental situations, including a brief spell as a former friend's lodger. At the time we met, Jonathan lived in a one-bed flat in Hackney Central with his girlfriend. It was small and expensive, but it was the nicest place he'd had in London. His parents had nonetheless communicated their dismay and disbelief at his material conditions. Like many White, middle-class people in British society, Jonathan's parents had experienced the social mobility of the postwar consensus. After growing up in public housing, they had become owner-occupiers with secure jobs and comfortable retirements. They struggled to understand what was between Jonathan and comparable 'success'. As a result, Jonathan mentally carried a readymade cache of facts and figures to include in conversations with them, which would inevitably arise whenever they visited:

'They'd come to London and go, "Whaaat how are you living here? Why is it costing you so much?" So I'd sit them down and say, "Let's have a look. Do you think that you could find somewhere better?" Once they actually get their head around that that is actually the new real, that it's not that you've just decided to. … Conditions have just got worse. There's something about just opening the door and going, "Yes this is where I live," when it's so much smaller and your relationship with it is so much less secure. I'll find myself pulling out random stats on London housing just so that everybody knows that this is the situation.'

Again, like Faiz, Jonathan felt pressed to educate his parents on London living costs, and the fact that conditions "have just got worse." Perennially chipping away at years of ballooning student debt, Jonathan also felt that he had to justify his consumer decisions to his parents, as if they reflected a lack of seriousness about wanting to change his circumstances. For Jonathan, what he wanted was irrelevant, because of the "margin between what you earn" and the cost of housing:

'When my mum and dad are like, "Well how come you went out for dinner the other night?", I'm like, "What am I going to do with it?

What literally am I going to do with it?" I want to pay my debts off but actually it doesn't matter if I have one pint a week or six pints a week, I still need to become an investment banker before I can actually buy a house somewhere that I want to live. A lot of people in [the] upper working class, lower middle class, whatever you want to call it, bracket, you're like well, I'm not in a situation where I've got nothing: I can have an iPhone and go out and get drunk and stuff like that, but there's not much point in me not doing any of that stuff because I could save a couple of grand every year. What am I gonna do with it? Go on holiday? You still don't actually have the prospect of materially changing your conditions, because the margin between what you earn and the cost of housing is too big.'

Working to make home

The stories outlined in this chapter thus far speak to the hard work of replenishing connection amidst precarity's generational disjunctures. This is not just about connection to family members, but about maintaining connection to the self amidst the compromised relational boundaries unfolding from economic inequality. Creating and maintaining a connection to the self – and to others – requires a durable connection to physical space. The inverse of this, according to philosopher Zygmunt Bauman (2003), is the 'liquid love' of our consumer age, exemplified by mobile connectivity. In a technocapitalist society built on digital connectivity, mobility and physical separation, the normalisation of transience has consequences for the durability of community infrastructures. The normalisation of relational transience is a disciplining facet of neoliberal life. This is evident, for example, in historical geographies of union militancy – Thatcher favoured North Sea oil extraction at least partly because of the seasonal work rhythms of oil rigs, because workers could never form the consistent relational bonds that miners did. The same thing is true of tenant organising. Private renters dealing with Assured Shorthold Tenancies, renting from individual landlords, and scared of complaining about anything face barriers to building mass power. Tenants living in the same block or estate for generations, renting from the same landlord, have more opportunities for building mass power; it is one of the reasons they are defamed, silenced, divided and ultimately displaced. As a researcher at the London Assembly, I met scores of housing estate residents who had been actively instructed to mistrust their neighbours, with conflicting interests between, for example, leaseholders and council tenants, relentlessly stoked by developers and councils. At Achilles Street in Lewisham, resident campaigners' anti-demolition banners had been taken down, but they didn't know by whom. Was it the council? Absentee landlords who were invested in regeneration schemes? Fractured interests and the stoking of inter-community mistrust lead to weaker relational bonds and thus weakened resistance.

Feeling like you belong somewhere is critical to the self-esteem required to build relationships. But in a rentier capitalist society in which the landlord is fed first, many private tenants spend more of their time working for the home they live in, than living in it. As a result, they don't often have the capacity to form community ties. Over the course of my research for this project, I spoke to some private renters that were high earners. One, Tom, was 27 and earned £57,000 per year working in marketing consultancy in the city. His hours were long and intense, and he didn't end up having very much time to spend in Hackney Downs, where he shared a flat with two friends. Instead, his work was his family:

'It's the most familial, because there's only nine of us, everyone likes to drink, it's the most fun, familial. It's always had that small vibe – you buy into the philosophy as well as what you do, especially in our space when they're that small, because they'll be led by someone like our founder, who's quite openly visionary and proselytises his vision.'

Tom was relationally satisfied by his work culture; it fulfilled his longing for kinship. While he was engaged in local arts and queer culture, he described spending most of his leisure time on consumption. My conversations with Tom took place about two years before the COVID-19 outbreak in Britain. In endless cycles of lockdown, many private renters like Tom suddenly encountered a very different relationship to their homes. Homes became workplaces, places of cultural consumption, care facilities, recreational spaces, studios.

The mutual aid networks that exploded in the wake of the first lockdown orders also illustrated the extent to which people actually wanted and were invested in community ties to their neighbours. With stronger community ties, there was greater investment in mutual defence. Neighbours I had met through the summer lockdowns of 2020 – usually while sunning myself in an empty parking space – turned up regularly while my partner and I were going through our eviction. They promised to locally circulate news of this injustice. We were invited for tea, given furniture and offered removal vans. Through their support, I was also able to contribute to neighbours in need. For example, with the van, I collected an unused mattress and delivered it to a family in temporary accommodation. With our eviction notice in the background, however, the work I had put into making my home in that fated basement flat was being concurrently squandered. As usual, it was easier to give away possessions than pay hundreds to move them all every one or two years. In Clapton, leave something on the street for five minutes and it will get picked up; I am thankful for this service because it is free. Over time, private renters learn that having as little as possible is more economical.

While writing this book, another tenancy came to an end. Looking around the flat I had loved for two years, I fought feelings of regret for the shelves I had erected, the drawings I had fixed to the walls, the string lights. Renters are not permitted to leave a trace of their habitation. I spent my final weekend at the flat with scraper in one hand and Polyfilla in the other, cleaning, scrubbing, mopping, plastering and painting, just as I had done at my eight previous Hackney abodes. This labour is carried out to protect the capital of landlords, and if it is not done, the landlord takes the entire protected tenancy deposit. I cleaned and repaired my flat to the highest standard, spending an additional £200 on professional cleaning help. My landlord still took over £600 of my deposit. The previous landlord (of Chapter 1's pandemic-courgette-eviction fame) even tried to take deposit money for furniture we had bought from the previous tenants.

Short-term leases in the private rented sector create a complex relationship to improving and bettering space. Rooting yourself somewhere is dangerous because of the grief and pain that comes with the inexorable uprooting. This hesitancy is carried into community relationships: why invest if your time is limited? We can therefore read longings for relational connection in renters' work to create a sense of belonging and home in their accommodation. Among respondents, such desires were nonetheless in tension with fears of losing deposits, or antipathy towards landlords who would reap the financial benefits of tenants' self-funded home improvements. Why would they contribute to the appreciation of an asset they do not own? Leon, who lived in a split-level flat in Haggerston with a friend, was plagued by the knowledge that he had all the construction acumen required to significantly improve his home, but that any improvements would simply furnish the wealth of his landlord:

'I work in construction so I know what you can do with some plasterboard and some paint. I always look around my house and think, if this was my house then blah blah blah blah and it'd be great. But honestly, because I'm renting it, even if I have those thoughts, I'm not gonna tell my landlord that, you know? It's his house. This isn't actually "my" place. I'm here for a certain amount of time.'

As we know from the previous chapter, Leon also had first-hand knowledge of what repair and refurbishment felt like when you had autonomy and security in durable space. He described his girlfriend's house, expressing admiration for the interior design. For Leon, the house was a source of escape from the alienated material reality of his own flat:

'It's a beautiful house. They bought an absolute wreck of a house a few years ago and then they did it up and it's this amazingly beautiful house. It's like a little escape from reality almost. It's beautiful, it's a beautiful place. It's like a townhouse in Stokey, it's a beautiful house, and it's just been done up. I was looking at all the pictures of the build and you know, they've done really cool work, I can't fault this work. The first time I went to her house, we'd been on a couple of dates and I ended up staying there for like three days, and I thought afterwards, "Fucking hell, that was a nice little escape from reality, I wonder if that will ever happen again".'

For Leon, the house was not only beautiful but also spoke to his own style and standard of construction work – these are features he would have created in a home that he also owned. The value of the work in his girlfriend's house wasn't wasted on improving someone else's asset, an asset he was effectively charged monthly for protecting. Instead, the beautiful work in this Stoke Newington house was part of a trajectory of growth, putting down roots, making everyday life sweeter. A place to invite people to, a place where relationships could be held and sustained. Jonathan was also frustrated that he couldn't work on his home as a private renter. Again, like Leon, not being able to work on his flat has relational ramifications. He felt like he was missing out on something with his dad:

'There's definitely something there in a gendered way I think, in terms of my relationship with my dad and my older brother who both have had the opportunity to have this kind of masculine rite of passage: "I'm gonna knock this wall down," or, "I've got enough space to do shit with bits of wood on a Saturday or whatever." If you live in rented accommodation, particularly in London, you have no opportunity like that to engage with your environment. And I've always lived in flats around here which are so badly designed. It's generally been in the 70s or 80s where people have gone, "Fantastic, let's knock up as many plasterboard walls as we can, let's just plug a bathroom in here and squeeze as many people as we can into these places," and that's the reality of most rented accommodation round here, isn't it? And you're like, "If only I could just start from scratch, rebuild this space in a better way".'

Jonathan and Leon both knew their accommodation could be a product of their own creative and constructive labour, rather than simply a place to pay for and keep in roughly the same shoddy condition they had found it in.

Sometimes, when tenancies are extremely insecure, there is paradoxically more freedom to make changes, even through the gritted teeth of knowing you are doing free work for your landlord's gain. For privately renting couple Joel and Alice, this was the case. In 2018, they lived with their one-year-old in a one-bed flat above a small grocery store in Clapton. The plumbing for the grocery store went right through their home, exposed pipes gurgling with astonishing vigour every time a tap was turned or toilet flushed. The bedroom was separated from the living room with plasterboard, and the kitchen was a small counter about three feet long. The couple had strong doubts about the legal existence of the flat. "There's four flats in the building," Alice told me. "We think we're a secret flat, and I think if every person who lives here registered to vote, there would be a bit of a problem – because we say we're Flat A and we don't know where's Flat A. We're probably Flat D or something." They paid their rent in cash to the landlord, who they described as "crooks": the rent had been raised a month before their first baby (they had another) was born. Alice recalled the shock of finding this out while heavily pregnant. Joel described the flat as "half-finished." To him, it felt like "they just decided there was a point where they were like, 'We can probably get someone to live in here'." Joel told me that he had discovered the flat was never registered as a property or applied to be a property with the council, so the landlords knew "they can probably get away with the bare minimum." There was no contract, "just some business cards with the money I've paid written on them."

Still, to them, the flat was still a steal at less than a grand a month. And they needed low rent, because Joel's freelance work had dried up, and Alice was doing a master's while working full-time in sign language interpreting. So, they sucked it up, and they found openings within the precarity: amidst the total indifference of her landlord, Alice felt like she had more freedom to change things without permission. "I literally think we could do whatever we wanted to this place," she said, "they wouldn't care. I don't think they'd realise. We put those shelves up there. My first week of maternity leave, I re-grouted the bathroom, because I was like: 'My baby is not coming into this room!'." But really, there was little joy for Alice and Joel in attempting to secretly baby-proof a flat through their own financial means, when the place offered them so little protection and belonging. With the stress of living in crowded, dilapidated space, Alice's mind and spirit were often clouded. Like Anzuli in the previous chapter, the moments when this really flared were when Alice couldn't make social reproduction work in the space. For example, there was nowhere to properly prepare food. "There's nowhere to actually chop anything," she said. There was no space to "put things away, like everything just seems to have to be out." Sometimes, Alice told me, the flat felt "really oppressively untidy," but she had become "depressingly accepting" of it. "I had a really depressing thought the other day when I was like, 'If I was terminally ill, I could die here'. That would be the saddest thing."

The informality of the private rented sector means that you never really know how hands-off, vengeful, invasive, agreeable, contactable or controlling a landlord will be. The 'Rogue Landlord Checker' – that Mayor Sadiq Khan is proud of – technically gives tenants the opportunity to suss out whether their prospective landlord has been prosecuted for misdeeds in the sector. But as the Green Group discovered at City Hall, the checker is not being used by many London councils, and enforcement is equally elusive. Offending landlords are wiped from records after two years, in line with criminal justice legislation, and there have been reports of fake names being employed to cover tracks and continue collecting rents from new tenants. Letting agents do not work on behalf of tenants – without the now-banned 'agent fees' that were previously added to new tenants' moving costs, their revenue comes from landlords – so they provide little protection if tenants rent their homes through such intermediaries. A benevolent, boundaried landlord is therefore all that a private renter can really hope for.

For Nasra, this was a welcome feature of her renting life, and one that meant she had been able to work on the flat, deepening her relationship to the place as her home, and fostering positive relationships with her neighbours. "It's a direct landlord, she lives down the road," Nasra told me in her bright and tidy living room.

> 'Her family live downstairs. She's quite hands-off in a way. She knows us, she trusts us, and she lets us do what we want with the house. So she's like, "Yeah, do the garden, yeah, put up pictures, yeah, do what you want, paint the wall whatever." She kind of trusts us to look after the house. I think she's seen we're quite homely in here, so she just lets us get on with it.'

With freedom from intervention, Nasra was able to garden. Growing up, she had never had a garden. This was first time she'd had access to green space in her life, and she was rapt by it.

> 'I feel like we've made it quite homely. Last year we really did the garden nicely. Everybody chipped in and we made a massive vegetable garden and we had fruit and veg and salad every single day. This is a picture of the garden in the summer. We were really living the good life. We didn't have to buy any fruit or veg for the whole summer. I've never had a garden before. It's the first time we all had green space. We had so many vegetables. We were giving them to everyone. The neighbour, we gave him tons of courgettes.'

By growing and sharing food, Nasra was able to connect with her neighbours, establishing a stronger bond to the community she lives in. It has been bittersweet returning to Nasra's thoughts after being forced to leave my home for doing far less of the very same thing. Having the capacity to do this work in a garden, for the first time in her life, increased Nasra's sense of security amidst the impermanence always lingering in the background of private rental life. She was literally grounded, rooted, nurtured by the capacity to nurture. And yet, just like Joel and Alice, no contract existed. "I think she just trusts us as people," Nasra said, "because we haven't paid a deposit and there's no guarantor." Again, it was this very insecurity that paradoxically gave Nasra a greater sense of freedom to do as she pleased in the flat. The only way to game the alienated labour of precarity was through doing it partly in secret – as Tsianos and Papadopoulos (2006) write, to become 'cunning' is an affective burden of precarious work.

In this chapter, I have woven together some of the more hidden affective labours involved in the reproduction of intimate relationships amidst precarity, focusing on the ways they are alienated by the twin forces of capital and state. For example, the intergenerational transmission of racialised state violence was seen to interlock with contemporary policies, mediating relationships through the sediments of cumulative precarity. This precarity intensified the affective labour of maintaining relationships, especially amidst unchosen, prolonged proximity to origin family members. My conversations with millennials renting in the private sector also demonstrated that the work of making a home and creating a sense of belonging within precarious, informally managed space involved confronting different attachments and accepting various realities. Trade-offs abounded: the dilapidation of an unlicensed flat was measured against cheap rent; a formal contract traded with the ability to grow vegetables outside. The need to justify, legitimate, bargain and scheme spoke to the alienation of lover's labours through capital's destruction of home. At the same time, there was little resentment or regret among respondents about the emotional work they practised. Nouman loved taking care of his brother's kids; Jonathan actively longed for a day of painting and decorating; Leon could see what needed to be worked on in his apartment, and exactly how to do it; Nasra raved about how much she loved growing food for her neighbours. All simply wanted the fruits of this labour to belong to their communities.

5

Feeling Space

In 2022, I had one of my first experiences of dating a homeowner. It was a world apart from relationships with people renting in shared flats and houses. I could speak after 10pm without being asked to keep it down, and we didn't need to book the living room days in advance to watch a film. There was less awkwardness, and more room for communication, experimentation, spontaneity. Our desire didn't feel confined, our voices didn't feel stifled. The flat was small for a two-bed: the kitchen and living room were the same room. It was nicely fitted out, but it wasn't palatial. The space nonetheless totally transformed my partner's opportunities to love and relate on their own terms.

The reality is that many people trapped in London's private rented sector are heading into middle age having never consistently experienced privacy or sovereignty regarding intimacy and sexual expression, because of the cost and quality of their housing. As adrienne maree brown's work so thoroughly outlines, this is a problem for our political power. Rentier capitalism suppresses our sexuality, and it therefore diminishes our erotic power. We need this power: it tells us what we really want. It guides us to the 'orgasmic yes,' in brown's words, that could undergird all the decisions we make in our lives. It gives us the confidence to show up for ourselves and for each other, and it refuses the enfeebling effects of shame, fear and self-minimisation. But in the thrown-togetherness of precarious renting in London, spaces are assembled by feelings, sensations and affects that are so often characterised by their constriction and constrictiveness.

In this chapter, I first look at the ways that affective politics circulate within precarious rental accommodation, as a result of constricted desires and difficulties in holding boundaries. Moving from a discussion of sexual constriction to feelings of 'displaced sovereignty' among respondents who are mistreated by, yet defend, controlling landlord behaviour, I aim to make connections between capital's constriction of embodied agency and the suppression of political subjectivity (see Taylor 2021b). In the second part of the chapter, I shift my engagement with desire to the efforts of queer collective households to realign their homes with desire for social and political transformation, and the tensions and challenges experienced along the way.

Thinking about precarious space as an assemblage of affects gives more agency to those who co-create that space. For geographers Colin McFarlane and Ben Anderson (2011), thinking about space as assemblage denotes an emergent plurality of power rather than a 'central governing power'. This gives us a way of thinking about precarious space that centres power without rendering it distant or monolithic: we can move beyond a vision of ourselves as simply navigating the impacts of things beyond our control. Space, in the words of theorist Henri Lefebvre, is not 'merely a political instrument for homogenising all parts of society' (1979: 191). Space isn't just happening 'to' us. The idea of space as affective assemblage can therefore enhance our understanding of the ways that biopower operates through networked life. Thinking with affective assemblage highlights our response-ability (see Haraway 2016; bergman and Montgomery 2017). Not our responsibility *for* unjust conditions, but our ability to respond to them from a place of political subjectivity: 'cramped space', in the words of Deleuze, forces each individual to 'connect immediately with politics' (1975: 17).

Thinking of space as networked feeling is implied by the ways that space metaphorically features in our descriptions of emotions. We sense distance, we feel isolated, our minds feel crowded, we need space, we want to be closer, we feel empty, our hearts desolate. We especially talk, write and sing about love as a place or space. 'I'm looking for a soft place to land', Kathleen Edwards sings, 'the forest floor, the palm of your hand' (2012). Our emotional imaginations are entwined with space, because we are animals living in nature, on Earth. The boundaries that we can and can't hold between ourselves and other objects and beings in space shape our nervous systems, our capacities, our beliefs, unfolding into the ways that we experience conscious reality. These boundaries are ignored by capital: for profits to consistently increase, the extractive relations of rentier capitalism require the spatial densification of people. The relationship of the tenant to their own identity is also commonly disregarded through proscriptions limiting the alteration of space. While needs and desires are constricted by involuntary proximities, identities are suppressed by blank magnolia walls.

Lauren Berlant described intimacy as emerging from 'mobile processes of attachment' in which 'contradictory desires mark the intimacy of daily life' (1998: 284–285). This is a fluid, unsanctified view of intimacy, but one that remains rooted in desire rather than circumstance. We must nevertheless account for the relationship between these contradictory desires and the materiality of precarious homes. Unwanted closeness obstructs the real closeness of intimacy, 'the sphere in which we become who we are, the space in which the self emerges' (Oswin and Olund 2010: 60). Our capacity to feel safe is directly tied to our capacity to establish and hold boundaries between ourselves and other people. In London, the precarity of renting has taken this safety away from people, splintering and fraying embodied sovereignty, consent and overall wellbeing. Zooming out, beyond the crumbling walls of privately rented terraces and overcrowded social homes, these dynamics bleed into the city's streets. In densely packed homes, with eroded green spaces and gutted youth services, many young people don't have anywhere to 'be' that they don't have to pay for (see Davies 2018). Claustrophobia, disenfranchisement, exclusion, poverty and policing have seen increases in violence among young people in London. Jackie, from the Peabody Trust on the Pembury Estate, explained more about these interconnections, and her own fears:

> 'Everything is flats, flats, flats. It's tightly closed. And the relationship between the police and the Black community is not very good. I'm not even sure they'd come out if you really needed them, anyway. It's sad, because when you're in that space where you're really frightened and your child's indoors all the time, in this very tight space, mentally it's not healthy. I make sure my grandson has an activity every single day. He's back home by about five thirty. It's sad, I grew up being able to play out, whereas children of today don't. I think everyone's really frightened because you're constantly hearing this bad news all the time – this has happened, this has happened, this has happened. There just isn't that respect. Mostly it's young people. I don't mean to be picking on them, but you just don't know what could happen. Anything can happen, say walking from here up to Stoke Newington. Anything could happen.'

Jackie's fears are the affective collateral of London's financialisation, where commercially driven regeneration schemes often mean that poor people of colour are forced to accept shrinking floorplans, spiralling rent inflation and the removal of public space and facilities. Young people from low-income backgrounds don't have room to breathe, play, connect, create, heal and grow. These conditions foment tension, as they do in privately rented house-shares where the same things are often lacking.

Since 2019, I have organised with a migrant-led mutual aid project called Akwaaba, working specifically with the children's project. During the first two years of the COVID-19 pandemic, there was an obvious and urgent scarcity of space for personal creativity among marginalised children spending successive lockdowns in overcrowded homes. Gaining a closer understanding of this motivated my decision to begin working at an adventure playground in Southeast Hackney. While the playground is desperately in need of more funding, it is land that belongs to Hackney children, and it is theirs to transform and reimagine according to their creative and playful desires. Through adventure playgrounds, children exercise their right to the city.

This can subvert the obstructive impact of housing injustice upon this right – an injustice that is often in close geographical proximity to adventure playgrounds, as they are commonly situated in or near estates where there is a higher level of deprivation, overcrowding and exclusion.

Children living in overcrowded homes are often eager for peace and solitude. The treehouses, dens, hammocks and shelters on adventure playgrounds can provide this. In these places of secret succour, young people are also more protected from police violence, and from the criminalised survival work that can envelop adolescent lives. In this way, an open-access, everyday place to play can be a second home for children living in overcrowded homes, and a refuge from some of the everyday violences of racial capitalism. The playspace dilutes the affective density experiences in overcrowded homes, releasing and transforming feeling into creative desire and expression.

Desiring space

Adults deserve places to play, too. We deserve dwellings that are conducive to recreation, and not just places to sleep after and before working. Sex is one of the ways that adults explore and play. It builds connection and creates attachment to place. In the absence of space and time to pursue pleasure – be it through physical intimacy or other forms of recreation – nervous system dysregulation heightens frustration, tension, resentment, control. Such feelings have energetic consequences for spaces, as affective atmospheres are assembled by members of the same household. In this way, the constrained and crowded spaces of London's rented accommodation are limiting of desire, because the corrosion and alienation of sexual desire is key to rentier capitalist accumulation.

In April 2018 I wandered through the post-industrial streets of Hackney Wick, confused by the absent door numbers and by my own lostness. Everything seems suspended in time yet in motion in this part of the city: always in the process of being unmade, remade (see Ferreri and Dawson 2018). As I reached the cusp of giving up, 28-year-old Maja popped out of a graffitied metal door. She led me into a warehouse building full of plants, chicken wire, a turntable, a projector. A long dinner table stood in the middle. Someone was cooking at a makeshift counter behind it. We snaked around and entered a small windowless room with magnolia walls and a brushed concrete floor. There was a mattress on it, and in the corner a few cardboard boxes yet to be unpacked. Maja got in touch with me earlier that year on the advice of her boyfriend, Brandon, who spotted one of my study advertisements. They'd been having relationship trouble and my poster seemed to speak to it. Brandon was staying elsewhere so they could have some distance from each other, but Maja said he would soon run out of money and have to move back in with her, and this room would house both of them. She said many of their arguments stemmed from sharing unaffordable space. There was never enough of it, and Brandon craved solitude. Their conflicts were cyclical and it had dampened desire. Their excessive proximity had cleaved sexual and romantic distance between them. They cuddled, but that was it. Could this new rented room in Hackney Wick be a space for rekindled desire? How might a desiring space be assembled when it is also a working space, a living space, a worrying space, an arguing space?

Maja showed me Polaroids of friends from her student days. She was a keen photographer with shoeboxes full of brooding cityscapes and snapshots of house parties, raves, dinners. "He takes up more space physically, like he has more stuff," she said, "and whenever we have shared a room, I can do my things in the kitchen, or I dunno, sometimes he'll be like, 'How can you agree, you know, to go halves on the room and let me take up the majority of the space?'" Their conflicts over space seemed to reflect other disparities in their relationship, where Maja's identity and passions were diminished. Maja explained this with an art reference, a memory of watching Lee Krasner shrink into her and Jackson Pollock's shared kitchen:

> 'She was mostly known as "Pollock's wife." And you know, there's a scene where he's splashing his thing to – you know, taking up that space. And she's in the kitchen with a little canvas. … And I remember watching that film as a teenager and being like "That's fucked up," but like you know, initially, that's probably exactly what I've been doing. I've been letting him take up more space and I've just been giving myself enough space to put one canvas down.'

She relayed this with a mixture of embarrassment and deflation, but she seemed glad to be on her own for a while. Maja was also wistful about previous homes with Brandon. Both artists – she a photographer, he a DJ – they had met at a warehouse rave and teamed up as promoters, putting on nights to help pay their rent. Brandon had been in and out of employment for the duration of their relationship, and spent much of his time making mixes on his laptop. Their experience of room-sharing was therefore one of constant proximity. Most of the week was spent job-seeking, working, eating and sleeping in the same shared room.

Before I visited Maja's new place, we met up and chatted in a café in Clapton. At that time, she and Brandon were still sharing a room. Touch was part of the day's choreography, but its embeddedness with production, consumption and rest left little room for sexual intimacy. Maja explained:

> 'There's just one chair and one bed, so someone winds up on the chair and the other person winds up on the bed. If you do work, you can

do a quick cuddle and then go back. That's a quite common cycle of work or just being – make two cups of tea, someone ends up there, someone ends up in the chair, eventually tea's finished, you cuddle, and then you go back to work.'

There was a sweet and parental quality to the image she painted. Maja elaborated on the topic of sex:

'I don't know if it is the thin walls that makes it a bit awkward. I know there's been times where we've just been more anxious and more stressed and then we've rarely touched and you know, we spoon but that's it. And I think at times our relationship has been very platonic. At one point he brought it up, like, "Maybe we should stop seeing each other because we don't, you know …" But I think just mentioning it, we were like, "Yeah, but: is that important?"'

Sharing constrained space amidst the anxiety of under-employment heightened anxious tension in their shared room, and this diminished sexual desire. Maja's anxieties about the thin walls added another layer of discomfort and pressure: the stress of people hearing her was a barrier to sexual intimacy. A platonic dynamic had felt almost easier to manage.

Thrown together by unaffordability and spatial scarcity, there was an overarching sense among many renting respondents that desire for physical intimacy was alienated, separated from the self. Twenty-five-year-old junior doctor Caitlin, for example, had started dating someone who needed a place to stay but couldn't afford short-term London rent. Amidst the abrupt closeness of his presence, Caitlin described her difficulties in asserting boundaries. He needed accommodation, but the only option was her single bed, and she wasn't ready to share it. "I feel like I do that really feminine thing of accommodating people," she remarked:

'He came on Thursday, and we'd be doing different things in the day or in the evening. But it got to Sunday morning and I was like, "You have to leave." I do think that his living situation might have changed the pace of my relationship. I think that I'm quite uncomfortable with being physically intimate but not being emotionally close, and I pushed the emotional closeness to make myself feel more comfortable with the physical intimacy.'

Caitlin privately rented a single room in a high-rise tower block on an estate in Stoke Newington, sharing the flat with two men. There was no outdoor space and, while the living room was a decent size and comfortable, there was nowhere to host guests other than her own private room. She didn't have the material means to hold the boundaries she needed. Caitlin was 'pushing' her feelings so they could catch up with physical circumstances.

These affects of awkwardness and discomfort, generated through excessive proximity and hastened romantic relationships, were mirrored in the lives of many of the renters I've met. Supply teacher Claire, for instance, had just moved out of a shared house where there was no communal living space. The only place she could socialise was her bedroom, which contained a single bed. At 34, Claire had struggled with dating. She said that since experiencing a break-up from a long-distance relationship, she mainly used apps for casual sex, but the lack of communal space in her home obstructed even that:

'Not only was there no sofa to go and crash on, but also just nowhere that isn't your bedroom, which is a bit awkward. It felt as though I couldn't really invite people back unless it was "bedroom-inviting" people back. Not the worst, better than sneaking someone into your parents' place, but I felt that it would be difficult to sustain a relationship without sharing the burden of whose space do we go to. Do you know what I mean? And also, if I tried to get with anyone in a similar situation to me, it's always gonna be slightly uncomfortable. I had one relationship, but it was long distance, so that was not a problem.'

The only autonomous space available in her shared household was her own bedroom, but this space was already coded as intimate, and Claire balked at the thought of bringing someone home that she didn't already know well. It was awkward to think of someone fielding implied sexual advances, so much so that a long-distance relationship was almost easier than risking mixed messages. For others, the impact of spatial constriction upon feelings of sexual desire was oriented around the absence of a site that was uncircumscribed with the practices and substances of other labours. This was especially true when the latter pertained to childcare. Joel, for example, mentioned that occasional changes to room layouts were welcome opportunities for "pop-up" sexual environments:

'All the rooms are one room, essentially. Sometimes the lack of space bugs me and that's the thing I always get most envious of when I'm round my friends' flats – kitchens, like, a surface. And because Sam sleeps in our bedroom, that's really impacted things for us in our sex life. There is nowhere else that is the "nice place" to have sex in this flat. When someone stays there's an inflatable mattress and then when they leave we're like, "Well let's not put this away straight away...".'

Discomforts could also stem from blurred spatial boundaries between housemates' sexual lives. Leon, for example, lamented his proximity to his housemate's sexual adventures. Like Maja, some of Leon's unease emerged from acoustic intrusion. His bedroom was below the living room, and, in his words, he "could actually hear shit going on. I'm talking like, he's rolling in at three in the morning with four girls and I'd be like mate I'm trying to sleep but I was also like I kind of respect what you're doing." Through the bravado, the blurring of these boundaries fed an unwanted affective exchange. Leon was passively brought into the sounds and movements of sex, and his stamp of "respect" seemed to mark a reclamation of agency over a situation that systematically disturbed his sleep.

Affective experiences of constriction as well as involuntary encounter run throughout these reflections. Among some of them are territorial claims, as residents jostle for embodied autonomy and privacy in homes that are sensorily busy with the continual proximity of people and things. In turn, the renters cited here each brought this sense of physical constriction and undesired proximity to broader narratives of their lives and identities: Maja shrank into corners as if Pollock's wife; Caitlin integrated her discomfort within a 'feminine' disposition towards accommodating people. There is a suggested relationship, then, between the affective dynamics of their living space and their political subjectivities: the latter are co-constructed through the *affectif* of their shared dwellings, where interacting bodies are attuned 'to the same interactive frequency' (Seyfert 2012: 42). Fundamentally, in all the homes discussed here, affective atmospheres were assembled through a lack of sovereignty over desire: how and when it was expressed, the pace at which it moved, and where it was felt and nurtured.

Displaced sovereignties

The impermanence of private renting assembles spaces that are fraught with feelings of unbelonging, instability and a loss of control over material, geographical and intimate destinies. In other words, precarity disrupts desires for the future. As Bhattacharyya et al observe of post-crash British society (2021), the sorrow of lost desire can activate a 'longing for authority'. In my conversations with millennial private renters, I could often identify this longing in micro-relational practices, especially among those who were 'downwardly mobile'. Frustration with circumstances and a sense of constricted agency could produce a desire to categorise cohabitants or identify with the authority of landlords or other powerful actors. However, there was also resistance to this authority. This resistance was not always direct: for example, it could involve manoeuvres to appease and bargain with landlords to buy more time in a home. In this section, I consider the affective politics of such identifications and strategies. Within these politics, I see different approaches to the grief of lost desire.

Geographers Christie, Smith and Munroe observe that attaining home ownership is 'as much about emotional returns as it is about financial investment; as much about affective ties … as about speculating on the prospects for wealth accumulation' (2008: 2302). Conversely, within the private rented sector, there are lost or displaced affective 'returns'. Here, I consider these heterogeneous affects as 'displaced sovereignties' owing to the discomfort, resentment and mistrust that circulate amidst quasi-voluntarily shared space, specifically in the absence of routes to 'chosen' household formations. These affects are generated by the relational and material encounters structuring everyday life in shared rental accommodation, but they are also a product of collective attachments to a 'good life' that has ebbed from realistic view. Among the millennial private renters I interviewed, this sense of displaced personal sovereignty was often generated through political-economic encounters. Frustrations, suspicions and fears about decision-making authority and bill-sharing within shared households could cut through cohabitant solidarities. Sara Ahmed writes that 'emotions do things, and they align … bodily space with social space – through the very intensity of their attachments' (2004: 119). Affects circulating between social bodies in shared rental accommodation may align individuals with actors that financially profit from their insecurity. For example, while describing a shared house where every room was individually rented out, Claire expressed both frustration and respect for the extensive rules her landlord devised. She read a litany of his directives from an email on her phone:

'You see your room number on all the doors and in the spaces, please make sure that you're using the correct space and use your space only. This way we can keep the flat without rubbish. This is your responsibility, to keep your stuff on your own space. For example, when Room 1 leaves, I'll check all Room 1 spaces and if I see any items, I will consider it left from Room 1 and will throw it away without asking. Once again, I won't take any responsibility if that happens. However, if Room 1 doesn't use her space properly, you can ask her to use it, but in that case make sure you take your stuff from there when Room 1 moves out. Otherwise, it might be thrown.'

Claire's landlord had designed rules to limit his tenants sharing space. The language is clinical: tenants referred to by numbers, any liabilities on his end denied. The technicity of the phone screen affectively deadens the dehumanising language, but consolidates his surveillant authority. Claire said she had been bothered by the email. But she was also sympathetic, because she saw herself as a good tenant (see also Naik's observations of tenants' sympathies with informal landlords in Gurgaon [2020]). "He wanted to make sure that everyone was having a good time," she said. "I was fine with him because I wasn't doing anything wrong. He was trying to look after us, but it was a little bit paternal. It's like, we're all adults, but I mean, he wanted to keep things tidy." While Claire remarked that he could have given the tenants some warning before discarding belongings, she mentioned that he was "quite naïve" and "just trying to run the household well for everyone." She rationalised his intrusions as part of the job of maintaining order amidst a rapid residential turnover. This was underpinned by low trust in her housemates. Indeed, Claire explained that most of the problems in the shared house were down to their inconsiderate behaviour. "I don't create trash but it would always be me that's taking it out," she remarked. "I don't know who it was – I had suspicions."

For others, generous assessments of landlords' intentions were muddied further by the flagrance with which affects of lost control were calibrated into punishments against tenants. Twenty-three-year-old barista Hannah, for example, recounted a time when her landlord, Carol, threatened eviction because of a complaint about the heating. Hannah described Carol as very nice, but "not overly professional" because she was "overly friendly." There had been a "weird blip," however, when the heating and hot water stopped working for a month and Hannah requested a slight rent reduction:

> 'So, in January we sent her an email being like, "We just were wondering, in light of not having proper working facilities for December, whether you'd consider a reduction on our rent this month," and she just flew off the handle. She was like, "I've treated you like family, this is so cold, we normally just text about things, you've betrayed my trust." It was mad. My contract was up for renewal at the end of January, and she was like, "I don't think I can renew your contracts."'

Carol's reactions kept oscillating. She called another housemate and "ranted to her for half an hour" about how she needed the rents because "that's part of my income: I use it to pay my bills." Shortly afterwards, she instructed all the tenants to leave because they had betrayed her trust. The following day, she changed her mind again, and Hannah texted her to say they all wanted to remain there but were "troubled" by her response. Once more, Carol U-turned, replying with: "Wow, well I don't know if I do want you to stay." The see-sawing continued – "it was this horrible, horrible, horrible weekend where we didn't know whether we'd be able to stay." Carol finally manipulated Hannah into remaining at the house by informing her that if she left (as she had been originally instructed), everyone would have to follow suit. "Either we all have to leave, or we all have to stay," Hannah said, "but the thing is, I don't think that's true. In many ways our landlady is quite reasonable and will try her best to make it work but it feels very unstable."

Hannah's and Claire's reflections reveal the affective politics assembling informal/ised relationships between private landlords and tenants. They were unwillingly drawn into their landlords' emotional worlds, their moods and whims. The good intentions of these landlords were nonetheless clung to, even amidst extraordinary boundary violations. This was partly owing to feared reprisals. But for Claire, it was also because of a perception of herself and cohabitants as potentially culpable. Such responses are survival mechanisms in the face of dehumanisation and the grief of lost sovereignty. In illuminating these mechanisms, however, we witness affect's 'social productivity' (Wissinger 2007: 232) and the agency undergirding it.

As these narratives convey, the informalisation of landlord–tenant relationships imbricates everyday personal practices of relating with surplus value extraction, and this can generate tension and fissure. This imbrication can be especially apparent in circumstances where tenants are 'lodging'. Under current law in Britain, lodgers have significantly fewer rights than assured shorthold tenants. If they live in the same home as their 'resident landlord' and share common spaces with them, they are considered 'excluded occupiers' and landlords only need to give 'reasonable', unwritten notice – defined as the length of the rental payment period – to evict them (HM Government 2019b). Jonathan remembered a time he was renting a room in a childhood friend's home, and thus technically lodging. "Initially it seemed like a really, really good scenario," he recalled, but there was a "change of dynamic" when the friend's family member had suggested raising the rent.

> 'Overnight it just went from this thing that was like, well we know we don't really have any rights, but that doesn't matter because we're all mates, to a sort of really awkward "OK so quite soon I think I'd like you to pay quite a lot more," and us being like, "Shit well we don't have any rights whatsoever," so there was a lot of tension.'

Jonathan elaborated on the awkward lexicon he developed to negotiate the situation:

> 'It becomes very complicated, a situation like that, because there's no rules to regulate really. You debate something transactional in a way that you wouldn't do if it was just a transactional relationship. So, it was sort of like, "You can do this but it's gonna be shit for us!" That kind of thing. But if you were talking to Foxton's [a letting agent company] it wouldn't come into the conversation. And it never fully ruptured, we came to a temporary compromise. Essentially, we started paying slightly more but then we were like, "We're gonna pay slightly more, and then we're gonna move out".'

Jonathan was resigned to finding alternative housing over 'rupturing' his friendship, after failing to elicit his resident-landlord's empathy. He admits his attempt to invoke this empathy was only possible because of the comparative intimacy of living with her, compared with the distanciated relations typically framing dealings with lettings companies. Jonathan described the tense affective atmosphere that had resulted from this proximity. His girlfriend "was a lot more affected by it. … She started to really feel like she couldn't feel at home there." She was anxious, he remarked, despite the absence of any "overt hostility," because the conversation about increasing the rent had "planted the seeds of a different set of relations. Even though we paid money into her bank account all that time, we'd never felt it until then." Thus affect makes the political economy of the relationship to his resident-landlord more visible: value extraction and payment are 'felt' only after Jonathan's watershed conversation about the rent hike, and his appeals for compassion muddy what was initially just a 'transactional' relationship. Again, this removal of agency was hurtful. He grieved the trauma of displacement and he grieved the loss of the friendship. While Jonathan activated some agency through deciding to leave after a period of slightly higher payments, the injury of a friend choosing profit over his wellbeing was a betrayal of solidarity and wasted desire for connection.

Affective politics also circulate around informal decision-making positions within shared households, especially where a 'lead tenant' role is assigned. Although they are not legally required, 'lead tenant' agreements are generally mandatory for Tenancy Deposit Schemes: a nominated tenant becomes the point of contact between the landlord and cohabitants regarding deposit divisions, professedly to avoid financial conflict. In warehouse districts like Hackney Wick, sometimes this role is confusingly known as 'leaseholder', despite said housemate remaining a private tenant. Maja discussed a turbulent scenario with a former housemate who had taken up this role. To her, the lead tenant had abused her position after a conflict, sending threatening text messages and turning off the household's utilities:

> 'So, there's a lead tenant in each unit. It's basically just based on trust. There's no contract and there's no written rules. So, she started having a problem with my partner. It was quite political, just about space. We had the party when they were gone and they said it was OK that we had the party. The flats next door was complaining, the police were gonna come, and when they came back from their trip, they had a huge argument and they were just yelling that we had to get the fuck out of there like in a few days, a week. They were like, "Everyone has to get out, the police will come!" They'd switched the mains off. I got told I had to, "OBEY AND RESPECT" her! Capital letters!'

Although the lead tenant had no legal power to evict Maja, her authority-by-proxy gave her power over tenants and their money. Maja expressed suspicions that the lead tenant had defrauded her and other housemates, limiting her financial capacity to leave:

'I dunno how long I'm gonna be here. I thought around Christmas I would have had enough because the girl who was the lead tenant kept jacking the rent up. All of a sudden there was this bill. We never paid bills in this place, British Gas didn't know they existed. All of a sudden there were bills. And then there was something else, and then we had to pay for something else, because we were all meant to chip in.'

Like Jonathan, Maja wanted out. And like Jonathan, the affective politics of informalised rental relations meant that she could not immediately afford to leave. Stories such as these speak to ways that the politics of feeling assemble precarious space. The accommodation described here is shared by multiple people through economic necessity, on the part of the tenant. In these spaces of forced togetherness, precarious intimacies abound between cohabiting tenants as well as between renters and landlords, as capital limits empathic capacities and poisons solidarities. In this way, capital is mycoparasitical: it germinates from the spores of rent-seeking, forming haustoria that weave through and attach onto cohabitant hosts, the strength of whose commonalities are subsequently obscured. And yet, amidst the mistrust and betrayal, the trauma and the fear, there are longings for safety and connection – sad passions that speak to the cradled flame of desire. For Susan Ruddick, the challenge is to engage these passions 'actively, to uncover the role they can play in the production of thought' (2010: 35). Through exploring the grief of displaced sovereignty, I have sought to examine this production and its relationship to political and economic subjectivity.

Queer conviviality and social reproduction

Throughout the COVID-19 'lockdowns', the family household was the only kinship formation that the British government's pandemic policy addressed. This meant that a year of epidemiological governance involved an implicit ban on sexual relations among single people. Intimacy was effectively banned outside of the family (and the infidelities of government ministers). Treating the heteromonogamous nuclear family household as default aligned with the 'traditional value' politics of Boris Johnson's government, which relied on jingoistic references to hard-working, patriotic families to push through the Brexit vote. This has been drilled further into the national psyche by his successors Truss and Sunak, and by the leader of the official opposition, who have all used transphobic rhetoric to shore up voter support. In an interview with the founder of online forum Mumsnet in 2022, Labour Party leader Keir Starmer defended the rights of parents to block trans teenagers from transitioning. 'And let's be clear', Keir said, 'it is a matter of biology, and we all understand that'.

This reinforcement of biological essentialism characterises what are popularly known as the 'culture wars' of our age. With an ageing population, low birth rates, slashed childcare budgets and housing unaffordability, these so-called wars are like so many typical nationalist projections and longings for authority. As the state realises the need for steady streams of new labour (through birth or migration) for the pensions and healthcare of an ageing right-wing electorate, 'natural' reproductive roles are returning to popular discourse. Constitutional rights to abortion have been overturned in the United States, and there is a real risk of similar regressions in Britain. While abortion was legalised in Northern Ireland in 2019, let us not forget that Stormont has continued to obstruct commissioning.

Culture wars are not fought on equal footings. We must therefore give voice to alternative kinships and care infrastructures to resist their violent erasure. Moreover, we need this tutelage to prepare for futures where financialised care cannot keep our ageing relatives, let alone ourselves, safe. Many are already living these futures. Paying attention to alternative social reproduction beyond the family is therefore part of surviving environmental and economic collapse: queer liberation is liberation for all. Geographical studies on queer practices of social reproduction are nonetheless scarce. This oversight became more noticeable during the COVID-19 pandemic, because splintered access to safe homes was laid bare. While droves of privately renting millennials exited London for the landing places of origin-family homes in other regions, access to comparable refuge with origin-families was not straightforward for the LGBTQIA+ community. So many of us have experienced familial homophobia, transphobia, violence and abandonment. The city is therefore often the safest place to be, because it is where queer kinship is most reliably found.

In this section, I explore the desires of queer millennial renters to reimagine their shared homes as spaces of alternative kinship and reproduction, focusing first on the affective politics of queer conviviality and the distribution of household labour and resources, and second on breakdown. Some of the experiences discussed are set against the backdrop of the COVID-19 pandemic. In these politics, I identify efforts towards building cohabitant cultures of pleasure, solidarity and care, and I also locate tensions unfolding from gendered and racialised inequalities. These inequalities are amplified by the spatial scarcity, unaffordability and precarity of private renting. Indeed, by looking at the 'micropolitical relationships and practices' of queer social reproduction in shared households, it is possible to inform on the ways that the 'macropolitical practices' of the state are both subverted and remade

(Heckert 2011). I argue, therefore, that the existence of these inequalities does not erase the creative desire at the heart of the queer reimagination of precarious space.

The sense of being economically obstructed from settling down and having children was not commonly voiced among the queer renters I spoke to for this project. Instead, there were often positive attitudes towards cohabitation with friends and strangers, with a view to collectivising social reproduction rather than containing it. Long-term house-sharing was sometimes entangled with visions for ethical praxes of inter-community care. For example, 25-year-old Anna-Lise contributed perspectives on shared living that were undergirded by a desire to care for more vulnerable members of their community. In 2018, when I interviewed them, Anna-Lise was an artist and sex worker, and they were keenly aware of the housing struggles that other trans sex workers endured. "I would like to one day get a mortgage," Anna-Lise told me. "Before sex work, I thought it would never happen – I thought I would be renting or struggling forever. Some of my friends are more vulnerable than me and I often think about buying a house for all of us that we could all live in." For Anna-Lise, the insecurity of private renting was a motivator for some-day ownership, but this goal was far removed from reproductive dreams of 'settling down' in a nuclear family household. They wanted to own a home to better care for their community: to do queer social reproduction.

For queer millennials already living in privately rented house-shares, there were nonetheless tensions between desires for households full of queer conviviality – socialising through queer events, for example, or watching LGBTQIA+ media together – and micropolitical dynamics that some household members found oppressive. Like Anna-Lise, desires for inter-community care and queer sociality anchored 27-year-old Tom's perspectives on his house-share. As we know from earlier in this book, Tom was a marketing consultant who shared a flat in a new-build tower block in Hackney Downs. His housemates were a couple, Melissa and Matthew. All three were young, White, middle-class professionals. Melissa worked for a charity, and Matthew also worked in marketing. Tom had become close friends with Matthew after they had both met while teaching English in Japan as fresh graduates. The two men shared an intimate bond, and Tom enthused about bringing Matthew into alignment with "non-traditional" masculinity via their shared housing experience, explaining that the flat had become a hub for male friends. "What weaves us together as friends, sexuality regardless, is this non-traditional male persona," Tom said. "One of the straight guys who was fully into drinking pints and going to the football now really likes coming over on Fridays and watching *RuPaul's Drag Race* in a way that he would never have been exposed to. ... We'll sometimes spoon in bed, after a night out." The homosociality of the shared home was a source of playfulness for Tom and Matthew, in which boundaries between social affection, touch and recreation were fluid.

Matthew similarly lauded this fluidity. He enjoyed hosting nights for their friends, and said he sometimes shared queer pornography with Tom. Melissa, too, echoed Matthew's laid-back attitude towards the blurring of homosociality and sexuality. Yet, cutting across this conviviality were tensions regarding household labour. Matthew voiced frustration regarding Melissa's "higher threshold" for cleanliness:

> 'She does the most cleaning – [her] threshold is much higher than mine. I think she definitely does way more than me and is happier to do that. She'll want to clean loads and she'll want me to help out, and I'm like, "Uhh but your threshold is just so much higher than mine!" Like, I don't really wanna carve out two hours of my weekend to clean when I'm happy with how it is.'

Tom was similarly disparaging, commenting that Melissa cleaned "to the extent where I feel bad." Melissa took on a martyrdom in this description ("She seems to take that burden on and not complain about it, so it's almost like silently suffering"), which seemed to interfere with the homo/sociality of the home. Tom and Matthew both expressed ambivalence towards the reproductive work Melissa undertook, because her contributions amplified their lesser involvement. Melissa was aware of this mismatch. For her, the 'threshold' argument was not "a fair excuse," since "cleaning once a week is not a high ask of a flat this small": "If I've just done everything then he's like, 'Well I don't need to do it!' Thus, the cycle continues."

Imbalanced labour also disrupted the "good vibes" of queer households in experiences shared by Leah, who I interviewed over Zoom in early 2021. Leah was an older millennial: she was 40 at the time, and worked part-time in book retail. We originally connected seven years ago, through political organising: Leah was active in several movements for gender and urban justice. Leah had struggled with housing for many years, and was homeless from 2017 to 2019. In those years, she had stayed on friends' couches and air mattresses. As a result of her experiences, Leah suffered from stress-related migraines and chronic pain. She put this down to a lifetime of living with the marginalisation of being Black and working class in a country built on racial capitalism.

After her years sofa-surfing, Leah found a shared house in Lewisham, South London, with five others, all "from marginalised backgrounds." There was one heterosexual Black woman, and "then everybody else that moved in was queer." Two of those were "queers of colour" with incomes that were "infrequent," and the other two were both White and in full-time employment. When we spoke in February 2021, Leah had moved out of this house three weeks prior. She described how her former household "inherited a spreadsheet" from previous tenants that calculated pro rata rents:

'We inherited this spreadsheet that calculated how much you were going to pay on rent, and it calculated it based on three things: the size of the room – like, your room, which is like, the better your room, the more you paid, so things like size, how much sunlight you got, where it was positioned in the house: if it was positioned on the ground floor next to the front door that's not a great room. And then also your income.'

Leah mentioned that the spreadsheet had become the foundation of the financial support system she and her housemates set up during the spring 2020 COVID-19 lockdown. At this time, only two people in the house stayed full-time employed, while everyone else either lost their income or it was dramatically reduced. In response, the housemates devised a plan where they "financially looked after each other" by redistributing a collectively negotiated rent reduction to housemates who had lost income. Leah praised the collective way money was redistributed, citing regular meetings and communication.

However, she mentioned that for others, the imbalance reinforced racialised power relations, since the only cohabitants who remained in full-time employment were White. While Leah had not been personally bothered, she said "Whiteness was playing out in the house" in other ways, and she drew attention to the dominance of a "good vibes only" approach to care and communicative labour among White housemates. Leah felt her need for quiet space at night was especially disrespected. While housemates were receptive to criticism and "said all the right things," patterns remained unchanged. Her bedroom was on the ground floor near the kitchen, and she suffered with the noise and spatial domination. Her frustrations with the lack of care peaked during the Black Lives Matter uprisings of June 2020, mentioning that her ill-health went virtually unnoticed by White housemates:

'I almost lost my fucking mind ... that was in the height of Black Lives Matter. And the combination of not being heard in that house with regards to noise and being able to sleep, Black Lives Matter, my mental, emotional and physical health hadn't been good for a long, long time. Like I've been officially diagnosed now with ADHD [attention deficit hyperactivity disorder] and complex PTSD [posttraumatic stress disorder]. The complex PTSD was not from the house. It was just ... a life. So I've got all of this stuff going on and then this kind of bullshit where people want to make signs saying "Black Lives Matter" but you don't want to check on the Black people you're living with when you haven't seen them for four days, you know?'

There are political tensions in Leah's experiences of queer social reproduction that are centred around the uneven politics of reproductive labour. These tensions cut through the hegemonic conviviality of the household as a project of queer relatedness. At the same time, they did not erase Leah's recognition of the efforts behind systems to re/distribute money and space. Rather, for Leah, the intentionality behind systemic efforts to transform the household's politics was in disjuncture with the lack of intentionality and racialised thoughtlessness surrounding the privileging of 'good vibes'.

Another queer renter, Kasia, similarly described employing a pro rata system of resource distribution in their home, which they shared with their partner Chloe and best friend Liz. Kasia was 28 at the time of our interview in 2021, and a migrant to England via Eastern Europe and North America. They worked full-time at a busy hospital. Echoing Anna-Lise's emphasis on non-biological kinship, Kasia explained that their house-share "actually felt like a little family" which was "not always something that queer house-shares manage to achieve." Resonating with Leah's experiences, Kasia outlined a weighted financial system:

> 'It's kind of on a model of "who can afford what," especially since the lower-earning one of the trio is my partner, so I'm still like, "You pay a fixed amount of like 400 a month and then I'll make up the difference." As far as bills go, we pretty much split it a bit tit for tat, so I'll pay council tax, for instance, and Liz pays for water and electric and whatever, so it's all based on what we can afford. We had a discussion about it because I think with queers and money – because queers don't often have a lot of money – that can be one of the really big sticking points for everyone getting along.'

Kasia's partner, Chloe, worked in municipal infrastructure. She was neurodiverse and trans, and had not had an easy time with workplace inclusion as a result. Describing Chloe's resultant job insecurity, Kasia said:

> '[A] lot of people who are neurodivergent, queer or whatever don't end up developing the kind of skills that let you just be a good little drone and work away behind a till or in an office and make enough just to get by, so there's a precarity that comes from that.'

In Kasia's current household, this pro rata household finance system felt workable owing to the strength of existing bonds. However, in their previous house-share, similar systems had not worked as well. Ivy, a 22-year-old trans woman, had moved into the house and did not have stable employment. Kasia and Liz had fronted her rent and bills but were never paid back. The household ended up dissolving, but Kasia explained that they harboured no resentment:

'So many of us have lived experience of what it's like to be absolutely like down in the dirt, frankly, that when you see someone – especially someone a bit younger than you – it's difficult for me to draw a line between queer praxis and socialist, communist, anarchist praxis, because so often they're the same thing. And I do definitely think that's because we have common cause with each other, like we all have this one thing that unites us, you know we're all queer, we all know what it's like to be marginalised. … And then unfortunately, the social contract that ends up being built there of like "I will front that for you, but you have to pay me back," it is easy to abuse because it's an honour system.'

Like Leah, Kasia's experience of practising queer social reproduction involved formalising strategies for the redistribution of resources, and approaching financial matters with flexibility and compassion. This came with risks, but it was necessary for community survival. Such strategies speak to collective desires for transformation that were experienced in tandem with tension, disappointment and hierarchy, but that nonetheless perdured.

Decomposition work

The accounts shared in this chapter demonstrate the affective politics circulating within precarious rental accommodation. These politics involve territorial claims over space, desires for embodied sovereignty and pleasure, and longings for social transformation stemming from shared visions of collective care. In this way, affect assembles space. Through its enunciation, it creates openings. These openings are so often formed through fissure, and through these fissures, the light of change sometimes pours.

My conversations with queer renters suggested resistance to the affective constriction of rentier capitalism could involve surrendering to the breakdown of households. In *Staying with the Trouble*, Donna Haraway uses the metaphor of compost to argue that 'critters – human and not – become-with each other, compose and decompose each other' (2016: 97). Compost is the state of decomposition, then, from which life is made and co-replenished. The stories I collected from queer shared households draw attention to the labour of household decomposition as a necessary facet of replenishment. This is not to say that unhoming, dissolution or displacement are not exhausting and violent processes. Rather, I want to draw attention to the political desires and reclaimed affective labours that can undergird unravelling, breaking down and death.

In Leah's and Kasia's stories, disparities in the distribution of space, labour and sustenance regularly threatened to 'kill the dream' of queer collectivity, and in several instances households did break down. Yet, these breakdowns were also often the accepted outcome of hard communicative and caring work: efforts to address power relations that were consciously departed from. Leah explained that in her former shared house, people of colour had devised strategies to try to address racialised inequalities:

> 'We tried everything. It even got down to we created Google Documents with different subject headings and one of them was "How to Create a Culture of Care," and I was like "Okay I'm gonna go with this because I've exhausted my means of trying to get shit to flow," but it wasn't only culture of care, there was lots of other things.'

Leah explained that these Google Documents had been created over direct conversation because of fear of Whiteness – in her words, because White people can be "passive aggressive as fuck and they avoid confrontation and it just ends up twisting people and situations up." The documents were therefore a form of protection against potential harm, but for Leah they also signalled the end of the household's attempts to work as a queer collective project. Household breakdowns had been repeatedly experienced by Kasia, too, who described collective efforts to mediate harm stemming from the cumulative precarities and traumas carried by the most marginalised household members. Kasia had formerly lived in a house with several other queer residents, including a former partner, Ali. Kasia explained that Ali was a trans woman of colour and had fled an abusive origin-family home. Her experiences had severely impacted her mental health, and she struggled with addiction. Unable to work, Kasia helped her to access benefits. However, Ali missed rent and bill payments, so the landlord refused to renew their fixed-term tenancy. Kasia described their efforts to mitigate harm throughout the household's dissolution, but the exigencies of private rental insecurity and the disparate economic positions of housemates meant that some of them were vulnerable to homelessness. One vulnerable housemate, Sky, decided she could not face the uncertainty of attempting to find another privately rented house-share. Like others in the household, Sky was neurodiverse, estranged from their family and did not have a reliable income. She decided that the better option would be to try to access social housing, but this required her to live in temporary accommodation while waiting to be allocated, where she was not allowed to keep her cat, Nina. Without Nina, Sky tragically took her own life. "Nina helped Sky to interface with the world when the world didn't make sense to her" said Kasia. Kasia was scarred by this loss.

But they did not hold Ali responsible for it. They blamed the government for its disinvestment in secure housing, and said that Sky's death motivated them to start organising in the feminist anti-austerity movement. Despite the painful aftermath of the household's dissolution, Kasia remained adamant about the importance of such spaces, even in their fleetingness:

'Blaming Ali personally isn't something that gives me peace, so I'm not going to, but it's a chain of events that shows how small a tether there is to keeping some households warm, functional and inviting versus an array of utter chaos that honestly we were all glad to have left. Except, you know, some of us didn't have anywhere else to go. A reason why we as queer people tolerate dysfunction from others – and sometimes don't hold ourselves to high standards also – is because it's not great, but it's what we've got. And it is very much *all* some of us have.'

Sky, may your memory be a blessing. May the warmth of your spirit light fires for us to gather around, so that we can share in this Earth's abundance differently, for the time we are granted.

There is no romance or nobility about the loss of queer comrades to the brutality of a capitalism that is premised on the differentiated value of living beings. But the surrender involved in accepting and grieving loss is a vital component of our relentless reclamation of power. This is because grief is an expression of love. Ericka Huggins said that "love is an expression of power. We can use it to transform our world." There is love in the queer work of transforming social reproduction amidst precarity, and this involves mourning endings. In the openings created by grief's collective practice is the oxygen for new flames of political desire.

Feminist engagements with social reproduction are still yet to fully reach beyond the role of mother as labouring subject. While not all research on mothers' social reproduction entrenches the heteromonogamous family as default kinship model, the emphasis is rarely on collective modes of social reproduction that do not centre the caring of children. But adults are somebody's children. Turning our attention to the ways that adults nurture, care for, indeed mother each other is key to understanding queer social reproduction, as well as to deconstructing the temporalities that hem care within the nuclear family (see Lewis 2019). Homing in on the everyday dimensions of queer relationality in shared households is also, in the words of Sarah Marie Hall, about 'seeing the world through a lens focused on acknowledging and recognising social difference' (2020: 83). While Hall applies this to her work on austerity, social difference is fundamental to studies of precarity more broadly, wherein scholarship on precarious housing, for example, requires careful consideration of the subjectivities, histories, circumstances and identities of those caught within it, as well as the institutions and actors that profit from its ongoing erosion. Turning our attention to queer shared housing practices can visibilise some of these differential experiences of precarity, while reaffirming, too, the ethical dimensions of precarity as a broader form of cohabitation and interdependence that is inexorable.

As these final empirical accounts speak to, queer cohabitants' practices of sharing and caring persist on uneven political terrain. The "common cause" of sexual or gender dissidence, in Kasia's words, was infused with power relations unfolding from classed, aged, racialised and gendered differentiation. As Leah's recollections demonstrate, the social reproduction of the household involved forms of communication, redistribution and interpersonal practice that could also solidify and replenish racialised power dynamics. Such stories make the relationship between micropolitical relationships and macropolitical practices undeniably clear, in that a queer praxis of kin-making cannot afford to see just one dimension of subjective difference or oppression. Freedom, in the words of June Jordan, is 'indivisible, and either we are working for freedom or you are working for the sake of your self-interests and I am working for mine' (1991/2014: 56).

These narratives convey the necessary affective politics of making and replenishing queer everyday life, wherein dealing with and naming feeling was a political claim on existence. Accounts discussed earlier in the chapter were not as directly shaped by radical engagement. Indeed, occasionally they conveyed subtle longings for hierarchy. But such longings were only revealed by their proximity to the grief of squandered futures, constricted desires and displaced sovereignties. It is this vulnerability that is worth focusing on. On Deleuze's interpretation of desire, Susan Ruddick writes that it is not 'the harmony of the senses that marks the possibility for thought, but their discord. Thought emerges in a cramped space, forced and under constraint, beginning with an overwhelming visceral refusal' (2010: 37). In the same vein, the discordant intimacies and affects I have discussed in this chapter speak to 'potentia' (a Spinozan term) for political transformation. This is because they are entwined with desires for emotional safety, relational harmony, privacy and personal sovereignty, even while they are also reflective of desires that are curtailed or alienated. This doesn't mean we should identify political potential when 'refusal' is not necessarily there, or when 'domination or alienation', in Ruddick's words (2010: 25) ('potestas' for Spinoza) diminishes, rather than enhances, affective capacities. The answer, for Ruddick, is in Deleuze's reading of Spinoza's 'sad passions': a 'reservoir of knowledge' that reflects desire's 'multiple sites of irruption' (2010: 36, 40). The intimate accounts shared in this chapter echo this ambivalence. They give voice to affects that are in/tense, awkward and resentful; they also convey desire.

Methods for calibrating sad passions into transformative change is a topic for another book. However, awareness of and resistance to hierarchy tracks throughout each narrative, even when survival mechanisms of internalisation and interpersonal blame are activated. As Jamie Heckert writes, if the anarchist argument that 'our subjectivities are the result of our practices is in any way true, then our capacity to develop egalitarian relational skills may be stunted by our participation in fixed hierarchies' (2010: 263). We resist this participation by teasing out the reasons why and the contexts within which it occurs. We resist it, too, in documenting the griefs and desires of endings. Joan Shelley sings: 'when it breaks down, oh babe let's try to see the beauty in all the fading.'

6

Conclusion

Since 2008, Britain's political and economic regime has successively proletarianised the public. As I described in the opening chapter, this has finally resulted in a shift in the way that economic 'crisis' is described. The 'cost-of-living crisis' describes the ontological impossibility of neoliberal life. This differs from 'health crisis' or 'housing crisis', both of which are still susceptible to neoliberal responses: privatised healthcare, for example, or 'affordable housing' quotas that are met through the demolition of existing homes. From the financial crash, austerity and the economic fallout of Brexit (see Sampson 2017) to COVID-19, Trussonomic meltdown, Sunak and Hunt's austerity 2.0 and climate poverty, cascading stages of state-led dispossession have perhaps finally led to a departure from the shame that has historically disciplined people in Britain to internalise their struggles, and to blame either themselves or minoritised members of their own communities. Through the movements that have born action against the cost of living, it seems that the shame is finally being assigned to the state. Within this, we can identify the emergent political potential of affect when it is collectively circulated. Constriction, resentment, anxiety, yes, but grief, longing and desire too: collectively generated affects assemble the precarious spaces of late capitalist Britain.

This book has investigated some of these spaces, focusing on the precarity of renting in the financialised city: overcrowded house-shares, dilapidated flats, warehouses, multigenerational households. By examining attitudes, experiences and practices of relationships among the inhabitants of these spaces, I have sought to show the ways that precarious intimacies hold up a mirror to the crisis of capitalism: they reflect the loss and pain of neoliberal precarity, but they also signal a turning point in a disease. This turning point is an inexorable result of the embedded reproductive contradiction of neoliberal rentier capitalism: the traditional owner-occupying family – an institution more likely to vote for regimes promising property appreciation – cannot be replenished without the adequate provision of housing. Engaging with the political potential of this crisis-as-turning-point requires loving attention to the discomfort, awkwardness, grief and anxiety of precarious intimacy. Tending to these sad passions, we can uncover the burnish of longing and desire. Some of the desires discussed in this book reflect a nostalgia for traditional models of kinship; urges for certainty and safety beyond the precarious city; separation and disconnection from collective experience. Others, however, speak to longings for relational repair, self-knowledge, community infrastructure, alternative constellations of care, pleasure and resistance.

This ambivalence also reflects the contradictory nature of precarity as a concept. As discussed in the theoretical part of Chapter 2, precarity connotes the loss of the economic entitlements associated with Keynesianism. In this way, to 'feel' precarity can involve longings for the modes of social and cultural organisation associated with that postwar consensus: job security or housing stability, for example. However, such entitlements were not evenly distributed, and indeed always relied on a global system of differentiated value for their existence. Indeed, to feel precarious is also to feel vulnerable, and thus aware of one's interdependence. While there is no romance in the insecurities that neoliberalism has unleashed upon populations, such vulnerability has the capacity to open our minds and hearts to solidarity with regions and communities whose dispossession funded the past economic health we now long for. And it provides us with a common enemy.

In this book, I have focused on millennial experience because of the specific generational disjunctures often framing millennials' economic engagement. The affective ambivalence of precarity is most salient for an age group that grew up in preparation for a society and economy that neoliberalism pulled apart. On an intergenerational level, these disjunctures have created cleavages in understanding between older people and millennials, engineering age-based class divisions that undermine solidarity. However, I have also sought to demonstrate the highly disparate nature of millennial economic experience: intra-generational inequality, for example, is also a feature of millennial life, especially as social inequality overall increases. As noted in Chapter 1, my interest in generation is imbricated with my interest in reproduction: from these disjunctures and ambivalences, from these feelings of obstruction and disparate generational understanding, what can be remade? What are the new generations of political subjects that can be born, and from what modes of reproduction?

The empirical narratives shared in this book speak to disparities in generational experience that are nonetheless born from the same imperialist system: a system, as I detailed in Chapter 2, that is historically rooted in the capture and enclosure of land for the production of wealth and power. Through this geo-historical account, I showed how contemporary experiences of precarity in London's rented accommodation are intimately connected to the colonial exploitation of land, resources and populations across centuries. This degree of contextualisation may seem overly extensive, but it is necessary grounding for a book that explores the differentiated value of human life under capitalism through people's real lives. These histories lived in the bodies and minds of renting respondents, who are still living in the same racial capitalist nexus. As we saw in Chapter 3, racialised experiences of market dis/enfranchisement produced distinctly different engagements with the city as an infrastructural resource for collective social reproduction. These same structures, bolstered by policies that discipline the composition of households through the bordering of welfare and citizenship, limited capacities to relate romantically, and to access pleasure and desire beyond origin-family homes. These structures were also generative of unequal burdens of affective labour among the respondents cited in this book. As discussed in Chapter 4, those dealing with cumulative precarity – sedimented experiences of insecurity transmitted across generations of imperialist violence – had intensified affective and relational workloads. Reflecting the economic and psychic disjunctures embedded within precarity, this labour involved preserving or renegotiating generationally divergent fantasies of future advancement.

Throughout this book, I have consistently shone light on the immaterial, unseen labours of social reproduction – as it pertains to the replenishment of intimate relationships, and to respondents' relationships to themselves. I have argued that the alienation of this labour is necessary for the accumulation of rentier capital, and that the corrosion of communities through housing injustice can be usefully read through this alienation. In so doing, I have sought to expand understandings of precarity as a signifier for neoliberal labour relations, uniting this understanding with the intimate experience of precariousness – of vulnerability – that all human subjects are party to, especially amidst the collapse of late capitalist economic infrastructure. I have homed in on the reproduction of relationships as a domain in which this conceptual reconciliation is most salient. As Chapter 4 explores, among the renting respondents cited in this book, precarious relational labour involved creating a sense of belonging in transient, privately rented homes. Here, longings for rootedness and identity through home improvement butted up against reluctance to self-fund the appreciation of property that did not belong to inhabitants. But the consequences of putting up with unaddressed disrepair created further psychic and physiological work. Respondents' experiences of unalienated creative or reproductive labour for privately rented homes were rare, but they gleamed: the simple act of growing food and sharing it with neighbours unfolded into a hitherto unexperienced sense of rootedness and community belonging.

In this way, seeds of community were watered by the feeling of reclaimed labour. Such feelings, as I have argued in Chapter 5, are part of the collateral of housing precarity, which too often denies residents access to the affects of recreation, play, pleasure and desire. Tracing this affective alienation through experiences of constricted sexual intimacy and uncomfortable physical proximities, this chapter explored the ways that desires for connection and embodied sovereignty are present in respondents' narratives. These desires, I propose, are also evident in recollections in which residents apologise for or identify with landlord authority, despite experiencing mistreatment and boundary violation. Reading these narratives through affect theory's attention to 'sad passions', I identified a 'cradled flame' of yearning for connection and safety, amidst predispositions towards resignation and occasionally blame. This flame is oxygenated by radical engagements with alternative care infrastructures, as a response to widening precarity. The latter part of this chapter delved into examples of queer renters' practices and visions of social reproduction in shared homes. Here, I identified the political potential of grief in the face of household disintegration and death. This potential, I suggested, is located in the tenacity of transformative desire born from collective engagement with loss.

By bringing these narratives to the surface, I wanted to shine a compassionate but critically engaged light on feelings, labours and practices that are so often sunk in the murkiness of our system's unforgiving waters. Unseen and undiscussed, these feelings and practices remain unvalued, and it is too easy to internalise the shame of capital's relational wreckage. But this is not our wreckage. Rather, renting respondents' efforts to form and replenish precarious intimacies speak to our persistent return to that surface. This, as far as I can see, is the persistence of social reproduction: the will to become, to regenerate. While housing unaffordability has materially gatekept the biological production of human life, the resulting fissures are potential openings to alternative engagements with reproduction – and thus, with labour.

This may seem a paradoxical conclusion for a book that has largely focused on the struggles that millennial renters face amidst economic imperatives to share constrained and insecure living space: to densify, but also to collectivise. But to write a book focusing on positive experiences of this imperative would be to do the work of neoliberalism for free. Of course, many people actively want to live in shared housing, and thrive in these environments. I count myself as one of them, and several of the respondents of this book would too. My point is not that access to private property or individually contained homes would mitigate feelings of obstruction, constriction and boundary-compromise attendant upon the housing landscape I have outlined. My point, rather, is that the primacy of private property as an ideological pillar of British rentier capitalist society has led to this very landscape, in which residents are thrown together, rather than intentionally choosing to communally cohabit. And, in this thrown-togetherness, they are also emotionally pulled apart from each other. Through identifying these heartbreaks, though, and giving them voice, we can work towards the recalibration of coercion into collective power.

The individual explication of sad passions is not itself necessarily politically mobilising. As Matt Wilde has observed of private renter organising strategies in London, resisting evictions and challenging local authorities constitute a 'mode of affective experience' in which 'the act of taking care for others constitutes not merely a vital survival strategy, but also a means of fashioning embryonic moral economies' (2019: 72). At the bedrock of these strategies are, nonetheless, solidarities forged through sharing feelings about individual experiences. London tells so many historical stories of this interconnection of feeling for collective reproduction and community survival. From Carpenters to Kilburn Square, collective kinship networks have been vital to the reproduction of everyday life on London's housing estates, and resistance to financialised development. Community ownership campaigns, exemplified by Wards Corner Community Benefit Society in North London's Latin Village, are galvanising intimate, social, familial networks of connected people with mutual investments in their economic and cultural survival. Private renters in house-shares are banding together and developing plans to cooperatively purchase their homes from willing landlords. Tenant unions are drawing together people of all backgrounds and generations, picketing letting agents and stopping evictions.

Such is the creativity of human resistance to capital's removal of space for relating: we persist in relating, despite and alongside the precariousness. This is because the labour possible beyond capitalism, in the words of Lola Olufemi, is only 'labour for the sake of life-making' (2022: 54). When the resources and space for life-making are removed from us, we fight for alternative visions of reproduction, and our right to a closeness that is chosen.

Bibliography

Abramovitz M (2012) The Feminization of Austerity. *New Labor Forum* 21(1): 30–39.

Ahmed S (2004) Affective Economies. *Social Text* 79, 22(2): 117–139.

Anagnost A (1995) A Surfeit of Bodies: Population and the Rationality of the State in Post-Mao China. In Ginsburg FD and Reiter RR (eds) *Conceiving the New World Order: The Global Politics of Reproduction* (pp 19–22). Berkeley: University of California Press.

Anderson B (2006) Becoming and Being Hopeful: Towards a Theory of Affect. *Environment and Planning D: Society and Space* 24(5): 733–752.

Anderson B (2010) Migration, Immigration Controls and the Fashioning of Precarious Workers. *Work, Employment and Society* 24(2): 300–317.

Anderson B (2014) *Encountering Affect: Capacities, Apparatuses, Conditions.* Farnham: Ashgate.

Aretxaga B (2003) Maddening States. *Annual Review of Anthropology* 32: 393–410.

Baer WC (2011) Landlords and Tenants in London, 1550–1700. *Urban History* 38(2): 234–255.

Barker J (2018) Decolonizing the Mind. *Rethinking Marxism* 30(2): 208–231.

Bauman Z (2003) *Liquid Love: On the Frailty of Human Bonds.* London: Polity.

Beck J (2018) The Concept Creep of 'Emotional Labor'. *The Atlantic,* 26 November.

Beckett A (2009) *When the Lights Went Out: Britain in the Seventies.* Kindle edition, London: Faber & Faber.

Benson M and Lewis C (2019) Brexit, British People of Colour in the EU-27 and Everyday Racism in Britain and Europe. *Ethnic and Racial Studies* 42(13): 2211–2228.

Benston M (1969) The Political Economy of Women's Liberation. *Monthly Review* 21(4): 13–27.

bergman c and Montgomery N (2017) *Joyful Militancy: Building Thriving Resistance In Toxic Times.* Chico: AK Press.

Berlant L (1998) Intimacy: A Special Issue. *Critical Inquiry* 24(2): 284–285.

Berlant L (2011) *Cruel Optimism.* Durham, NC: Duke University Press.

Berry S (2022) Estate Resident Ballots: Are They Working Well? https://www.london.gov.uk/sites/default/files/2022_07_12_ballot_research_sian_berry_final_1.pdf (last accessed 30 September 2023).

Beswick J and Penny J (2018) Demolishing the Present to Sell off the Future? The Emergence of 'Financialized Municipal Entrepreneurialism' in London. *International Journal of Urban and Regional Research* 42(4): 612–632. https://doi.org/10.1111/1468–2427.12612

Bezanson K and Luxton M (2006) *Social Reproduction: Feminist Political Economy Challenges Neo-Liberalism.* Montreal/Kingston: McGill-Queen's Press.

Bhattacharya T (2017) *Social Reproduction Theory: Remapping Class, Recentering Oppression.* London: Pluto Press.

Bhattacharyya G (2018) *Rethinking Racial Capitalism: Questions of Reproduction and Survival.* London: Rowman & Littlefield.

Bhattacharyya G, Elliott-Cooper A, Balani S, Nişancıoğlu K, Koram K, Gebrial D, El-Enany N and de Noronha L (2021) *Empire's Endgame: Racism and the British State.* London: Pluto.

Bichler S and Nitzan J (1996) Military Spending and Differential Accumulation: A New Approach to the Political Economy of Armament – The Case of Israel. *Review of Radical Political Economics* 28(1): 51–95.

Bissell D (2014) Transforming Commuting Mobilities: The Memory of Practice. *Environ Plan A* 46(8): 1946–1965.

Blackman L (2012) *Immaterial Bodies: Affect, Embodiment, Mediation.* London: SAGE.

Blunt A and Dowling R (2006) *Home.* New York: Routledge.

Blunt A and Sheringham O (2018) Home-City Geographies: Urban Dwelling and Mobility. *Progress in Human Geography* 43(5): 815–834.

Böll-Stiftung H and Schönenberg R (2014) *Transnational Organized Crime: Analyses of a Global Challenge to Democracy.* London: Transcript Verlag.

Bondi L (2003) Empathy and Identification: Conceptual Resources for Feminist Fieldwork. *ACME: An International Journal for Critical Geographies* 2(1): 64–76.

Bondi L (2007) *Emotional Geographies.* London: Routledge.

Bondi L (2009) Teaching Reflexivity: Undoing or Reinscribing Habits of Gender? *Journal of Geography in Higher Education* 33(3): 327–337.

Bondi L (2013) Research and Therapy: Generating Meaning and Feeling Gaps. *Qualitative Inquiry* 19(1): 9–19.

Bondi L and Davidson J (2011) Lost in Translation. *Transactions of the Institute of British Geographers* 36(4): 595–598.

Boterman WR and Bridge G (2015) Gender, Class and Space in the Field of Parenthood: Comparing Middle-Class Fractions in Amsterdam and London. *Transactions of the Institute of British Geographers* 40(2): 249–261.

Bouchal P and Norris E (2012) Implementing Sure Start Children's Centres. https://www.instituteforgovernment.org.uk/sites/default/files/publications/Implementing%20Sure%20Start%20Childrens%20Centres%20-%20final_0.pdf (last accessed 25 September 2019).

Boughton J (2018) *Municipal Dreams: The Rise and Fall of Council Housing*. London: Verso.

Bourdieu P (1980) *The Logic of Practice*. Cambridge: Polity.

Bourdieu P (1994) Rethinking the State: Genesis and Structure of the Bureaucratic Field. *Sociological Theory* 12(1): 1–18.

Bowlby S (2011) Friendship, Co-Presence and Care: Neglected Spaces. *Social & Cultural Geography* 12(6): 605–622.

Boyer K (2009) Of Care and Commodities: Breast Milk and the New Politics of Mobile Biosubstances. *Progress in Human Geography* 34(1): 5–20.

Brickell K (2015) Towards Intimate Geographies of Peace? Local Reconciliation of Domestic Violence in Cambodia. *Transactions of the Institute of British Geographers* 40(3): 321–333.

Brickell K (2017) *Geographies of Forced Eviction: Dispossession, Violence, Resistance*. London: Palgrave Macmillan.

British Medical Journal (2017) Health and Social Care Spending Cuts Linked to 120,000 Excess Deaths in England. https://www.bmj.com/company/newsroom/health-and-social-care-spending-cuts-linked-to-120000-excess-deaths-in-england/ (last accessed 27 February 2019).

brown am (2017) *Emergent Strategy: Shaping Change, Changing Worlds*. Chico: AK Press.

brown am (2019) *Pleasure Activism: The Politics of Feeling Good*. Chico: AK Press.

brown am and Imarisha W (2015) *Octavia's Brood: Science Fiction Stories from Social Justice Movements*. Chico: AK Press.

Brown JN (2007) Response: 'In the Eye of the Beholder: Placing Race and Culture'. *Antipode* 39(2): 376–381.

Burn G (2006) *The Re-Emergence of Global Finance*. London: Palgrave Macmillan.

Butler J (1992) Contingent Foundations: Feminism and the Question of 'Postmodernism'. In Butler J and Scott JW (eds) *Feminists Theorize the Political* (pp 3–22). New York: Routledge.

Butler J (1993) *Bodies that Matter: On the Discursive Limits of 'Sex'*. London: Psychology Press.

Butler J (1997) *The Psychic Life of Power*. Stanford: Stanford University Press.

Butler O (1998) *The Parable of the Talents*. New York: Seven Stories Press [Kindle Edition].

Butler J (2004) *Precarious Life: The Powers of Mourning and Violence*. London: Verso.

Butler J (2012) Precarious Life, Vulnerability, and the Ethics of Cohabitation. *Journal of Speculative Philosophy* 26(2): 134–151.

Butler P (2019) Sure Start Numbers Plummet as Cuts Hit Children's Centres. *The Guardian*, 16 June.

Bywaters P, Kwahli J, Brady G, Sparks T and Bos E (2017) Out of Sight, Out of Mind: Ethnic Inequalities in Child Protection and Out-of-Home Care Intervention Rates. *The British Journal of Social Work* 47(7): 1884–1902.

Cahill K (2002) *Who Owns Britain and Ireland: The Hidden Facts Behind Landownership in the UK and Ireland*. London: Canongate.

Canning V (2016) Immigration Detention: What's the Problem with Privatisation? *Open Learn*. https://www.open.edu/openlearn/people-politics-law/immigration-detention-whats-the-problem-privatisation (last accessed 10 March 2019).

The Care Collective (2020) *The Care Manifesto: The Politics of Interdependence*. London: Verso.

Cassidy K (2019) Where Can I Get Free? Everyday Bordering, Everyday Incarceration. *Transactions of the Institute of British Geographers* 44(1): 48–62.

Castle S (2019) Of Civil Wars and Family Feuds: Brexit Is More Divisive Than Ever. *The New York Times*, 9 March.

Cavallero L and Gago V (2021) *A Feminist Reading of Debt*. London: Pluto Press.

Chapman B (2019) Millennials More Like to Face Working-Age Poverty That Any Previous Generation, Report Finds. *The Independent*, 22 May.

Chapman RR (2010) *Family Secrets: Risking Reproduction in Central Mozambique*. Nashville: Vanderbilt University Press.

Chartered Institute of Housing (2019) UK Housing Review. https://www.ukhousingreview.org.uk/ukhr18/index.html (last accessed 25 September 2019).

Chodorow N (1978) *The Reproduction of Mothering: Psychoanalysis and the Sociology of Gender*. Berkeley: University of California Press.

Christie H, Smith SJ and Munro M (2008) The Emotional Economy of Housing. *Environment and Planning A: Economy and Space* 40(10): 2296–2312. doi:10.1068/a39358

Christophers B (2018) *The New Enclosure: The Appropriation of Public Land in Neoliberal Britain*. London: Verso.

Christophers B (2019) Putting Financialisation in its Financial Context: Transformations in Local Government-Led Urban Development in Post-Financial Crisis England. *Transactions of the Institute of British Geographers* 44(3): 571–586.

Clark A (1997) *The Struggle for the Breeches: Gender and the Making of the British Working Class*. Berkeley: University of California Press.

Clarke C (2007) Race, Place and Space: Liverpool's Local-Born Blacks. *Antipode* 39(2): 367–369.

Cloke P, May J and Williams A (2017) The Geographies of Food Banks in the Meantime. *Progress in Human Geography* 41(6): 703–726.

Clough NL (2012) Emotion at the Center of Radical Politics: On the Affective Structures of Rebellion and Control. *Antipode* 44(5): 1667–1686.

Cobain I (2011) Jersey: Haut de la Garenne Children's Home Abuse Scandal Ends with One Last Conviction. *The Guardian*, 7 January.

Cockayne DG (2016) Entrepreneurial Affect: Attachment to Work Practice in San Francisco's Digital Media Sector. *Environment and Planning D: Society and Space* 34(3): 456–473.

Cohen S Humphries B and Mynott E (2014) *From Immigration Controls to Welfare Controls*. London: Routledge.

Cole M (2017) *New Developments in Critical Race Theory and Education: Revisiting Racialized Capitalism and Socialism in Austerity*. London: Palgrave Macmillan.

Collinson P (2015) The Other Generation Rent: Meet the People Flat-Sharing in Their 40s. *The Guardian*, 25 September. https://www.theguard ian.com/money/2015/sep/25/flatsharing-40s-housing-crisis-lack-homes-renting-london (last accessed 20 September 2023).

Collinson P (2018) One in Three UK Millennials Will Never Own a Home – Report. *The Guardian*, 17 April.

Conrad R (2014) *Against Equality: Queer Revolution, Not Mere Inclusion*. Chico: AK Press.

Constable, N (2009) The Commodification of Intimacy: Marriage, Sex, and Reproductive Labor. *Annual Review of Anthropology* 38(1): 49–64.

Cooke M (1950) The Bronx Slave Market Pt I. *The New York Compass*, 8 January.

Coombe-Whitlock C (2022) 'People can't afford to raise families': Gen Z Not Planning on Having Children Due to a Lack of Money. *The Independent*, 22 March.

Coppola M, Curti L, Fantone L, Laforest MH and Poole S (2007) Women, Migration and Precarity. *Feminist Review* 87: 94–103.

Corporate Watch (2018) Tidemill: Peabody Housing Association – From Social Landlord to Big Business. https://corporatewatch.org/tidemill-peabody-housing-association-from-social-landlord-to-big-business/ (last accessed 23 September 2019).

Cosslett RL (2018) Priced Out of Parenthood: No Wonder the Birthrate is Plummeting. *The Guardian*, 20 July.

Coulthard G (2014) From Wards of the State to Subjects of Recognition? Marx, Indigenous Peoples, and the Politics of Dispossession in Denendeh. In Simpson A and Smith A (eds) *Theorizing Native Studies* (pp 56–99). Durham, NC: Duke University Press.

Craig G, Waite L, Lewis H and Skrivankova K (2015) *Vulnerability, Exploitation and Migrants: Insecure Work in a Globalised Economy*. London: Palgrave Macmillan.

Cresswell T (2012) Mobilities II: Still. *Progress in Human Geography* 36(5): 645–653.

Critical Art Ensemble (2012) Reinventing Precarity. *The Drama Review* 56(4): 49–61.

Curwen PJ (1994) *Understanding the UK Economy*. London: Palgrave Macmillan.

Cusicanqui SR (2012) Ch'ixinakax utxiwa: A Reflection on the Practices and Discourses of Decolonization. *South Atlantic Quarterly* 111(1): 95–109.

Cusicanqui SR (2023) *A Ch'ixi World is Possible: Essays from a Present in Crisis*. London: Bloomsbury.

Davies B (2018) *Austerity, Youth Policy and the Deconstruction of the Youth Service in England*. London: Palgrave Macmillan.

Davies H (2020) Revealed: Sheikh Khalifa's £5 bn London Property Empire. *The Guardian*, 18 October. https://www.theguardian.com/uk-news/ng-interactive/2020/oct/18/revealed-sheikh-khalifas-5bn-london-property-empire (last accessed 30 September 2023).

Davis M (2007) *Planet of Slums*. London: Verso.

Dawney L, Kirwan S and Walker R (2018) The Intimate Spaces of Debt: Love, Freedom and Entanglement in Indebted Lives. *Geoforum* 110: 191–199.

De La Cadena M (2015) *Earth Beings: Ecologies of Practice Across Andean Worlds*. Durham, NC: Duke University Press.

De Leeuw S (2016) Tender Grounds: Intimate Visceral Violence and British Columbia's Colonial Geographies. *Political Geography* 52: 14–23.

Deleuze G (1975) *Kafka: Toward a Theory of Minor Literature*. Minneapolis: University of Minnesota Press.

Deleuze G (1978) Gilles Deleuze, Lecture Transcripts on Spinoza's Concept of 'Affect'. https://www.gold.ac.uk/media/images-by-section/departments/research-centres-and-units/research-centres/centre-for-invention-and-social-process/deleuze_spinoza_affect.pdf (last accessed 17 October 2022).

Deleuze G and Guattari F (1987) *A Thousand Plateaus: Capitalism and Schizophrenia*. London: Continuum.

Delgado Wise R (2015) Migration and Labour under Neoliberal Globalziation. In Schierup C, Munck R, Likic-Brboric B and Neergaard A (eds) *Migration, Precarity, and Global Governance: Challenges and Opportunities* (pp 25–45). Oxford: Oxford University Press.

DeLoughrey E, Didur J and Carrigan A (2015) *Global Ecologies and the Environmental Humanities: Postcolonial Approaches*. New York: Routledge.

Delph-Janiurek T (2001) (Un)consensual Conversations: Betweenness, 'Material Access', Laughter and Reflexivity in Research. *Area* 33(4): 414–421.

Demertzis N (2013) *Emotions in Politics: The Affect Dimension in Political Tension*. London: Palgrave Macmillan.

Department of Health (2016) Equality Analysis on the New Contract for Doctors and Dentists in Training in the NHS. https://assets.publishing.service.gov.uk/government/uploads/system/uploads/attachment_data/file/512696/jd-eia.pdf (last accessed 25 September 2019).

Department for Levelling Up, Housing & Communities (2022) A Fairer Private Rented Sector. https://assets.publishing.service.gov.uk/governm ent/uploads/system/uploads/attachment_data/file/1083378/A_fairer_ private_rented_sector_web_accessible.pdf (last accessed 2 October 2023).

Department for Work and Pensions (2010) Universal Credit: Welfare That Works. https://assets.publishing.service.gov.uk/government/uploads/sys tem/uploads/attachment_data/file/48897/universal-credit-full-docum ent.pdf (last accessed 23 September 2019).

Derrida J (2005) *Politics of Friendship*. London: Verso.

Dewey S and Kelly P (2011) *Policing Pleasure: Sex Work, Policy, and the State in Global Perspective*. New York: New York University Press.

Digby T (2014) *Love and War: How Militarism Shapes Sexuality and Romance*. New York: Columbia University Press.

Disability Rights UK (2022) Care Home Discharges During Covid 'Unlawful'. https://www.disabilityrightsuk.org/news/2022/may/ care-home-discharges-during-covid-ruled-'unlawful' (last accessed 2 October 2023).

Dittmer J (2010) Comic Book Visualities: A Methodological Manifesto on Geography, Montage and Narration. *Transactions of the Institute of British Geographers* 35(2): 222–236.

Dixon D (1983) Thatcher's People: The British Nationality Act 1981. *Journal of Law and Society* 10(2): 161–180.

Dorling D (2017) Austerity and Mortality. In Cooper V and Whyte D (eds) *The Violence of Austerity* (pp 44–50). London: Pluto.

Doty RL (1996) Immigration and National Identity: Constructing the Nation. *Review of International Studies* 22(3): 235–255.

Doward J (2016) UK Weapons Sales to Oppressive Regimes Top £3bn a Year. *The Observer*, 28 May.

Doward J (2019) UK Elderly Suffer Worst Poverty Rate in Western Europe. *The Observer*, 18 August.

Dowling, E (2020) *The Care Crisis: What Caused It and How Can We End It?* London: Verso.

Eddo-Lodge R (2018) *Why I'm No Longer Talking to White People about Race*. London: Bloomsbury.

Edwards K (2012) A Soft Place to Land. From the album *Voyageur*, track 3, MapleMusic Records.

Edwards N and Beng Huat C (1992) *Public Space: Design, Use and Management*. Singapore: National University of Singapore University Press.

Ehrenreich B and Hochshild A (2003) *Global Woman: Nannies, Maids, and Sex Workers in the New Economy*. London: Granta.

Elden S (2007) *Space, Knowledge and Power: Foucault and Geography*. London: Routledge.

Eleftheriou-Smith L (2019) London's Property Hotspots: Hackney and Islington Named as the Capital's Most In-Demand Boroughs for Home Buyers. *Homes & Property*, 24 May.

El-Enany N (2020) *(B)ordering Britain: Law, Race and Empire.* Manchester: Manchester University Press.

Elliott-Cooper A, Hubbard P and Lees L (2019) Moving beyond Marcuse: Gentrification, Displacement and the Violence of Un-Homing. *Progress in Human Geography* 44(3): 1–18.

Ettlinger N (2007) Precarity Unbound. *Alternatives* 32(3): 319–340.

Federici S (1975) *Wages Against Housework.* London: Falling Wall Press [for] the Power of Women Collective.

Federici S (2014) Foreword. In Mies M (ed) *Patriarchy and Accumulation on a World Scale: Women in the International Division of Labour* (pp ix–xiii). London: Zed Books.

Ferguson S (2017) Social Reproduction Theory: What's the Big Idea? https://www.plutobooks.com/blog/social-reproduction-theory-ferguson/ (last accessed 2 February 2019).

Fernandez B (2018) Dispossession and the Depletion of Social Reproduction. *Antipode* 50(1): 142–163.

Ferreri M and Dawson G (2018) Self-Precarization and the Spatial Imaginaries of Property Guardianship. *Cultural Geographies* 25(3): 425–440.

Fortier AM (2003) Making Home: Queer Migrations and Motions of Attachment. In Ahmed S, Castañeda C and Fortier AM (eds) *Uprootings/Regroundings: Questions of Home and Migration* (pp 115–135). Oxford: Berg.

Fortunati L (1995) *The Arcane of Reproduction: Housework, Prostitution, Labor and Capital.* New York: Autonomedia.

Foundation for Common Land (2019) Rights of Common. http://www.foundationforcommonland.org.uk/rights-of-common (last accessed 23 September 2019).

Franklin S and Ragoné H (1998) *Reproducing Reproduction: Kinship, Power, and Technological Innovation.* Philadelphia: University of Pennsylvania Press.

Fraser N (2016) Capitalism's Crisis of Care. *Dissent.* https://www.dissentmagazine.org/article/nancy-fraser-interview-capitalism-crisis-of-care (last accessed 9 February 2019).

Gaines P (1998) For Steve Michael, One Final Act of Protest. *Washington Post*, 5 June.

Garavini G (2011) Completing Decolonization: The 1973 'Oil Shock' and the Struggle for Economic Rights. *The International History Review* 33(3): 473–487.

Garthwaite N, Hatter M, Jonn J, Maxwell S, Benson F and Friedli L (2020) A Commentary on Encountering Austerity: The Experiences of Four Men Living in a London Hostel. *Geoforum* 110: 252–260. https://doi.org/10.1016/j.geoforum.2018.10.007

Gill S and Bakker I (2003) *Power, Production and Social Reproduction: Human In/security in the Global Political Economy*. London: Springer.

Gillespie T, Hardy K and Watt P (2018) Austerity Urbanism and Olympic Counter-Legacies: Gendering, Defending and Expanding the Urban Commons in East London. *Environment and Planning D: Society and Space* 36(5): 812–830.

Gilman-Opalsky R (2020) *The Communism of Love: An Inquiry into the Poverty of Exchange Value*. Chico: AK Press.

Gilmore RW (1999) You Have Dislodged a Boulder: Mothers and Prisoners in the Post Keynesian California Landscape. *Transforming Anthropology* 8: 12–38.

Gilmore RW (2007) *Golden Gulag: Prisons, Surplus, Crisis, and Opposition in Globalizing California*. Berkeley: University of California Press.

Gimenez ME (2018) *Marx, Women, and Capitalist Social Reproduction: Marxist Feminist Essays*. Leiden: Brill.

Ginsburg F and Rapp R (1995) *Conceiving the New World Order: The Global Politics of Reproduction*. Berkeley: University of California Press.

Gopal P (2019) *Insurgent Empire: Anticolonial Resistance and British Dissent*. London: Verso.

Gorman-Murray A (2015) Men at Life's Work: Structural Transformation, Inertial Heteronormativity, and Crisis. In Meehan K and Strauss K (eds) *Precarious Worlds: Contested Geographies of Social Reproduction* (pp 65–81). Athens, GA: University of Georgia Press.

Gould DB (2012) Political Despair. In Thompson S and Hoggett P (eds) *Politics and the Emotions: The Affective Turn* (pp 95–115). New York: Continuum.

Grande S (2004) *Red Pedagogy: Native American Social and Political Thought*. Lanham: Rowman & Littlefield.

Green WN and Estes J (2019) Precarious Debt: Microfinance Subjects and Intergenerational Dependency in Cambodia. *Antipode* 51(1): 129–147.

Gregg M (2011) *Work's Intimacy*. Cambridge: Polity.

Gregg M and Seigworth GJ (2010) *The Affect Theory Reader*. Durham, NC: Duke University Press.

Griffiths M (2017) Hope in Hebron: The Political Affects of Activism in a Strangled City. *Antipode* 49(3): 617–635.

Guex S (2000) The Origins of the Swiss Banking Secrecy Law and Its Repercussions for Swiss Federal Policy. *Business History Review* 74(2): 237–266

Hackney Council (2019) A Profile of Hackney, its People and Place. https://www.hackney.gov.uk/media/2665/Hackney-profile/pdf/Hackney-Profile (last accessed 23 September 2019).

Hackney Gardens (2019) Uncover the Hidden Hackney. https://hackneygardens.com/ (last accessed 23 September 2019).

Hackney History (2011) Hackney's Anarchic Nineties. https://hackneyhist ory.wordpress.com/2011/05/26/hackneys-anarchic-nineties/ (last accessed 23 September 2019).

Hall SM (2018) Everyday Austerity: Towards Relational Geographies of Family, Friendship and Intimacy. *Progress in Human Geography* 43(5): 769–789.

Hall SM (2020) *Everyday Life In Austerity: Family, Friends and Intimate Relations.* London: Palgrave Macmillan.

Hall S and Grossberg L (1985/2018) On Postmodernism and Articulation. In *Essential Essays: Volume I* (pp 45–60). Durham, NC: Duke University Press.

Haraway D (2016) *Staying with the Trouble: Making Kin in the Chthulucene.* Durham, NC: Duke University Press.

Harding V (2002) Space, Property, and Propriety in Urban England. *The Journal of Interdisciplinary History* 32: 549–569.

Hardt M (1999) Affective Labor. *Boundary* 26(2): 89–100.

Harker C (2009) Spacing Palestine through the Home. *Transactions of the Institute of British Geographers* 34(3): 320–332.

Harris E and Nowicki M (2020) 'GET SMALLER'? Emerging Geographies of Micro-Living. *Area* 52: 591– 599. https://doi.org/10.1111/area.12625

Harris E, Nowicki M and Brickell K (2019) On-Edge in the Impasse: Inhabiting the Housing Crisis as Structure-of-Feeling. *Geoforum* 101: 156–164.

Hartman S (2002) The Time of Slavery. *The South Atlantic Quarterly* 101(4): 757–777.

Hartman S (2008) Venus in Two Acts. *Small Axe* 12(2): 1–14.

Hartsock N (1983) *Money, Sex and Power: Towards a Feminist Historical Materialism.* Dartmouth: Northeastern University Press.

Harvey D (2003) *The New Imperialism.* Oxford: Oxford University Press.

Harvey D (2007) *A Brief History of Neoliberalism.* Oxford: Oxford University Press.

Harvey D (2014) *Seventeen Contradictions and the End of Capitalism.* London: Profile Books.

Health Foundation (2021) 6 Out of 10 People Who Have Died of COVID-19 are Disabled. *Health Foundation*, 11 February. https://www.health. org.uk/news-and-comment/news/6-out-of-10-people-who-have-died-from-covid-19-are-disabled#:~:text=Worryingly%2C%20today%27s%20 data%20confirms%20this,for%20more%20and%20better%20support (last accessed 29 September 2023).

Heckert J (2010) Love without Borders? Intimacy, Identity and the State of Compulsory Monogamy. In Barker M and Langdridge D (eds) *Understanding Non-Monogamies* (pp 255–266). New York: Routledge.

Heckert J (2011) Sexuality as State Form. In Rouselle D and Evren S (eds) *Post-Anarchism: A Reader* (pp 195–203). London: Pluto.

Hellema D (2018) *The Global 1970s: Radicalism, Reform, and Crisis.* London: Routledge.

Hendrickse R (2020) Neoliberalism is Over: Welcome to Neo-Illiberalism. *Open Democracy*, 7 May.

Hill D (2016) Sadiq Khan Sets Out Key Plans for More 'Genuinely Affordable' London Homes. *The Guardian*, 29 November.

Hill S (2017) Precarity in the Era of #BlackLivesMatter. *Women's Studies Quarterly* 45(3–4): 94–109.

HM Government (2011) Laying the Foundations: A Housing Strategy for England. https://www.housing.org.uk/resource-library/browse/laying-the-foundations-a-housing-strategy-for-england (last accessed 23 September 2019).

HM Government (2018) PM Speech to the National Housing Federation Summit. https://www.gov.uk/government/speeches/pm-speech-to-the-national-housing-federation-summit-19-september-2018 (last accessed 23 September 2019).

HM Government (2019a) Family Visas: Apply, Extend or Switch. https://www.gov.uk/uk-family-visa/proof-income (last accessed 25 September 2019).

HM Government (2019b) Rent a Room in Your Home. https://www.gov.uk/rent-room-in-your-home/your-lodgers-tenancy-type

HM Treasury (2012) Consultation on Reforms to the Real Estate Investment Trust Regime. https://assets.publishing.service.gov.uk/government/uploads/system/uploads/attachment_data/file/81552/condoc_reforms_to_reit.pdf (last accessed 2 October 2023).

Hochschild AR (1983) *The Managed Heart: Commercialization of Human Feeling.* Berkeley: University of California Press.

Hollibaugh A and Weiss M (2015) Queer Precarity and the Myth of Gay Affluence. *New Labor Forum* 24(3): 18–27.

Holloway SL and Pimlott-Wilson H (2016) New Economy, Neoliberal State and Professionalised Parenting: Mothers' Labour Market Engagement and State Support for Social Reproduction in Class-Differentiated Britain. *Transactions of the Institute of British Geographers* 41: 376–388.

Holmes C (2003) *Housing, Equality and Choice.* London: Institute for Public Policy Research.

Home (2019) Hackney Market Rent Summary. https://www.home.co.uk/for_rent/hackney/current_rents?location=hackney (last accessed 25 September 2019).

Home Office (2015) A Short Guide on Right to Rent. https://assets.publishing.service.gov.uk/government/uploads/system/uploads/attachment_data/file/823111/short_guide_on_right_to_rent_v001.pdf (last accessed 3 March 2019).

Home Office (2016) Code of Practice on Illegal Immigrants and Private Rented Accommodation. https://www.gov.uk/government/publications/right-to-rent-landlords-code-of-practice/code-of-practice-on-illegal-immigrants-and-private-rented-accommodation-for-tenancies-starting-on-or-after-1-february-2016 (last accessed 2 March 2019).

hooks b (2000a) *Feminism is for Everybody*. Boston: South End Press.

hooks b (2000b) *All About Love: New Visions*. New York: Harper.

Housing Act (1988) http://www.legislation.gov.uk/ukpga/1988/50/contents (last accessed 23 September 2019).

Housing Act (1996) http://www.legislation.gov.uk/ukpga/1996/52/contents (last accessed 23 September 2019).

Housing Moves (2014) Welcome to Housing Moves. https://www.housingmoves.org/ (last accessed 23 September 2019).

Housing and Planning Act (2016) http://www.legislation.gov.uk/ukpga/2016/22/contents/enacted (last accessed 23 September 2019).

Housing and Regeneration Act (2008) http://www.legislation.gov.uk/ukpga/2008/17/contents (last accessed 23 September 2019).

Hubbard P (2001) Sex Zones: Intimacy, Citizenship and Public Space. *Sexualities* 4(1): 51–71.

Hubbard P and Wilkinson E (2015) Welcoming the World? Hospitality, Homonationalism, and the London 2012 Olympics. *Antipode* 47(3): 598–615.

Hunter S (2015) *Power, Politics, and the Emotions: Impossible Governance?* London: Routledge.

Hutcheson G and Longhurst R (2017) I'm Here, I Hate It and I Can't Cope Anymore: Writing about Suicide. In Donovan C and Moss P (eds) *Writing Intimacy into Feminist Geography* (pp 41–47). London: Routledge.

Ingram GB (1997) *Queers in Space: Communities/Public Spaces/Sites of Resistance*. Seattle: Bay Press.

Jackson B and Saunders R (2012) *Making Thatcher's Britain*. Cambridge: Cambridge University Press.

Jeraj S and Walker R (2016) *The Rent Trap: How We Fell Into It And How We Get Out Of It*. London: Pluto.

Johnson RL and Woodhouse M (2018) Securing the Return: How Enhanced US Border Enforcement Fuels Cycles of Debt Migration. *Antipode* 50(4): 976–996.

Jordan J (1991/2014) A New Politics of Sexuality. In Jordan J and Davis A (eds) *Life as Activism: June Jordan's Writings from the Progressive* (pp 54–59). Sacramento: Litwin.

Joyner C (1975) The Petrodollar Phenomenon and Changing International Economic Relations. *World Affairs* 138: 152–176.

Judt T (2008) *Reappraisals: Reflections on the Forgotten Twentieth Century*. London: Penguin Books.

Kalia A (2021) 'It is devastating': The Millennials Who Would Love to Have Kids – But Can't Afford a Family. *The Guardian*, 13 October.

Kalleberg AL (2009) Precarious Work, Insecure Workers: Employment Relations in Transition. *American Sociological Review* 74(1): 1–22.

Katz C (2001) Vagabond Capitalism and the Necessity of Social Reproduction. *Antipode* 33(4): 709–728.

Katz C (2008) Childhood as Spectacle: Relays of Anxiety and the Reconfiguration of the Child. *Cultural Geographies* 15: 5–17.

Katz C (2011) Accumulation, Excess, Childhood: Toward a Countertopography of Risk and Waste. *Documents d'Anàlisi Geogràfica* 57(1): 47–60.

Katz C, Marston S and Mitchell K (2015) Conclusion: Demanding Life's Work. In Meehan K and Strauss K (eds) *Precarious Worlds: Contested Geographies of Social Reproduction* (pp 174–188). Athens, GA: University of Georgia Press.

Katz C (2017) The Angel of Geography: Superman, Tiger Mother, Aspiration Management, and the Child as Waste. *Progress in Human Geography* 42(5): 723–740.

Kaufman P (2005) Middle-Class Social Reproduction: The Activation and Negotiation of Structural Advantages. *Sociological Forum* 20(2): 245–270.

Kerschbaum S, Eisenman L and Jones J (2017) *Negotiating Disability: Disclosure and Higher Education*. Ann Arbor: University of Michigan Press.

Kersley A (2023) With Their Bosses Earning Twice That of Other Charities, Have Housing Association 'Lost Their Social Purpose?'. *Byline Times*, 17 July. https://bylinetimes.com/2023/07/17/with-their-bosses-earning-twice-that-of-other-charities-have-housing-associations-lost-their-social-purpose/ (last accessed 2 October 2023).

Kosofsky-Sedgwick E (2003) *Touching Feeling: Affect, Pedagogy, Performativity*. Durham, NC: Duke University Press.

Lai KP (2017) Unpacking Financial Subjectivities: Intimacies, Governance and Socioeconomic Practices in Financialisation. *Environment and Planning D: Society and Space* 35(5): 913–932.

Lambert R and Herod A (2016) *Neoliberal Capitalism and Precarious Work: Ethnographies of Accommodation and Resistance*. Cheltenham: Edward Elgar.

Landlords Guild (2010) Lead Tenant Agreement. https://www.landlords guild.com/lead-tenant-agreement/ (last accessed 25 September 2019).

Law CM (1967) The Growth of Urban Population in England and Wales, 1801–1911. *Transactions of the Institute of British Geographers* 125–143.

Leahy S, McKee K and Crawford J (2018) Generating Confusion, Concern, and Precarity through the Right to Rent Scheme in Scotland. *Antipode* 50(3): 604–620.

Lefebvre H (1979) Space: Social Product and Use Value. In Brenner N and Elden S (eds) *State, Space, World: Selected Essays by Henri LeFebvre* (pp 185–196). Minneapolis: University of Minnesota Press.

Lewis H, Dwyer P, Hodkinson S and Waite L (2015) Hyper-Precarious Lives: Migrants, Work and Forced Labour in the Global North. *Progress in Human Geography* 39(5): 580–600.

Lewis S (2019) *Full Surrogacy Now: Feminism Against Family*. London: Verso.

Linebaugh P (2014) *Stop, Thief! The Commons, Enclosures, and Resistance*. Oakland: PM Press.

London Gardens (2014) Record: St John's Churchyard Gardens. http://www.londongardensonline.org.uk/gardens-online-record.php?ID=HAC 039 (last accessed 23 September 2019).

López TM (2014) *The Winter of Discontent: Myth, Memory, and History*. Oxford: Oxford University Press.

Lorde A (1978) Uses of the Erotic: The Erotic as Power. In brown a (ed) *Pleasure Activism: The Politics of Feeling Good* (pp 30–39). Chico: AK Press.

Lorde A (1981) Uses of Anger. In Lorde A *Sister Outsider* (pp 124–133). Berkeley: Ten Speed Press.

Lorimer H (2008) Cultural Geography: Non-Representational Conditions and Concerns. *Progress in Human Geography* 32(4): 551–559.

Lowe L (2015) *The Intimacies of Four Continents*. Durham, NC: Duke University Press.

Luke N and Kaika M (2019) Ripping the Heart Out of Ancoats: Collective Action to Defend Infrastructures of Social Reproduction against Gentrification. *Antipode* 51(2): 579–600.

Lund B (2016) *Housing Politics in the United Kingdom*. London: Policy.

Macdonald BJ (1999) Marx and the Figure of Desire. *Rethinking Marxism* 11(4): 21–37.

Manitowabi E (2011) Our Theory is Personal. In Simpson L (ed) *Dancing On Our Turtle's Back* (pp 72–76). Chico: AK Press.

Marx K (1967/1887) *Capital, Vol. 1: A Critical Analysis of Capitalist Production*. London: Lawrence & Wishart.

Mason R (2019) No-Deal Brexit: Key Points of Operation Yellowhammer Report. *The Guardian*, 18 August.

Massumi B (1995) The Autonomy of Affect. *Cultural Critique* 31(2): 83–109.

Mayor of London (2014) Homes for London: The London Housing Strategy. https://www.london.gov.uk/sites/default/files/gla_migrate_files_destinat ion/Housing%20Strategy%202014%20report_lowresFA.pdf (last accessed 29 September 2023).

Mayor of London (2017a) Affordable Housing and Viability Supplementary Planning Guidance (SPG). https://www.london.gov.uk/what-we-do/planning/implementing-london-plan/planning-guidance-and-practice-notes/affordable-housing-and-viability-supplementary-planning-guida nce-spg (last accessed 23 September 2019).

Mayor of London (2017b) Homes for Londoners – Affordable Homes Programme 2016–21. https://www.london.gov.uk//decisions/md2125-homes-londoners-affordable-homes-programme-2016-21 (last accessed 23 September 2019).

Mayor of London (2017c) The London Plan: The Spatial Development Strategy for Greater London. https://www.london.gov.uk/sites/defa ult/files/new_london_plan_december_2017.pdf (last accessed 23 September 2019).

Mazoyer M and Roudart L (2006) *A History of World Agriculture: From the Neolithic Age to the Current Crisis.* New York: New York University Press.

McFarlane C and Anderson B (2011) Thinking with Assemblage. *Area* 43(2): 162–164.

Mearns A (1883) *The Bitter Cry of Outcast London: An Inquiry into the Condition of the Abject Poor.* London: Cass.

Medhurst J (2014) *That Option No Longer Exists: Britain 1974–76.* Alresford: John Hunt Publishing.

Meehan K and Strauss K (2015) *Precarious Worlds: Contested Geographies of Social Reproduction.* Athens, GA: University of Georgia Press.

Meek J (2014) *Private Island: Why Britain Now Belongs to Someone Else.* London: Verso.

Millar KM (2017) Toward a Critical Politics of Precarity. *Sociology Compass* 11(6): 1–11.

Ministry of Housing, Communities & Local Government (2011) Localism Act 2011: Overview. https://www.gov.uk/government/publications/local ism-act-2011-overview (last accessed 23 September 2019).

Ministry of Housing, Communities and Local Government (2019) *English Private Landlord Survey 2018: Main Report.* https://assets.publishing.serv ice.gov.uk/government/uploads/system/uploads/attachment_data/file/ 775002/EPLS_main_report.pdf (last accessed 2 October 2023).

Ministry of Justice (2023) *Mortgage and Landlord Repossession Statistics.* https:// www.gov.uk/government/statistics/mortgage-and-landlord-possession-statistics-october-to-december-2022/mortgage-and-landlord-possession-statistics-october-to-december-2022 (last accessed 2 October 2023).

Minton A (2017) *Big Capital: Who Is London For?* London: Penguin.

Mitchell J (1971) *Woman's Estate.* London: Penguin Books.

Mitchell K, Marston SA and Katz C (2004) *Life's Work: Geographies of Social Reproduction.* Hoboken: Wiley.

Mohanty CT (1991) Cartographies of Struggle. In Mohanty CT and Russo Torres L (eds) *Third World Women and the Politics of Feminism* (pp 1–51). Bloomington: Indiana University Press.

Moos M, Pfeiffer D and Vinodrai T (2018) *The Millennial City: Trends, Implications and Prospects for Urban Planning.* London: Routledge.

Morrison CA, Johnston L and Longhurst R (2013) Critical Geographies of Love as Spatial, Relational and Political. *Progress in Human Geography* 37(4): 505–521.

Moss P and Donovan C (2017) *Writing Intimacy Into Feminist Geography*. London: Routledge.

Mullings B (1991) *The Colour of Money: The Impact of Housing Investment Decision Making on Black Housing Outcomes in London*. London: London Race and Housing Research Unit.

Naik M (2020) Negotiation, Mediation and Subjectivities: How Migrant Renters Experience Informal Rentals in Gurgaon's Urban Villages. *Radical Housing Journal* 1(2): 45–62.

Nash C (2005) Geographies of Relatedness. *Transactions of the Institute of British Geographers* 30(4): 449–462.

Nash CJ and Bain A (2007) 'Reclaiming Raunch'? Spatializing Queer Identities at Toronto Women's Bathhouse Events. *Social & Cultural Geography* 8(1): 47–62.

National Landlords Association (2019) London Rental Standard. https:// landlords.org.uk/lrspartner/accreditation (last accessed 23 September 2019).

Neale A and Lopez N (2017) Suffer the Little Children and their Mothers: A Dossier on the Unjust Separation of Children from their Mothers. *Legal Action for Women* http://legalactionforwomen.net/wp-content/uploads/ 2017/01/LAW-Dossier-18Jan17-final.pdf (last accessed 2 October 2023).

Neilson B and Rossiter N (2008) Precarity as a Political Concept, or, Fordism as Exception. *Theory, Culture & Society* 25(7–8): 51–72.

Newhouse LS (2017) Uncertain Futures and Everyday Hedging in a Humanitarian City. *Transactions of the Institute of British Geographers* 42(4): 503–515.

OECD (Organisation for Economic Co-operation and Development) (2023) Net Childcare Costs (Indicator). https://data.oecd.org/benwage/ net-childcare-costs.htm (last accessed 2 October 2023).

Olechnowicz A (1997) *Working-Class Housing in England Between the Wars: The Becontree Estate*. Oxford: Clarendon.

Olufemi L (2022) *Experiments in Imagining Otherwise*. London: Hajar Press.

Olusoga D (2016) *Black and British: A Forgotten History*. Kindle edition, London: Pan Macmillan.

ONS (Office for National Statistics) (2019) Births, Deaths and Marriages. https://www.ons.gov.uk/peoplepopulationandcommunity/birthsdeathsa ndmarriages (last accessed 25 September 2019).

ONS (Office of National Statistics) (2020a) Living Longer: Changes in Housing Tenure Over Time. https://www.ons.gov.uk/peoplepopulation andcommunity/birthsdeathsandmarriages/ageing/articles/livinglonger/ changesinhousingtenureovertime (last accessed 2 October 2023).

ONS (Office of National Statistics) (2020b) Living Longer: Implications of Housing Tenure in Later Life. https://www.ons.gov.uk/peoplepopulat ionandcommunity/birthsdeathsandmarriages/ageing/articles/livinglon ger/implicationsofhousingtenureinlaterlife (last accessed 2 October 2023).

ONS (Office for National Statistics) (2020c) Births by Parents' Country of Birth. https://www.ons.gov.uk/peoplepopulationandcommunity/births deathsandmarriages/livebirths/bulletins/parentscountryofbirthengland andwales/2019 (last accessed 26 October 2022).

Oswin N (2008) Critical Geographies and the Uses of Sexuality: Deconstructing Queer Space. *Progress in Human Geography* 32(1): 89–103.

Oswin N and Olund E (2010) Governing Intimacy. *Environment and Planning D: Society and Space* 28(1): 60–67.

Pain R (2015) Intimate War. *Political Geography* 44: 64–73.

Palan R (2003) *The Offshore World: Sovereign Markets, Virtual Places, and Nomad Millionaires.* Ithaca: Cornell University Press.

Palan R, Murphy R and Chavagneux C (2009) *Tax Havens: How Globalization Really Works.* Ithaca: Cornell University Press.

Panayi P (2010) *An Immigration History of Britain: Multicultural Racism since 1800.* London: Routledge.

Paton K and Cooper V (2017) Domicide, Eviction and Repossession. In Cooper V and Whyte D (eds) *The Violence of Austerity* (pp 164–170). London: Pluto Press.

Pedersen S (1995) *Family, Dependence, and the Origins of the Welfare State: Britain and France, 1914–1945.* Cambridge: Cambridge University Press.

Perkin MR, Heap S, Crerar-Gilbert A, Albuquerque W, Haywood S, Avila Z, et al (2020) Deaths in People from Black, Asian and Minority Ethnic Communities From Both COVID-19 and Non-COVID Causes in the First Weeks of the Pandemic in London: A Hospital Case Note Review. *BMJ Open* 10: e040638. doi: 10.1136/bmjopen-2020-040638

Pettifor A (2018) *The Production of Money: How to Break the Power of Bankers.* London: Verso.

Phoenix A and Phoenix A (2012) Racialisation, Relationality and Riots: Intersections and Interpellations. *Feminist Review* 100: 52–71.

Pile S (2010) Emotions and Affect in Recent Human Geography. *Transactions of the Institute of British Geographers* 35(1): 5–20.

Pratt G and Rosner V (2012) *The Global and the Intimate: Feminism in Our Time.* New York: Columbia University Press.

Price PL (2013) Race and Ethnicity II: Skin and Other Intimacies. *Progress in Human Geography* 37(4): 578–586.

Pring J (2017) Welfare Reforms and the Attack on Disabled People. In Cooper V and Whyte D (eds) *The Violence of Austerity* (pp 51–58). London: Pluto.

Puar JK (2007) *Terrorist Assemblages: Homonationalism in Queer Times*. Durham, NC: Duke University Press.

Reid-Musson E (2014) Historicizing Precarity: A Labour Geography of 'Transient' Migrant Workers in Ontario Tobacco. *Geoforum* 56: 161–171.

Rich A (1976) *Of Woman Born: Motherhood as Experience and Institution*. New York: W.W. Norton.

Richardson L (2018) Feminist Geographies of Digital Work. *Progress in Human Geography* 42(2): 244–263.

Ritchie J (2015) Pinkwashing, Homonationalism, and Israel–Palestine: The Conceits of Queer Theory and the Politics of the Ordinary. *Antipode* 47(3): 616– 634.

Roberts D (1997) *Killing the Black Body: Race, Reproduction, and the Meaning of Liberty*. New York: Pantheon.

Robinson C (1983) *Black Marxism: The Making of the Black Radical Tradition*. Chapel Hill: University of North Carolina Press.

Rodger R (1987) Political Economy, Ideology and the Persistence of Working-Class Housing Problems in Britain, 1850–1914. *International Review of Social History* 32: 109–143.

Rose G (1993) *Feminism and Geography: The Limits of Geographical Knowledge*. Cambridge: Polity Press.

Rose G (1995) *Love's Work*. New York: New York Review Books.

Ruddick S (2010) The Politics of Affect: Spinoza in the Work of Negri and Deleuze. *Theory, Culture & Society* 27(4): 21–45. doi:10.1177/0263276410372235

Ryan F (2019) *Crippled: Austerity and the Demonization of Disabled People*. London: Verso.

Sabbagh D and McKernan B (2019) UK Arms Sales to Saudi Arabia Unlawful, Court of Appeal Declares. *The Guardian*, 20 June.

Saberi P (2019) Preventing Radicalization in European Cities: An Urban Geopolitical Question. *Political Geography* 74: np.

Salih R (2017) Bodies That Walk, Bodies That Talk, Bodies That Love: Palestinian Women Refugees, Affectivity, and the Politics of the Ordinary. *Antipode* 49(3): 742–760.

Sampson T (2017) Brexit: The Economics of International Disintegration. *The Journal of Economic Perspectives* 31(4): 163–184.

Savills (2023) First-time buyer funding and the Bank of Mum and Dad. https://www.savills.co.uk/blog/article/302871/residential-property/first-time-buyer-funding-and-the-bank-of-mum-and-dad.aspx (last accessed 28 September 2023).

Sassen S (2014) *Expulsions: Brutality and Complexity in the Global Economy*. Cambridge, MA: Harvard University Press.

Schram S (2015) *The Return of Ordinary Capitalism: Neoliberalism, Precarity, Occupy*. Oxford: Oxford University Press.

Schumacher D (1985) *Energy: Crisis or Opportunity? An Introduction to Energy Studies*. London: Macmillan International Higher Education.

Sedgwick EK (2003) *Touching Feeling: Affect, Pedagogy, Performativity*. Durham, NC: Duke University Press.

Seyfert R (2012) Beyond Personal Feelings and Collective Emotions: Towards a Theory of Social Affect. *Theory, Culture & Society* 29(6): 27–46.

Sharma A and Gupta A (2006) *The Anthropology of the State: A Reader*. Oxford: Blackwell.

Sharpe C (2010) *Monstrous Intimacies: Making Post-Slavery Subjects*. Durham, NC: Duke University Press.

Shelley J (2019) The Fading. From the album *Like the River Loves the Sea*, track 6, No Quarter.

Shepherd J (2015) *Crisis? What Crisis? The Callaghan Government and the British 'Winter of Discontent'*. Manchester: Manchester University Press

Shilliam R (2018) *Race and the Undeserving Poor: From Abolition to Brexit*. New York: Columbia University Press.

Shrubsole G (2019) *Who Owns England? How We Lost Our Green and Pleasant Land, and How to Take It Back*. Kindle edition, New York: HarperCollins.

Slater T (2014) The Myth of 'Broken Britain': Welfare Reform and the Production of Ignorance. *Antipode* 46(4): 948–969.

Smart-Grosvenor V (1970) The Kitchen Crisis. In Bambara TC (ed) *The Black Woman: An Anthology* (pp 149–155). New York: Washington Square Press.

Smith M and Mac J (2018) *Revolting Prostitutes: The Fight for Sex Workers' Rights*. London: Verso.

Soaita AM and McKee K (2019) Assembling a 'Kind of' Home in the UK Private Renting Sector. *Geoforum* 103: 148–157.

Spratt V (2022) *Tenants: The People on the Frontline of Britain's Housing Emergency*. London: Profile.

Standing G (2011) *The Precariat: The New Dangerous Class*. London: Bloomsbury.

Steinbach SL (2016) *Understanding the Victorians: Politics, Culture and Society in Nineteenth-Century Britain*. London: Routledge.

Stenning A (2020) Feeling the Squeeze: Towards a Psychosocial Geography of Austerity in Low-to-Middle Income Families. *Geoforum* 110: 200–210.

Stewart K (2007) *Ordinary Affects*. Durham, NC: Duke University Press.

Stoler AL (2006) *Haunted by Empire: Geographies of Intimacy in North American History*. Durham, NC: Duke University Press.

Strathern M (1995) Future Kinship and the Study of Culture. *Futures: Anthropological Perspectives on the Future of Culture and Society* 27(4): 423–435.

Strauss K (2013) Unfree Again: Social Reproduction, Flexible Labour Markets and the Resurgence of Gang Labour in the UK. *Antipode* 45: 180–197.

Strauss K (2018) Labour Geography 1: Towards a Geography of Precarity? *Progress in Human Geography* 42(4): 622–630.

Swanson M (1977) The Sanitation Syndrome: Bubonic Plague and Urban Native Policy in the Cape Colony, 1900–1909. *The Journal of African History* 18(3): 387–410.

Szreter S and Mooney G (1998) Urbanization, Mortality, and the Standard of Living Debate: New Estimates of the Expectation of Life at Birth in Nineteenth-Century British Cities. *The Economic History Review* 51: 84–112.

Taylor FM (2021a) Cumulative Precarity: Millennial Experience and Multigenerational Cohabitation in Hackney, London. *Antipode* 53: 587–606. https://doi.org/10.1111/anti.12689

Taylor FM (2021b) Desiring Space: The Affective Politics of Intimacy in Shared Rental Accommodation. *Radical Housing Journal* 3(2): 47–64.

Thomas T (2022) Total Fertility Rates Rise for the First Time in a Decade in England and Wales. *The Guardian*, 9 August. https://www.theguardian.com/uk-news/2022/aug/09/total-fertility-rate-rises-first-time-decade-england-wales (last accessed 2 October 2023).

Thom KC (2017) Righteous Callings: Being Good, Leftist Orthodoxy, and the Social Justice Crisis of Faith. *Medium*, 8 August.

Thom KC (2019) *I Hope We Choose Love: A Trans Girl's Notes from the End of the World*. Vancouver: Arsenal Pulp Press.

Tolia-Kelly D (2004) Locating Processes of Identification: Studying the Precipitates of Re-Memory through Artefacts in the British Asian Home. *Transactions of the Institute of British Geographers* 29(3): 314–329.

Tomaszczyk A and Worth N (2018) Boomeranging Home: Understanding Why Millennials Live with Parents in Toronto, Canada. *Social & Cultural Geography* 21(8): 1103–1121.

Tomlinson J (2012) Thatcher, Monetarism and the Politics of Inflation. In Saunders R and Jackson B (eds) *Making Thatcher's Britain* (pp 78–95). Cambridge: Cambridge University Press.

Tsianos V and Papadopoulos D (2006) Precarity: A Savage Journey to the Heart of Embodied Capitalism. *Transversal* 10: 1–11.

Vasudevan P (2019) An Intimate Inventory of Race and Waste. *Antipode* 53(2/3): 770–790.

Veldstra C (2018) Bad Feeling at Work: Emotional Labour, Precarity, and the Affective Economy. *Cultural Studies* 34(1): 1–24.

Vogel L (1983) *Marxism and the Oppression of Women: Toward a Unitary Theory*. Leiden: Brill.

Waitt G and Gorman-Murray A (2011) 'It's About Time You Came Out': Sexualities, Mobility and Home. *Antipode* 43(4): 1380–1403.

Waitt G and Harada T (2019) Space of Energy Well-Being: Social Housing Tenants' Everyday Experiences of Fuel Poverty. *Transactions of the Institute of British Geographers* 44(4): 794–807.

Walker R and Jeraj S (2016) *The Rent Trap: How We Fell Into It and How We Get Out of It*. London: Pluto Press.

Weeks K (2011) *The Problem With Work: Feminism, Marxism, Antiwork Politics and Postwork Imaginaries*. Durham, NC: Duke University Press.

Weinbaum AE (2019) *The Afterlife of Reproductive Slavery: Biocapitalism and Black Feminism's History of Philosophy*. Durham, NC: Duke University Press.

Welch G (2001) Everything is Free. In *Time (The Revelator)*, 9, Acony Records

Welfare Reform Act (2012) http://www.legislation.gov.uk/ukpga/2012/5/contents/enacted (last accessed 25 September 2019).

West E and Knight RJ (2017) Mothers' Milk: Slavery, Wet-Nursing, and Black and White Women in the Antebellum South. *Journal of Southern History* 83(1): 37–68.

White T (2018) Build-to-Rent: How Developers are Profiting from Generation Rent. *The Guardian*, 11 April.

Wightman AD (1996) *Who Owns Scotland?* London: Canongate.

Wilde M (2019) Resisting the Rentier City: Grassroots Housing Activism and Renter Subjectivity in Post-Crisis London. *Radical Housing Journal* 1(2): 63–80.

Wilkinson E and Ortega-Alcázar I (2018) The Right to be Weary? Endurance and Exhaustion in Austere Times. *Transactions of the Institute of British Geographers* 44: 155–167.

Wills J, Datta K, Evans J, Herbert J, May J and McIlwaine C (2010) *Global Cities At Work: New Migrant Divisions of Labour*. London: Pluto.

Wilson A (2015) The Infrastructure of Intimacy. *Signs: Journal of Women in Culture and Society* 41(2): 247–280.

Wissinger E (2007) Always On Display, Affective Production in the Modeling Industry. In Clough P and Halley J (eds) *The Affective Turn: Theorizing the Social* (pp 231–261). Durham, NC: Duke University Press.

Wood A (2007) *The 1549 Rebellions and the Making of Early Modern England*. Cambridge: Cambridge University Press.

Yelling J (1982) L. C. C. Slum Clearance Policies, 1889–1907. *Transactions of the Institute of British Geographers* 7(3): 292–303.

Index

A

abortion 114
academia, experience of participating in 15–16
adventure playgrounds 20, 103–104
affect 28–31
    intimacy and 32–33
    theory 37, 127
affective assemblage of space 102, 104–108
affective attachments 29
affective labour 31, 32–33, 43
    alienated 31, 43, 44, 45, 80
    of children 88–89
    in educating parents on economic
        realities 91–92, 93–94
    of maintaining relationships in cumulative
        precarity 84–86, 86–89, 100
affective politics 15–18, 101–102, 124
    of informal decision-making
        positions 112–113
    of queer millennial households 114–119, 122
    and relationship between tenants and
        landlord 109–112
'affordable housing' 28, 52, 54–56, 57, 63,
    67, 124
Affordable Rent 55
AIDS Coalition to Unleash Power (ACT
    UP) 29–30
Akwaaba 103
Alice's story 62, 72, 98
alienated labour 30–31, 43–44, 45, 80, 100
Anna-Lise's story 115
Anzuli's story 68–69, 70
Assured Shorthold Tenancies (AST) 53, 94, 96
austerity 20, 24–25, 66, 124
    attacks on women 73

B

ballots, estate 20, 67
Bedroom Tax 66, 73–74, 91
belonging, sense of 34, 35, 94–100, 126
bergman, carla 27, 29, 37, 102
Berlant, Lauren 25, 26, 30, 102
Bhattacharya, Tithi 39, 42, 80, 108
biopower 31, 102

birth rates 61
Black communities, postwar housing
    discrimination 48, 49, 51
bodies 3, 81
bordering 36, 126
Bourdieu, P. 44, 76
Brexit 20, 26, 29, 51, 113
British Nationality Act 1981 53–54
brown, adrienne maree 36–37, 101
Build to Rent 54
Butler, Judith 27, 40
buy-to-let investors 13, 54

C

Caitlin's story 106–107
capital 38, 80, 113
    accumulation 10, 21, 25, 29, 41, 51, 80
capitalism 10
    contradiction 41
    crisis 8, 14, 21
    crisis-as-turning-point 8–9, 124–125
    differentiated value systems 40, 41–42, 44,
        52, 57–59, 81–82
    Keynesian welfare 24, 25
    late 8, 24, 25, 72–73
    modes of value 81
    patriarchy and 8, 10, 39
    uncompensated reproductive labour 9,
        10–11, 38–39
    see also racial capitalism; rentier capitalism
care capacities, neoliberal depletion of 39
Caribbean, migration from 48–49
Catherine's story 58
Chandice's story 67–68, 69, 70
child benefit cap 66
childcare 8, 81–82
children
    affective labour of 88–89
    having a child 60–62
    impact of disrepair and overcrowding on 68–69
    landlords' bans on 62
    private renting with 62–63, 64, 79
    removal from family home 84–85
    spaces for 20, 103–104

see also reproduction, obstructing
citizenship, types of 53–54
Claire's story 63–64, 107, 109–110, 111
comic strips 17
communicative labour 91–92, 93–94
community ownership campaigns 128
community, sense of 70, 94–96, 126
  barriers to 10, 96
  urban regeneration and erosion of 14, 58, 67, 94
connectivity 94–95
cost-of-living crisis 21, 61, 73, 124
COVID-19 pandemic 20–21, 29, 41–42
  ban on sexual relations among single people 113
  changing relationships to home 95
  evictions 6–7, 95–96
  housemates' financial support system 117
  queer kinship 114
  renting during 6–7
  social inequalities 41–42, 72–73
crisis
  of capitalism 8, 14, 21
  cost-of-living 21, 61, 73, 124
  etymology of 8
  reproduction 8, 14–15, 44
  as-turning-point 8–9, 124–125
culture wars 114
cumulative precarity 82–84, 100, 126
  legacies of 84–89

D

Daily Star 73
dating
  economic obstruction and 73–78
  lack of space a constriction on 106–107
death of a housemate 120–121
debt industry 39
Deleuze, G. 27, 28, 102, 122
demolition of housing estates 20, 26, 28, 57, 63
  estate ballots 20, 67
deposits 96, 112
desire 27–28
  space for 104–108
differentiated value, systems of 40, 44, 52, 57–59, 81–82
  in COVID-19 pandemic 41–42
disabled people 20, 41
  demonisation of 80–81
displaced sovereignties 108–113
disrepair, practical and psychological effects of 68–69
Dowling, Emma 16

E

economic
  necessity, households formed through 8, 113
  obstruction of intimate lives 72–79
  realities, educating parents on 91–92, 93–94

embodied
  epistemologies 37
  experience 32, 37–38
emotional labour 43
  see also affective labour
emotions, describing 102
enclosure movements 45–46
energy efficiency 13
English Private Landlord Survey 13
erotic power 101
evictions 62–63
  during COVID-19 pandemic 6–7, 95–96
  of lodgers 111
  and maintaining family relationships 84, 85, 86
  'under-occupier' 66, 73
  Section 21 6, 62

F

Faiz's story 73–75, 90–92
families
  abolition of 9
  future dreams of 76–78
  intrafamilial dependencies 5
  moving outside London 70, 71–72
  nuclear 11, 26, 36, 113
    anachronism of 1, 9
    rentier capitalism and 14–15
    thinking beyond 7–11, 14, 115
fantasies of future advancement 43, 89–94
fertility rates 61
financial industry 39, 49–50
  deregulation 51, 52
financialised life, impossibility of 20–22
foreign direct investment (FDI) 51
Fraser, Nancy 39
fuel poverty 13, 21

G

gardening 6, 99–100
general election 2019 20
generational disjunctures 91–93, 125
Gillespie, T. 39
Gilman-Opalsky, Richard 3, 10, 27, 38, 81
Ginsburg, F.D. 44
Green Group. City Hall 56, 99
Grenfell Tower fire 29, 47, 67
  safety concerns following 70–71
grief 29–30, 120–121
Grossberg, L. 16

H

Hackney
  children's services 85
  diversity 35
  growing unaffordability 65
  home and belonging 35
  moving to nine homes in 4–7, 95–96

Pembury Estate 57–58
  Shared Ownership experience 60–61
  space for young people 20, 103–104
  research based in 18–19
  St John's Church 57
  urban regeneration 57–58
Hall, Sarah Marie 25, 121
Hall, Stuart 16
Hannah's story 110–111
Haraway, Donna 102, 119
Hardt, Michael 31, 92
Harvey, David 49, 50, 52, 65–66
'Help to Buy' scheme 55
hierarchisation of private and social
  tenants 56–57, 57–59
histories 45–59, 125–126
  of housing and empire 45–52
  of precarious renting in London 52–57
  of urban regeneration 57–59
home
  attachment to materiality of 34–36
  moving 95–96
  politics of 33–34
  working to make 94–100, 126
home owners
  age-stratification 12, 14
  dating 75–76, 101
  savings and investments 12–13
home ownership 65, 109
  community 128
  educating parents on impossibility of 91–92,
    93–94
  'Help to Buy' schemes 55
  shared ownership schemes 55, 60–61, 63
hooks, bell 42, 84, 86
house prices 12, 52–53
  declining birth rates and rising 61
house-shares, privately rented
  displaced sovereignties 108–113
  excessive proximity 105, 106–107, 107–108
  household cleaning tensions 116
  lacking communal space 106–107
  'lead tenants' 40, 112–113
  obstruction to reproduction 63–65
  racialised power relations 117–118
  sharing a room in 5, 78, 105–106
  through economic necessity 8, 63, 113
  see also queer millennial renters
housing
  'affordable' 28, 52, 54–56, 57, 63, 67, 124
  benefit 53
  demolition of estates 20, 26, 28, 57, 63, 67
  in election campaigns 80
  history of empire and 45–52
  and immigration status 5, 40, 58, 87–88
  inequality 4, 11, 14–15, 40, 45
  informal contracts 98, 100
  insecurity and difficulties in maintaining
    family contact 84–86

overcrowded 47–48, 58, 67, 69, 103, 104
postwar discrimination 48, 49, 51
repairs and refurbishment 68–69, 91,
  96–98, 110
unlicensed 98
Housing Act 1930 48
Housing Act 1980 53
Housing Act 1988 53
  Section 21 6, 62
housing associations 53, 54–55, 57, 68
  executive pay 56
Housing of the Working Classes Act 1890 48

I

immigration policy
  and cumulative precarity 86–89
  'Hostile Environment' model 5, 36, 83, 87
  postwar 48–49
immigration status and housing 5, 40, 58,
  87–88
indigenous resurgence 37
inflation 50, 51, 52
  house-price 52–53
intergenerational
  collaboration 3, 4
  disjunctures 91–93, 125
  inheritance 9, 10, 14, 23
intimacy 31–38, 102–103
  economic obstruction of 72–79
  leaving a partner 73
  political power of 32, 36–37, 38
  sexual 105–108, 107–108
  state-sanctioned practices of 14, 35–36
  see also precarious intimacy
'investment zones' 12
invisibilised labour 42–43

J

Joel's story 98, 107
Johnson, Boris 20, 21, 29, 55, 113
Jonathan's story 65, 93–94, 97, 111–112

K

Kasia's story 118–119, 120–121
Katz, Cindi 16, 17, 24, 33, 39, 43, 44, 61,
  64, 67, 72
Keynesian society 11, 24, 25, 28, 82
Khan, Sadiq 20, 55, 99
Krasner, Lee 105
Kwarteng, Kwasi 12

L

labour 80–100, 126
  alienated 30–31, 43–44, 45, 80, 100
  communicative 91–92, 93–94
  cumulative precarity and 82–84, 100, 126
    legacies of 84–89
  devaluation of 40–41
  digitalisation of 41

fantasies of future advancement 43, 89–94
invisibilised 42–43
market, women in 82
reproductive 9, 10–11, 38–39, 81–82
security 25
working to make homes 94–100, 126
see also affective labour
land ownership 45–46
landlords 5–6, 12, 69–70
  bans on children 62
  controlling behaviours 109–112
  demographics of 13
  deposits 96, 112
  early modern 46
  encouraging of private 53, 54
  friends as 111–112
  informal contracts 98, 100
  origins 45
  repossessions 21
  'Rogue Landlord Checker' 99
  see also evictions
'lead tenants' 40, 112–113
Leah's story 116–118, 120
leaving a partner, difficulties of 73
Lefebvre, Henri 102
Leon's story 64–65, 75–76, 96–97, 107–108
letting agents 5, 99
Localism Act 2011 49, 54
lodgers 111–112
London
  desire to leave 70–72
  family life as incompatible with renting
    in 62–66
  history of precarious renting in 52–57
  racialised experiences of 70–72
  see also Hackney
London Living Rent 55
Lorde, Audre 37–38, 40
loss and grief 29–30, 120–121
love relations 10, 38, 81, 121

M

Maja's story 78, 104–106, 112–113
Manitowabi, Edna 37
Mariam's story 67, 69, 70
Marx, Karl 27–28, 38, 43, 45–46
Marxist-feminism 8, 32
Massumi, Brian 28
Matthew's story 64, 115–116
Melissa's story 63, 116
methods 1, 18–20
middle-class
  affordable housing products 57, 63
  aspirations of middle-class security 91,
    92, 93
  concerns over raising middle class
    children 77–78
  downward mobility 25, 26
  nuclear family 26

reproductive obstruction 44, 51–52
striving for home ownership 62
Middle East 50, 51
migrant family, cumulative precarity
    of 86–89
migration from Caribbean 48–49
millennial generation 1, 2, 3, 26, 125
  'generation rent' 2, 11–15
Minton, Anna 52, 53
monogamy 9, 10
Montgomery, Nick 27, 29, 37
mortgages 12, 21
  religious bans on 91, 92
moving
  home, possessions and 95–96
  out of London 70–72
multigenerational households 15
  being trapped in 73–74, 75, 84, 88–89, 90,
    91–92
  and cumulative precarity 84–89
  and issue of underoccupancy penalties
    73–74, 91
  maintaining intimate relationships 74–76
  protecting parental fantasies 89–90,
    91–92

N

Nash, Catherine 35
Nasra's story 65, 76–78, 99–100
National Health Service (NHS) 29, 81
neoliberalism 8
  decentralisation of public services 22, 40
  depletion of care capacities 39
  deregulation 25, 52
  networked life 27
  paradox 14, 124–125
  precarity 23–24, 43–44, 125
  racism a tool of 53–54
Nishnaabeg theory 37
Nouman's story 86–90
nuclear family 11, 26, 36, 113
  anachronism of 1, 9
  rentier capitalism and 14–15
  thinking beyond 7–11, 14, 115

O

oil prices 50
Organization of the Petroleum Exporting
    Countries (OPEC) 50
outdoor space 6, 20, 69, 99–100, 103
overcrowded living spaces 47–48, 58, 67, 69,
    103, 104

P

parenthood, obstructions to *see*
    reproduction, obstructing
parents, adult children living with *see*
    multigenerational households
partnership 81

patriarchy
  and capitalism 8, 10, 39
  power of 81–82
Pembury Estate, Hackney 57–58
  Shared Ownership experience 60–61
  space for young people 20,
    103–104
Penny's story 60, 71
Philomena's story 81
Pollak, Leo 56
polyamory 9–10
positionality 19–20
power
  collective 40, 94–95
  erotic 101
  of intimacy 32, 36–37, 38
  plurality of 102
  relations, racialised 117–118, 122
'precariat' 24
precarious intimacy 23–59
  histories 45–59, 125–126
  intimacy 31–38
  precarity 24–31
  reflecting crisis of capitalism 124–125
  reproduction 38–45
  theories 23–24
precarity 3–4, 23, 24–31, 43–44, 81–82,
    108, 125
precarity, cumulative 82–84, 100, 126
  legacies of 84–89
Pregnant then Screwed 82
private renters 2, 11, 62, 127–128
  age of 13–14
  author's experiences 4–7, 95–96
  barriers to building mass power 94–95
  dating outside class habitus 75–78
  deposits 96, 112
  displaced sovereignties 108–113
  generational disjunctures 92–93
  hierarchisation of social tenants and 56–57,
    57–59
  housing costs 11–12, 13
  improving living space 96–98
  obstructions to parenthood 62–66
  organising strategies 128
  paradox of very insecure tenancies 97–99
  savings and investments 13
  short-term leases 53, 94, 96
  see also house-shares, privately rented; queer
    millennial renters
property market, urban 46, 47, 51, 52, 54

Q

queer millennial renters
  breakdown of households 119–123, 127
  conviviality and social reproduction
    114–119, 121, 122
  pro rata systems of resource
    distribution 115–119, 117

sense of home and belonging 35
state delegitimisation of household
    structures 14, 35–36

R

Rachel's story 69–70, 71
racial capitalism 21, 29, 32, 36, 40, 72, 126
  alienation from labours of love 82
  in COVID-19 pandemic 41–42
  differentiated value systems 40, 44, 57–59, 80
  systems of devaluation 80
racialised experiences of London 70–72
racism 53–54
Rapp, R. 44
relational work 84, 91–92
  cumulative precarity and 85–86, 86–89
relationship anarchism 9–10
renters see house-shares, privately rented;
    private renters; queer millennial renters
Renters Reform Bill 62, 63
rentier capitalism 3, 23, 31–32, 127–128
  in context 51–57
  nuclear family and 14–15
  and renting with children 64
  reproductive contradiction of 124–125
  and spatial densification of people 102
  suppression of sexuality 101, 104
repairs and refurbishment 68–69, 91,
    96–98, 110
reproduction
  crisis in 8, 14–15, 44
  see also social reproduction
reproduction, obstructing 51–52, 60–79, 126
  dependentless private renting 62–66
  difficulties in imagining and planning family
    lives 66–72
  economic obstructions to intimacy 72–79
  having a child 60–62
  moving outside London 70, 71–72
  planning financial workarounds 65
  social tenants and 66–69
reproductive labour 9, 10–11, 38–39, 81–82
resource distribution, pro rata 117, 118–119
'Right to Buy' scheme 13, 53, 54
'Rogue Landlord Checker' 99
Rose, Gillian 81
Ruddick, Susan 113, 122
Ryan, Frances 80–81

S

sad passions 113, 122, 125, 127, 128
safe, feeling 70–72, 102–103
Saudi Arabia 51
savings and investments 12–13
sex workers 14, 42, 115
sexual intimacy 105–108
shame 3, 74, 75, 90, 124
shared ownership schemes 55, 60–61, 63
Sharpe, Christina 83, 89

single mothers 14, 35–36, 39
Sisters Uncut 73
Sky, death of 120–121
slavery 25, 42, 83, 89
slum demolition 47, 48
social housing 2
  Bedroom Tax 66, 73–74, 91
  in early 20th century 48
  estate ballots on demolition of 20, 67
  hierarchisation of tenants in private and 36,
    56–57, 57–59
  impact of disrepair and
    overcrowding 68–69
  invested labours in 91
  obstruction to reproduction in 66–69
  postwar building of 48, 49
  'Right to Buy' scheme 13, 53, 54
  urban regeneration and threats to 36,
    56–57, 58, 67
social mobility 44, 66, 90, 93
social reproduction 38–45, 126
  mothers' 121
  queer 114–119, 121, 122
  value differentiation and 42
sovereignties, displaced 108–113
space 101–104
  for bodies to relate 3
  for children and young people 20, 103–104
  desiring 104–108
  displaced sovereignties 108–113
  outdoor 6, 20, 69, 99–100, 103
St John's Church, Hackney 57
stamp duty 54
Standing, Guy 24
state violence 40, 83, 86, 100
  removal of children from family home 84–85
Strauss, Kendra 25, 39, 81
subsistence
  on the 'edge lands' of 40, 41
  privatised through family unit 5, 11
Sunak, Rishi 50, 113

T

Thatcherism 52–54
Themba's story 84–86
Thom, Kai Cheng 16, 35
Tom's story 95, 115–116
Truss, Liz 21, 50, 113

U

union militancy, geographies of 94
urban regeneration 14, 33, 36, 56–57,
  57–59, 67
  and demolition of housing estates 20, 26,
    28, 57, 63

V

value, systems of differentiated 40, 44, 52,
  57–59, 81–82
  in COVID-19 pandemic 41–42
Vasudevan, Pavithra 32

W

warehouse, living in a 104–106
wealth disparities in intimate relationships 73–78
weapons deal 51
welfare reform 36, 66
  Bedroom Tax 66, 73–74, 91
  cuts to disability benefits 80–81
Welfare Reform Act 2012 66
welfare state, retrenchment from 11, 81
Wilde, Matt 128
women
  austerity and attacks on 73
  in labour market 82
  value of work of 81
working-class
  constriction of reproduction 66
  disenfranchised, angry White 26
  early council housing for 48
  housing experiences from 1700s to
    1900s 46–48
writing with and without the university 15–18